Praise for *Coaching for Leadership*

"*Coaching for Leadership* explores powerful new ways to motivate your entire organization. Individuals at every level of the company will benefit from the concepts in this book."

—Ken Blanchard, coauthor of *The One Minute Manager*® and
Leading at a Higher Level

"This is a book by experienced coaches . . . As useful to the experienced coach as it is to the novice, it's a book worth owning!"

—William Bridges, author, *Managing Transitions* and *Creating You & Co.*

"*Coaching for Leadership* is an exceptional work on a vital subject in today's business environment that you don't want to miss."

—Elmer B. Harris, president and CEO, Alabama Power Company

"This book is the single best collection of first-rate articles on executive coaching. It covers every base from leading change to strategy and should be on the bookshelf of every student and practitioner of leadership and organizational development."

—Warren Bennis, University Professor and Distinguished Professor
of Business, University of Southern California, and author,
On Becoming a Leader, and coauthor, *Geeks and Geezers*

"What a resource! In *Coaching for Leadership*, the world's best coaches come together to present an advanced tutorial on the art of coaching. Anyone interested in becoming an executive coach, either as an individual practice or within his or her organization, must immediately buy and read this essential hands-on guide"

—Sally Helgesen, author, *The Female Vision: Women's Real Power at Work*,
The Female Advantage, and *The Web of Inclusion*

"This exceptional book is a must read for individuals at all levels of organization. Coaches, HR managers, and executives hoping to become coaches will benefit greatly from the concepts, practices, and techniques brought to light in *Coaching for Leadership*."

—Vijay Govindarajan, professor at Tuck School of Business at
Dartmouth and best-selling author of *The Other Side
of Innovation: Solving the Execution Challenge*

"This book is very important and valuable for executives who are reaching retirement and moving into another important area of contribution: coaching others to become effective executives. It is no less significant for corporate HR executives who are increasingly called upon to manage coaching interventions on behalf of their companies' leaders."

—D. Quinn Mills, professor, Harvard Business School

"Coaching is a critical business skill in today's fast-changing world. *Coaching for Leadership* pulls together insightful contributions from several renowned coaches. This book is a must read for leaders and future leaders."

—Dr. Homa Bahrami, senior lecturer, Haas School of
Business, University of California, Berkeley

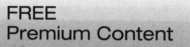

FREE Premium Content	Pfeiffer® An Imprint of ⊕ WILEY

This book includes premium content that can be
accessed from our Web site when you register at
www.pfeiffer.com/go/GoldsmithCF3
using the password *professional*.

COACHING FOR LEADERSHIP

COACHING FOR LEADERSHIP, THIRD EDITION

Writings on Leadership
from the World's
Greatest Coaches

Editors
Marshall Goldsmith, Laurence S. Lyons,
and Sarah McArthur

Pfeiffer
A Wiley Imprint
www.pfeiffer.com

Published by Pfeiffer
An Imprint of Wiley
One Montgomery Street, Suite 1200, San Francisco, CA 94104-4594
www.pfeiffer.com

For additional copies/bulk purchases of this book in the U.S. please contact 800-274-4434.

Pfeiffer books and products are available through most bookstores. To contact Pfeiffer directly call our Customer Care Department within the U.S. at 800-274-4434, outside the U.S. at 317-572-3985, fax 317-572-4002, or visit www.pfeiffer.com.

Pfeiffer also publishes its books in a variety of electronic formats and by print-on-demand. Not all content that is available in standard print versions of this book may appear or be packaged in all book formats. If you have purchased a version of this book that did not include media that is referenced by or accompanies a standard print version, you may request this media by visiting http://booksupport .wiley.com. For more information about Wiley products, visit us at www.wiley.com.

Library of Congress Cataloging-in-Publication Data

Coaching for leadership: writings on leadership from the world's greatest coaches / editors, Marshall Goldsmith, Laurence Lyons, Sarah McArthur. —3rd ed.
    p. cm.
  Includes bibliographical references and index.
  ISBN 978-0-470-94774-6 (hardback)
    1. Executives—Training of. 2. Leadership—Study and teaching.
3. Mentoring in business. 4. Business consultants. I. Goldsmith, Marshall.
II. Lyons, Laurence. III. McArthur, Sarah.
HD30.4.C63 2012
658.4'07124—dc23   2011052828

Acquiring Editor:	Matthew Davis
Director of Development:	Kathleen Dolan Davies
Production Editor:	Dawn Kilgore
Editor:	Donna Weinson
Editorial Assistant:	Michael Zelenko
Manufacturing Supervisor:	Becky Morgan

Printed in the United States of America
Printing   10 9 8 7 6 5 4 3 2 1

TABLE OF CONTENTS

FOREWORD

By Dave Ulrich

A Brief Trek Toward the Next Agenda for Coaching

Like many professions, business coaching began in bits and drabs with individuals here and there being and using coaches. In the last twenty years, as use of business coaches has mushroomed, the range of coaching expectations and services has exploded, for both the good and the bad. I believe that most change efforts like coaching go through the flow depicted by a diamond (Figure I.1). At the top, the early adopters, innovators, and experimenters (like Marshall Goldsmith and other authors in this volume) begin with a zealot's passion and great anticipation. As the field evolves, the widest part of the diamond depicts a host of coaching alternatives ranging from users of coaching who want to join the bandwagon but are not committed to change, to coaches who are passing from one job to another without a serious attempt at coaching rigor, to those want to increase the professionalization of the coaching movement. But, as the field evolves, coaching moves to the bottom part of the diamond, where rigor and clarity begin to emerge around three issues:

1. What are the outcomes of coaching?
2. What are the requirements of one being coached?
3. What are the skills of an effective coach?

FIGURE I.1. EVOLUTION OF THE COACHING MOVEMENT TO A PROFESSION

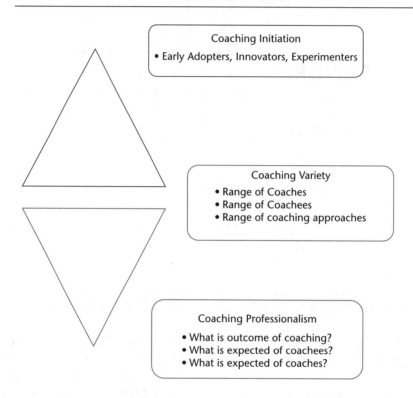

In this volume, Marshall, Laurence, and Sarah have done a marvelous job sourcing material from thoughtful coaches and observers of coaches about these important questions. With these answers, coaching will move down the diamond to become a more rigorous, relevant, and professional endeavor. Having had the privilege of previewing these outstanding essays, let me synthesize the messages they offer (with some of my flavoring) on these important questions.

What Are the Outcomes of Coaching?

One of my shortest and most memorable coaching experiences was with a high-potential family member on an executive team. I was honored to be invited to coach him as he prepared for his likely succession to run a large family business. When we began our conversation, I asked why he wanted to be coached and what he wanted out of the experience. He seemed surprised by the question and replied in an off-hand manner, something like, "I just need to tell the board that I am being coached by someone reputable so that I can be seen as ready to move into my next leadership role." When I probed what he wanted in terms of business or personal outcomes, he deferred to me, saying, "You tell me." It was not a long engagement. He was not ready to be coached and was totally unaware of the outcomes of coaching.

Individuals and companies engage in coaching for a host of reasons that often seem disconnected and disjointed:

These outcomes are well discussed in the chapters throughout this book with great examples and definitions of what coaching can and should accomplish.

As the coaching profession moves forward (down the diamond), it will become increasingly important to create a more rigorous typology of coaching outcomes that are not subject to the whims of the coachee, the coach, or the organization contracting for coaching. Let me offer a possible typology of coaching outcomes based on two dimensions: [1] does the coaching focus primarily on changing behaviors or on delivering results and [2] does the coaching focus more on the individual or the organization? With these two dimensions in mind, the coaching outcomes above might be categorized in Figure I.3. As coaching evolves to more professional standards, having clear outcomes will help the individual being coached know why she or he is engaging in coaching. It will help the coach have clear expectations so that the engagement can be monitored and monetized. It will help the sponsoring organization recognize the value of the coaching investment. This set of essays clearly articulates these potential coaching outcomes.

FIGURE I.2. DISJOINTED COACHING OUTCOMES

FIGURE I.3. A TYPOLOGY OF COACHING OUTCOMES

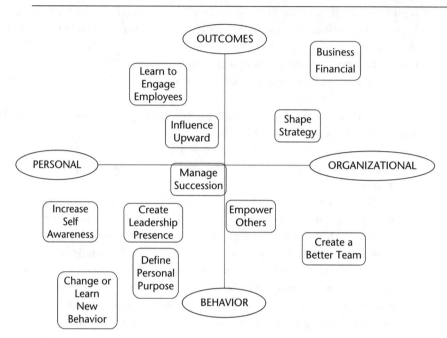

What Are the Requirements of the One Being Coached?

In the above case of coaching calamity, the individual was not ready to be coached. There are two broad issues relevant to the coachee.

First, who can and should be most open to coaching. This volume offers marvelous examples of when and for whom coaching might be most appropriate, for instance:

- Business leaders facing new and unforeseen business challenges who may require new behaviors
- Leaders throughout the company who may have a derailer behavior or style that keeps them from accomplishing what they desire (e.g., lack of self-awareness or ability to influence upward)
- Leaders who have had little exposure to or experiences outside their home organization
- Professionals (e.g., law students) who must have both emotional and social skills as well as technical expertise to succeed in their career
- High-potential employees who need to refine skills to prepare for future career opportunities

Coaching may be adapted to each of these target groups and offer the outcomes summarized above.

Second, obviously, the individual being coached has to be open to change. Every good coach I know has walked away from an engagement because the commitment of the coachee was not adequate for the change required. This volume lays out "tells" or "signals" to look for in the prepared coachee:

- Open to change
- Willing to experiment with ideas
- Able to reflect and acknowledge mistakes
- Willing to listen to what others say with a sense of inquisitiveness and humility
- Open to learning
- Focused on the future (feed *forward*) rather than the past (feedback)
- Able to adapt a style to the requirements of the situation
- Has a sense a personal mission and passion

Not all coachees will ever be fully prepared for coaching, but they should be aware that it is more than casual conversation and dialogue; it is serious and hard work to reflect, define behaviors, identify required behavior changes, and sustain those changes. It means a candor and openness that many hard-core and hard-shelled executives don't want to admit or face.

But, as the joke goes with psychologists (how many psychologists does it take to change a light bulb. . . one, but the light bulb has to want to be changed), so it goes with coaching. Unless and until the coachee is open, receptive, and willing to invest, the experience won't work well.

We may need for the profession a prescreening test for those who want to contract for coaches so that they recognize the commitment required of them to engage in the effort.

What Are the Skills of a Good Coach?

There are many types of coaches. This volume suggests that leaders, peers, HR professionals, social networks, and external experts can all participate in some form of coaching. Each role may have different coaching outcomes, but there are some common coaching skills that are required for anyone who wants to coach.

I know coaches with all kinds of styles: some are extroverts, others introverts; some are intuitive, others data-driven; some focused on cognitions, others on feelings; some who see the big picture, others who revel in details. Coaching style is not as important as following some guidelines on both the content and process of coaching. Again, the essays in this volume offer wonderful tips and insights as to how to be a more effective coach through both content and process.

Content means that the coach has a point of view about what it means to be an effective leader. This point of view is likely to be tied to the situation of the organization's business context, strategy, and team and to the gender and background of the individual being coached, but the coach needs to have a mental model about what makes an effective leader. In a clever essay, Sarah McArthur argues that when ideas are put into writing, they become clearer. It may be useful for coaches to craft their views about what makes an effective leader. Once they know their personal views, they may be better able to help the person they coach define their personal leadership point of view.

Process refers to the engagement between the coach and coachee. Again, the collective wisdom of these thought leaders offers some tried, tested, and true suggestions for managing the coaching engagement. Let me summarize some of what is talked about:

- Focus on the future, not the past (feed*forward*)
- Build a trusting relationship where the coachee knows you care about him or her as a person
- Recognize, discover, and build on the passion, meaning, and desires of the coachee
- Listen for understanding
- Ask probing questions that surface deeper issues
- Respect and build on the strengths of the coachee, but do not hesitate to label and run into the weaknesses
- Be candid without being punishing
- Use data from many sources (e.g., 360) to help the coachee recognize unintended consequences
- Find the right physical setting to coach
- Use time wisely (not too much or too little)
- Build sustainability into the coaching engagement by follow up and accountability
- Be very sensitive to unique qualities (e.g., gender, religious orientation, global experience, personal history) of the coachee and be open to talk about these sensitive areas

I was privileged very early in my career to observe Bill Ouchi, an incredible mentor and advisor, coach a senior business leader for two hours. I was able to see him create a professional and personal intimacy where the business leader put down his defenses and was able to hear Bill's thoughtful and caring counsel. Coaches need to pay attention to the process of coaching and nurturing those they coach, and then consulting, as appropriate, to build the organization infrastructure to sustain the personal changes.

Conclusion

Investments in coaching show few signs of slowing down. Hopefully, it is not another fad in the management heritage of fads. Coaching may shift from a movement to a profession with discipline and rigor around three questions:

1. What are the outcomes of coaching?
2. What are the requirements of one being coached?
3. What are the skills of an effective coach?

This outstanding volume offers thoughtful, innovative, and applicable insights on each of these questions. This is a trek worth pursuing!

Dave Ulrich

We have a duty to pass on our learning . . .

"I am pleased and thankful that in the consulting world I am considered a 'wise person.' My commitment is to use that gift to help other practitioners continue to develop their impact on their clients and on the world."
—*Richard Beckhard*

This book is dedicated to Dick Beckhard, a wonderful coach, a professional colleague, and a personal friend and mentor to many of the authors of this book. His inspiration reaches further than his companions might ever have expected.

PREFACE TO THE THIRD EDITION

When it was published in 2000, *Coaching for Leadership* became an instant classic in the field of executive coaching. The second edition in 2006 was aimed at the large number of retiring leaders who saw coaching as a way of passing on their learning. Coming twelve years after the book's inception, this third edition is aimed squarely at the intended recipients of that legacy—the bright young leaders and coaches of the Hi-Po (High-Potential) Generation of the twenty-first century who hold high expectations of our distressed world.

Leadership coaching has changed dramatically since the last edition. The supply side is now overwhelmed with practitioners from myriad disciplines crowding into the coaching space. Perhaps the most vociferous come with a psychology background, a discipline which itself is undergoing change, gradually shifting its focus from the study of dysfunctional toward a science of success. This nudges psychology even further into the realm of business, the home territory of our book.

Of the many other disciplines laying claim to the sphere of leadership coaching, we consider philosophy to be highly significant. In offering alternative models for the foundations of thought, philosophy offers a platform on which our entire subject may rest. Within philosophy lies the often-neglected topic of ethics, the science of doing good, which surely ought to be a central theme in any teaching of leadership.

Today's Hi-Po coaches are challenged with the recurring task of weaving threads from several disciplines into a tapestry that is fit for purpose in helping their clients learn and succeed. In this sense, the coach has to become a *discriminating eclectic,* developing a keen sense of judgment to select which threads are best woven into the fabric and those that it would be better simply to throw away. This book is intended to be a cherished companion in that learning journey.

Today's younger generation of leaders is comfortable with new ways of working and prefers a different style of learning. This book reflects that change. Building on the strong foundations of earlier editions, we have added new contributors while aiming for a fresh style. Without loss of rigor, the chapters are deliberately short and to the point. Wherever possible we have given preference to a punchy, fast-paced storytelling style.

Two significant additions to this third edition are the *The Coaching for Leadership Case Study Workbook: Featuring Dr. Fink's Leadership Casebook* and the premium web content section. *Dr. Fink's Leadership Casebook* authored by coeditor Laurence S. Lyons, has been written to help those who want to be successful leaders, business coaches, and agents of change to understand organizational life. This companion workbook is unique in that its lessons are told in narrative form with illustrations, exercises, and highly entertaining stories that, practically without effort on the part of its readers, engrain into them the complex learnings and theories of management and leadership.

With this edition we've also included a number of articles in our Premium Web Content section that we find specifically pertinent to people new to the subject of business coaching. Three of these articles are new and can be found only at www.pfeiffer.com/go/GoldsmithCF3 (password: professional). The others were in previous editions of *Coaching for Leadership* and are foundational articles that we hope will give readers a taste of what executive coaching is all about. And, with that brief introduction to this latest edition of *Coaching for Leadership,* a description of the sections you'll find in this book follows.

Structure of the Book

Our subject, *Coaching for Leadership,* has grown so much since our first book was published. With such a vast and expanding topic, even an experienced coach or leader may find it difficult to know what is important to spend precious time learning about now. We suggest that readers approach our book by picking a contribution that seems interesting or familiar and progress through the book in any order. Ours is an ideal book to use as a resource when looking for an approach, technique, or inspiration about the subject. For those who prefer a more structured approach, we have divided the book into parts, each representing an important aspect of coaching for leadership. These are:

Part I: Foundations of Coaching. Included here are elements that we see as foundational, classic, must-knows for our readers. These articles help make our subject accessible to readers from any background.

Part II: Portrait of a Leader. Here you will find a collection of chapters which illustrate leadership today. Essays about what are and may always have been valued characteristics and talents of high-potential leaders are included.

Part III: Challenges and Forces of Change. It is a given that the world is changing at a rapid, heretofore unseen pace. This collection of essays explores challenges brought about by today's forces of change and solutions based on the best practices of coaching pioneers.

Part IV: Recognizing and Developing High-Potentials. The hugely important issue for those in leadership and coaching, recognizing and developing high-potentials, is explored in the articles in this section. These authors provide a compendium of case studies and ideas which can make a significant contribution to the achievement of success in this highly critical area.

Part V: Into Action. In this part of the book, we focus on what high-potentials may need to do as they develop into the leaders of tomorrow. This certainly isn't exhaustive, and we hope to expand this section in subsequent editions of *Coaching for Leadership*.

Part VI: Coaching Models and Tools. In this part you will find some of the best, tried-and-tested practical approaches to coaching. Contributions in this section explain what works and also what might derail effective coaching.

Part VII: Coaching for Leadership: Premium Web Content. As mentioned previously, essays in this section will be found only on the web, and include articles we recommend for those new to the subject of leadership coaching.

PREFACE TO THE SECOND EDITION

It is happening. Executive coaching is exploding. The hope expressed in the first edition of this book is being accomplished.

The Practice of Leadership Coaching is the name we have given to this second edition of *Coaching for Leadership: How the World's Greatest Coaches Help Leaders Learn*. It builds on the success of the original work, acclaimed by many authorities as the definitive text on executive coaching. The original work, written as our subject was dawning, has to date inspired well in excess of twenty thousand English-speaking readers; it has since become available in a further four languages.

When Matthew C. Davis, senior editor at Pfeiffer, commissioned this new work, he most likely expected to receive lightly updated scripts culled to appeal to the important emerging audiences he had identified. We have surpassed this ambition. Readers of the first edition will not be surprised at the approach we have taken in producing this latest work. We remain committed to the research approach. So we went back to our authors and asked how they would like to present their ideas, now that our subject has moved on. Once again, their response was amazing.

The book you now hold is more like a separate volume than a second edition. It expounds a well-accepted leadership practice, not a rapidly emerging bright idea. This book contains fourteen brand-new chapters; another ten chapters have been significantly revised. We include new detailed case studies, which we know are highly valued by our readers. We are deeply grateful to all our authors for sharing our motivation, and to the leading companies who have been so generous in sharing their experiences.

Our audiences are expanding. This indicates an expansion of needs beyond a mere growth in numbers. We hope in this edition to address those emerging needs. We have expanded and updated our book to include two clearly important groups. The first is the rapidly growing number of executives who are reaching retirement and aspire to become executive coaches.

Within the next five years, it is likely that more than 30 percent of U.S. executives will be retiring.* In Canada, where the retirement rate of executives is nearly 40 percent, "executive failure" is estimated at a staggering 50 percent. In this context, the possibility of growing the skills of developing leaders makes an attractive corporate investment. Perhaps uniquely, executive coaching has the potential to satisfy this need to up-skill incumbent young leaders. The necessary supply of experienced leadership talent clearly exists, albeit in retirement. A fantastic opportunity has opened up to those leaders who are "officially" retired and are thinking about executive coaching as a "second career." Our authors have much to say to them.

The second emerging audience consists of people in Human Resouce departments who are now addressing the challenge of introducing and managing coaching programs. We have included case studies to demonstrate what has worked in particular instances. We suggest that coaching is better seen as a change management program than a training activity. We hope that the collective views throughout this book give HR sponsors a sense for the coaching opportunity and an indication of the different approach that it requires.

Our book delivers the well-researched best practices of the world's finest coaches to those entering and studying this exciting field. By "best practice" we do not mean that we asked our authors to research different approaches and then select a benchmark. As a matter of fact, we want to discourage our readers from simply copying something that worked for someone else somewhere else. We share with our audience—practitioners, leaders who are transitioning from line manager to executive coach, and HR sponsors—the distilled principles of best practice and an understanding of where and how to apply these principles.

We believe this book to be an invaluable contribution to the growing field of coaching, and we are sure you will find the authors' insights, practices, and experiences useful as you navigate the global business environment. Coaching is the better way.

---

*DDI, Executive Resource White Paper, 2002.

What to Expect from *The Practice of Leadership Coaching*

Our book begins by explaining and defining its subject, coaching, and then leads into the essential parts of the coaching process, the strategy of executive coaching as a change activity, and finally case studies and core applications—in other words, how executive coaching works in the real world. Of course, you may read the chapters in any order. Just pick a subject that you are interested in and find your author. Each article is valuable in its own right and can easily stand alone from the rest.

Our Hope

We hope you enjoy this new volume. We hope you will gain more understanding of coaching as it grows to meet with our changing times. We believe coaching can have an incredibly dramatic impact on leaders and organizations, and it is our sincere wish that you find within these pages a theory, method, and strategy to apply coaching within your own organization, or with the executives of organizations that you coach.

Marshall Goldsmith   Laurence S. Lyons
Rancho Santa Fe, California   *Reading, England*
May 2005

PREFACE TO THE FIRST EDITION

Motivation: Toward a Better Way

Every so often—perhaps once in a lifetime—we have a chance to anticipate a radical and pervasive change that is truly fundamental in nature. This book exists because we are at this very moment at the pinnacle of such change in the world of work. With the passage of every business day, yesterday's "management" approach becomes less relevant while we struggle to find better way.

Peter Drucker's "knowledge worker" is replacing the factory worker at such a rate as to become today's stereotypical worker. The flatter, shamrock organization typified by Charles Handy is evolving as modern networks are becoming as familiar as traditional pyramids. Whereas in the past we were taught how to work with managers, now we must ask: How can we learn to work with peers?

Ideas stemming from Edgar Schein's "process consulting" are escaping from the closed professional consulting world to reach a much wider group of practitioners—that growing number of people doing all sorts of work who now recognize themselves as leaders. Business is going global. Work is more turbulent and stressful. The "job for life" has disappeared, thus challenging each individual to take care of career and personal development—paradoxically at a time when organizational memory, knowledge, and learning are becoming more valuable and sought after. Consumers are pressing for products that deliver more value and continue to demand more service. Even the "office" is redefining itself in new places, allowing us to work at all times of the day as technology offers to make our style of work more flexible. The "better way" must somehow accommodate all these major shifts and offer some answers to the really hard questions.

We were motivated to write this book because we could see that a number of individuals and organizations had found a better way. At a time when managers were being urged to re-engineer the processes of their businesses, we noticed that some organizations were making even greater strides by focusing on people. Their approach is coaching. It is far too easy to dismiss coaching as yet another technique in the management toolbag. The editors see coaching quite differently. For us, a leadership attitude is essential if individuals and organizations are to flourish in the new business world: good coaching offers both dialogue and etiquette, which together provide the structure and process in which leadership can work well. For us, coaching is the style of choice that rehumanizes the modern worker.

The goal of the editors, then, was simply to bring together the thinking of the world's greatest coaches at a critical time when leaders and managers need to learn about good coaching. This need has been met in this book with tested guidelines that promote responsible and effective coaching. We feel we have a duty as a progressive group to articulate our experiences, ideas, theories, and practices into one book that consolidates and positions the coaching subject into mainstream leadership and management topics.

Our Audience

Naturally, there are many audiences for this book. Those who already recognize themselves as leaders will find valuable reference material to help develop and improve their own leadership style. All those who see themselves as "managers" will find here a route along which to explore and experiment in leadership activities. Our book is for those who sponsor coaching, those who provide or receive coaching, the designers of coaching programs, and anyone who will integrate coaching into his or her own personal style whenever relating to others in the workplace.

Our Authors

We did not expect to write this book alone. At the outset it was clear that we needed to consolidate the thoughts, experiences, and insights of the world's greatest coaches and thinkers on management and leadership. We feel that their generosity in contributing chapters and their enthusiasm toward this ambitious project has validated our own beliefs about the importance of coaching. We take this opportunity to thank our authors warmly, for their willingness to share, for their perseverance in keeping to deadlines, for working with us on making changes to their chapters, and for their unanimous encouragement and support. Their response has built this book into a unique collection of chapters offering an entry point into our subject to readers from all backgrounds.

We have read and edited all the chapters. In areas where we have found different authors writing about the same idea, we have tried to adjust the language so that the same word or expression in one place will refer to the same idea in another place, in a uniform way throughout the book.

We have been editors, never censors. While we have diligently applied a uniformity of language, we have deliberately avoided any insistence on a uniformity of ideas beyond a commitment to coaching. Ours is an emerging subject in which specific situations can be as important as tested techniques in determining outcomes. Practice concepts that today might appear to us as ambiguous, paradoxical, or even contradictory will compete in the real world of experience; they will synthesize, and our collective thinking will make progress into the future.

Our Subject

In order to describe our subject area, we make a few general comments. There is something fundamental about coaching that enables it to fit into organizations of all kinds. Coaching is a behavioral approach of mutual benefit to individuals and the organizations in which they work or network. It is not merely a technique or a one-time event; it is a strategic process that adds value both to the people being coached and also to the bottom line of the organization.

Coaching establishes and develops healthy working relationships by surfacing issues (raw data gathering), addressing issues (through feedback), solving problems (action planning), and following through (results)—and so offers a process in which people develop and through which obstacles to obtaining business results are removed. Coaching can also be looked at as a peer-to-peer language expressed in a dialogue of learning.

Coaching is transformational. Through a behavioral change brought about in individuals, a leader may transform the organization and gain commitment. Coaching can offer a new propellant to organizational change. In coaching, people are offered the chance to align their own behavior with the values and vision of the organization. By helping people understand how they are perceived when they are out of alignment—and then putting these individuals back into alignment, one person at a time—coaching can make real impact and build healthy organizations—top-down, and from the grass roots up.

As to a formal definition of "coaching," how it relates to "leadership," and questions such as the difference between coaching and "mentoring," or whether the "sports metaphor" is appropriate—here we have let our authors speak for themselves. Of course, each of us has a personal view, and we take the opportunity to share this in our own individual chapters, which open the book.

Our Hope

Our hope is that, through the reading of this book, the reader will gain an understanding of the importance of coaching as a preferred and tested route to achieve leadership; the dramatic impact that can be achieved through coaching; why managers need to develop into leaders; and how coaching fits in with other techniques and approaches (consulting, therapy, organizational development, and so forth).

You will gain a thorough grasp of how—and for whom—coaching should be applied in your own organization and in your career, and also how to perform in your role as a coach, a person being coached, a sponsor, or as a buyer or supplier of a coaching service. Last, you can return to this reference work when you need to see how the world's top forty-five leading professionals have successfully responded to difficult coaching problems and successfully applied their own ideas in diverse situations.

Ultimately it is you—our reader—who we hope will complete the quest of this book by bringing good coaching practice into the world of work for the benefit of all.

May 2000

ACKNOWLEDGMENTS

Coaching for Leadership: Writings on Leadership from the World's Greatest Coaches has been a group effort that wouldn't have been possible without the extraordinary efforts, care, and expertise of many people.

First, we are deeply indebted to our contributing authors. All of these authors are busy people, leaders in the arena, who have taken time from their full lives to share their knowledge with us. We appreciate their effort and wisdom immensely. We are especially grateful to Dr. Paul Hersey. Many of us rely and build on his theory of Situational Leadership in our work. Also, many thanks to renowned human resources thought leader Dave Ulrich for not only contributing chapters, but also for writing the foreword to our book.

We give our special thanks to the exceptional team at Jossey-Bass, Matthew Holt, Dawn Kilgore, and Michael Zelenko, whose skills and knowledge have made the publication and production process a breeze and a pleasure. Also, we are very grateful for the wonderful editorial assistance of Lorraine Fisher and Kathy Hyatt Stewart. Their editing skills—and their delightful attitudes—make both of them a joy to work with!

Finally, we are deeply grateful to our families whose support through the intense book writing and editing process is invaluable and at times challenging!

We owe our utmost appreciation to Lyda, Kelly, Bryan, Judi, Nathan, Rachael, Scott, Sally, and Homer. Without them, *Coaching for Leadership: Writings on Leadership from the World's Greatest Coaches* would not have been possible.

Marshall Goldsmith	Laurence S. Lyons	Sarah McArthur
Rancho Santa Fe, California	*Reading, England*	*San Diego, California*

ABOUT THE EDITORS

Dr. Marshall Goldsmith has recently been recognized as the most influential leadership thinker in the world in the Thinkers50/HBR global biannual study. He has also been described in *American Management Association* as one of the top fifty thinkers and leaders who have influenced the field of management over the past eighty years; in the *Wall Street Journal* as one of the top ten executive educators; in *Forbes* as one of the five most-respected executive coaches; in the *Economic Time (India)* among the top CEO coaches of America; in *Fast Company*, called America's preeminent executive coach. Marshall is one of a select few executive advisors who have been asked to work with over 120 major CEOs and their management teams. He is the million-selling author of numerous books, including *New York Times* best-sellers *MOJO* and *What Got You Here Won't Get You There* (also a *Wall Street Journal* #1 business book and winner of the Harold Longman Award for business book of the year).

Laurence S. Lyons was formerly senior vice president at Executive Coaching Network in California, European Practice Director of The Alliance for Strategic Leadership, and a member of the Worldwide Association of Business Coaches International Advisory Committee. In his early career Larry worked for start-up, small, and large organizations including Digital Equipment Corp (DEC), where he was Technical Director of European Hardware Engineering.

Larry is the creator of the fictional Dr. Fink and his business associates whose adventures are related in the companion volume *The Coaching for Leadership Case Study Workbook.*

His clients include Agilent Technologies, Aventis, BAE Systems, BBC, British Airways, Belgacom, BT Benelux, Deutsche Bank, Lufthansa, Oracle, Pitney-Bowes, Sasol, SITA-Equant, and Unilever. Larry is co-author of *Creating Tomorrow's Organization* (Pitman) and is founding editor of the *Coaching for Leadership* series (Jossey-Bass).

A library of his work is available at www.lslyons.com.

Sarah McArthur is founder of *sdedit, a writing and editing firm based in San Diego, California. With nearly two decades of experience in the publishing field, Sarah has worked with such influential clients as Marshall Goldsmith and Anthony Robbins. She has played significant roles in the best-sellers *What Got You Here Won't Get You There, Mojo: How to Get It, How to Keep It, and How to Get It Back If You Lose It,* and *Coaching for Leadership.* In 2009, she coedited *The AMA Handbook of Leadership* with Marshall Goldsmith and John Baldoni. This book received the Top 10 Business, Management, and Labour Title award of 2010 by Choice. As managing and developmental editor of numerous highly successful business and leadership titles, Sarah is a highly sought-after freelance editor and writing coach.

Sarah has held editorial and management positions at *The San Diego Reader,* Harcourt Brace & Company, and The Anthony Robbins Companies. She is former editor of *Business Coaching Worldwide,* and was graduated from the University of Oregon with degrees in English and Environmental Studies. Contact Sarah at sarahmc@sdedit.com and www.sdedit.com.

PART I

FOUNDATIONS OF COACHING

Part I, Foundations of Coaching, sets the stage for coaching as an approach to successful leadership. This section is comprised of foundational pieces, "classics" if you will, that explain how and why leadership coaching is relevant, valid, and necessary in today's post-management business arena. We begin our book with an updated version of Marshall Goldsmith's article, "Coaching for Behavioral Change," in which Marshall describes his proven process for behavioral change and explains the importance of integrating a practical, behavioral change mechanism as a vital foundation element that must be at the root of successful coaching. In order to flourish within an enterprise or nonprofit organization, coaching must support the creation of core value in delivering genuine measurable economic business results. Chapter Two, "Coaching at the Heart of Strategy" by Laurence S. Lyons, introduces a new and broader way of thinking about strategy to incorporate the ambitions of the individual as well as the work team and organization. We see this idea of mutual strategy as one of the foundations of coaching, and in describing this important connection, this chapter provides invaluable direction for coaches, individuals, teams, and organizations. Chapter Three, "Situational Leadership and Performance Coaching" by Paul Hersey and Roger Chevalier, reminds us once again that coaching is situational. In their article, they reveal how Situational Leadership® provides the necessary structure to guide executive coaches in working with their clients. In his article, "Coaching and Consultation Revisited: Are They the Same?" Edgar H. Schein raises and answers fundamental questions about the purpose and nature of coaching and shows how it can be regarded as a branch of process consulting. Setting forth critical descriptions of each, he compares the two and defines their differences. Finally, Dave Ulrich and Jessica K. Johnson demystify coaching in their article, "Demystifying the Coaching Mystique." With explanations of the various types, needs for, and methods of coaching, Dave and Jessica's article is a must-read for established and potential coaches and those looking to work with a coach for whatever reason.

CHAPTER ONE

COACHING FOR BEHAVIORAL CHANGE

By Marshall Goldsmith

My mission is to help successful leaders achieve positive, long-term, measurable change in behavior: for themselves, their people, and their teams. When the steps in the coaching process described below are followed, leaders almost always see positive behavioral change—not as judged by themselves, but as judged by preselected, key stakeholders. This process has been used around the world with great success—by both external coaches and internal coaches.[1]

Our "Pay for Results" Executive Coaching Process

Our coaching network (Marshall Goldsmith Group) provides coaches for leaders from around the world. All of the coaches in our network use the same proven process. We first get an agreement with our coaching clients and their managers on two key variables: (1) what are the key behaviors that will make the biggest positive change in increased leadership effectiveness and (2) who are the key stakeholders that can determine (six to eighteen months later) if these changes have occurred.

We then get paid only after our coaching clients have achieved positive change in key leadership behaviors—and become more effective leaders—as determined by their key stakeholders.

I believe that many leadership coaches are paid for the wrong reasons. Their income is a largely a function of "How much do my clients *like me*?" and "How much *time* did I spend in coaching?" Neither of these is a good metric for achieving a positive, long-term change in behavior.

In terms of liking the coach—I have never seen a study that showed that clients' love of a coach was highly correlated with their change in behavior. In fact, if coaches become too concerned with being loved by their clients, they may not provide honest feedback when it is needed.

In terms of spending clients' time—my personal coaching clients are all executives whose decisions have an impact on billions of dollars—their time is more valuable than mine. I try to spend *as little of their time as necessary* to achieve the desired results. The last thing they need is for me to waste their time!

Qualifying the Coaching Client

Because we use a "pay only for results" coaching process, we have had to learn to *qualify* our coaching clients. This means that we only work with clients who we believe will greatly benefit from our coaching process.

Knowing When Behavioral Coaching Won't Help

We do not work with leaders who are not really motivated to change. Have you ever tried to change the behavior of a successful adult that had no interest in changing? How much luck did you have? Probably none! We only work with executives who are willing to make a sincere effort to change and who believe that this change will help them become better leaders. Our most successful coaching clients are executives who are committed to being great role models for leadership development and for living their company's values.

I have personally worked with several of the world's leading CEOs. One reason that they are so effective in leading people is that they are always trying to improve themselves—not just asking everyone else to improve. Our best coaching clients are dedicated to be great role models in consistently working to improve themselves.

Some large corporations "write people off." Rather than just fire them, they engage in a pseudo-behavioral coaching process that is more "seek and destroy" than "help people get better." We only work with leaders who are seen as potentially having a great future in the corporation. We only work with people who will be given a fair chance by their management. We do not work with leaders who have been "written off" by senior management.

There are several different types of coaching. We only do behavioral coaching for successful executives—not strategic coaching, life planning, or organizational change. I have the highest respect for the coaches who do this kind of work. That is just not what our coaches do. Therefore, we *only* focus on changing leadership behavior. If our clients have other needs, we refer them to other coaches.

Finally, I would never choose to work with a client who has an integrity violation. We believe that people with integrity violations should be *fired*, not coached.

When will our approach to behavioral coaching work? If the issue is leadership behavior, the coaching clients are given a fair chance and they are motivated to improve, the process described in this article will almost always work. If these conditions do not exist, this process should not be used.

Involving Key Stakeholders

In my work as a behavioral coach, I have gone through three distinct phases.

In phase one—I believed that my clients would become better because of *me*. I thought that the coach was the key variable in behavioral change. I was wrong. We have published research on leadership development that involved input from over 86,000 respondents.[2] In our research we have learned that the key variable for successful change in leadership behavior is *not* the coach, teacher, or advisor. The key variables that will determine long-term progress are the leaders being coached and their coworkers.

I learned this lesson in a very humbling way. The client that I spent the *most* amount of time with did not improve and I did not get paid! This was a painful reminder to me that I was not the key variable in my clients' improvement.

The client that I spent the *least* amount of time with improved more than anyone I ever coached—and he was great to start with! He was later recognized as the CEO of the Year in the United States.

When I asked my "most improved" client, what I could learn about coaching from him, he taught me a great lesson. He told me that I needed to: (1) pick the right clients and (2) keep the focus of my coaching on my clients and their teams (not my own ego and need to prove how smart I was).

In phase two—I spent most of my time focusing on my coaching clients. I slowly learned that a motivated, hard-working client was more important than a brilliant coach! I learned that their ongoing efforts meant more than my clever ideas. My results improved!

In phase three (where I am now)—I spend most of my time not with my coaching client but with the key stakeholders around my client. I focus on helping my clients learn from everyone around them. By making this change, my clients' results have improved even more dramatically.[3]

How do I involve key stakeholders? I ask *them* to help the person that I am coaching in four critically important ways:

Let go of the past. When we continually bring up the past, we demoralize the people who are trying to change. Whatever happened in the past happened. It cannot be changed. By focusing on a future that can get better (as opposed to a past that cannot), the key stakeholders can help my clients improve. (We call this process feed*forward,* instead of feedback.[4])

Be helpful and supportive, not cynical, sarcastic, or judgmental. As part of our coaching process, my clients involve key coworkers and ask them for help. If my clients reach out to key stakeholders and feel punished for trying to improve, they will generally quit trying. I don't blame them! Why should any of us work hard to build relationships with people who won't give us a chance? If my clients' coworkers are helpful and supportive, my clients' experience increased motivation and are much more likely to improve.

Tell the truth. I do not want to work with a client, have him or her get a glowing report from key stakeholders, and later hear that one of the stakeholders said, "He didn't *really* get better, we just said that." This is not fair to my client, to the company, or to me.

Pick something to improve yourself. My clients are very open with key stakeholders about what they are going to change. As part of our process, our clients ask for ongoing suggestions. I also ask the stakeholders to pick something to improve and to ask my client for suggestions. This makes the entire process "two-way" instead of "one-way." It helps the stakeholders act as "fellow travelers" who are trying to improve, not "judges" who are pointing their fingers at my client. It also greatly expands the value gained by the corporation in the entire process.[5] In one of my most successful case studies, I was asked to coach one top executive—and about two hundred people ended up improving.

Steps in the Leadership Coaching Process

The following steps describe the basics of our behavioral coaching process. Every coach in our network has to agree to implement the following steps. If the coach will follow these basic steps, our clients almost always achieve positive change!

1. *Involve the leaders being coached in determining the desired behavior in their leadership roles.* Leaders cannot be expected to change behavior if they don't have a clear understanding of what desired behavior looks like. The people that we coach (in agreement with their managers, if they are not the CEO) work with us to determine desired leadership behavior.
2. *Involve the leaders being coached in determining key stakeholders.* Not only do clients need to be clear on desired behaviors, they need to be clear (again in agreement with their managers, if they are not the CEO) on key stakeholders. There are two major reasons why people deny the validity of feedback—wrong items or wrong

raters. By having our clients and their managers agree on the desired behaviors and key stakeholders in advance, we help ensure their "buy-in" to the process.

3. *Collect feedback.* In my coaching practice, we personally interview all key stakeholders. The people who I am coaching are all CEOs or potential CEOs, and the company is making a real investment in their development. However, at lower levels in the organization (that are more price sensitive), traditional 360-degree feedback can work very well. In either case, feedback is critical. It is impossible to get evaluated on changed behavior if there is no agreement on what behavior to change!

4. *Reach agreement on key behaviors for change.* As I have become more experienced, my approach has become simpler and more focused. I generally recommend picking only one to three key areas for behavioral change with each client. This helps ensure maximum attention to the most important behavior. My clients and their managers (unless my client is the CEO) agree upon the desired behavior for change. This ensures that I won't spend a year working with my clients and have their managers determine that we have worked on changing the wrong behavior!

5. *Have the coaching clients respond to key stakeholders.* The person being reviewed should talk with each key stakeholder and collect additional "feed*forward*" suggestions on how to improve on the key areas targeted for improvement. In responding, the person being coached should keep the conversation positive, simple, and focused. When mistakes have been made in the past, it is generally a good idea to apologize and ask for help in changing in the future. I suggest that my clients *listen* to stakeholder suggestions and not *judge* the suggestions.

6. *Review what has been learned with clients and help them develop an action plan.* As was stated earlier, my clients have to agree to the basic steps in our process. On the other hand, outside of the basic steps, all of the other ideas that I share with my clients are *suggestions.* I just ask them to listen to my ideas in the same way they are listening to the ideas from their key stakeholders. I then ask them to come back with a plan of what *they* want to do. These plans need to come from them, not me. After reviewing their plans, I almost always encourage them to live up to their own commitments. I am much more of a facilitator than a judge. My job is to help great, highly motivated executives get better at what *they* believe is most important—not to tell them what to change.

7. Develop *an ongoing follow-up process.* Ongoing follow-up should be very efficient and focused. Questions like, "Based upon my behavior last month, what ideas do you have for me next month?" can keep a focus on the future. Within six months conduct a two- to six-item mini-survey with key stakeholders. They should be asked whether the person has become more or less effective in the areas targeted for improvement.

8. *Review results and start again.* If the person being coached has taken the process seriously, stakeholders almost invariably report improvement. We then build on that success by repeating the process for the next twelve to eighteen months. This type of follow-up will ensure continued progress on initial goals and uncover additional areas for improvement. Stakeholders almost always appreciate follow-up. No one minds filling out a focused, two- to six-item questionnaire if they see positive results. The person being coached will benefit from ongoing, targeted steps to improve performance.

9. *End the formal coaching process when results have been achieved.* Our goal is not to create a dependency relationship between coach and client. Although I almost always keep in touch with my coaching "graduates" for the rest of their lives, we do not have an ongoing business relationship.

The Value of Behavioral Coaching for Executives

Behavioral coaching is only one branch in the coaching field, but it is the most widely used type of coaching. Most requests for coaching involve behavioral change. Although this process can be very meaningful and valuable for top executives, it can be just as useful for high-potential future leaders. These are the people who have great careers in front of them. Increasing effectiveness in leading people can have an even greater impact if it is a twenty-year process, instead of a one-year program.

People often ask, "Can executives *really* change their behavior?" The answer is definitely yes. If they didn't change, we would never get paid (and we almost always get paid). At the top of major organizations even a small positive change in behavior can have a big impact. From an organizational perspective, the fact that the executive is trying to change leadership behavior (and is being a role model for personal development) may be even more important than what the executive is trying to change. One key message that I have given every CEO that I coach is "To help others develop—start with yourself."

Dr. Marshall Goldsmith has recently been recognized as the most influential leadership thinker in the world in the Thinkers50/HBR global biannual study. He has also been described in *American Management Association* as one of the top fifty thinkers and leaders who have influenced the field of management over the past eighty years; in the *Wall Street Journal* as one of the top ten executive educators; in *Forbes* as one of the five most-respected executive coaches; in the *Economic Time (India)* among the top CEO coaches of America; in *Fast Company*, called America's preeminent executive coach; and he has received a lifetime achievement award (one of two ever awarded) from the *Institute for Management Studies*. Marshall is one of a select few executive advisors who have been asked to work with over 120 major CEOs and their management teams. He is the million-selling author of numerous books, including *New York Times* best-sellers *MOJO* and *What Got You Here Won't Get You There* (also a *Wall Street Journal* #1 business book and winner of the Harold Longman Award for business book of the year). Contact Marshall at marshall@marshallgoldsmith.com and www.marshallgoldsmith.com.

CHAPTER TWO

COACHING AT THE HEART OF STRATEGY[1]

By Laurence S. Lyons

Observing the Coaching Scene

Imagine them, perched at the corner of a highly polished mahogany table in some elegant boardroom. They appear to be business colleagues, come together to clinch a deal. The observer may suppose them to be friends—or perhaps adversaries—working through some evidently complex problem. They take turns at drawing on a whiteboard, one passionately elaborating on a point, the other deep in thought. A fresh pattern of thought sparks insight: highly animated, they evaluate every possible angle, moving toward a considered plan of action.

To the casual observer, the practice of executive coaching may appear to involve little more than holding an animated conversation. But behind the immediate "here-and-now" setting in which such an exchange takes place, many worlds are to be found. One describes the executive's career that stretches beyond today, well into the past and future. Any modern career is set within a world of work in which the ground rules are in a state of flux. Central to this, we find the immediate present, the world of today, populated by colleagues in various teams: managers, direct reports, associates, suppliers, and customers. The specific configuration of relationships can include government, trade unions, banks, shareholders, stock markets, and so forth. Permeating this is the competitive or purposeful world of the organization in which the executive works. And then again, there is a world beyond the boundary—one all too often neglected in management

---

[1]Laurence S. Lyons © 2005.

books—desperately needing to be acknowledged, although not explored, during the coaching process. This is the nonbusiness, nonwork, social, personal, family world. We must accept that there is life beyond work.

In order to be fully effective, a coaching dialogue must be able to integrate these worlds. Good coaching has the capacity to help an executive or team develop competencies and business effectiveness within any or all of the domains.

To complicate this picture, membership in the work teams to which the executive belongs (for example, project team, task force, or committee) is often fluid: people come and go. Team, personal, and organizational objectives also change over time. In addition, the organization itself is often in a state of reformulating its own identity, mission, and structure.

Yet this apparently simple coaching dialogue does take place. Our research shows that it is consistently successful when performed well. Amazingly, a seemingly simple "coaching conversation" accommodates turbulence and uncertainty, yet repeatedly succeeds in producing outstanding results. For the practitioner who has a limited perception of coaching as simply a collegial conversation, coaching will undoubtedly fail to deliver durable success. But coaching will be successful both in a strategic sense and over time when acted out as a structured dialogue of emerging purpose.

Dialogue

Good coaching is difficult to do. Perhaps the greatest challenge is to engage the executive in a dialogue of emerging purpose. The disarmingly simple question, "What should we talk about?" can be hard to answer well. Thus, the coach often works with the executive as a kind of scout, together selecting an appropriate path. Coaching is potentially both high-impact and high-risk. Dire consequences can result from setting off in the wrong direction—disappointing to both the executive and the business. In contrast, identifying the right path will reap high reward.

Dialogue is at the heart of coaching. In an interview, we find two people. One is typically a senior executive of a large corporation, responsible for a significant part of the business, the other an executive coach—neither an employee of nor a technical consultant to that corporation. The executive has million-dollar spending authority. The coach has no corporate authority whatever. But through dialogue alone, the external coach exercises considerable influence. With neither formal authority nor direct accountability, the coach's greatest ambition is to profoundly affect the way that the executive thinks and behaves.

Rapport is vital to make sure that the dialogue gets off the ground. The "chemistry" of the pair must quickly establish trust and credibility; the executive must have confidence that the coach is not simply wasting time. Good listening skills on the part of the coach, together with the ability to deliver honest feedback, are crucial to keeping the dialogue grounded in reality—not on fabricated supposition or unsupported beliefs. Between them, coach and executive need to agree on how to separate transient, situational factors from those that are innate and require attention. This sifting can often require delicate judgment when the setting is a turbulent corporate environment. Every effort made in teasing out fact from raw data is well rewarded: carefully validated data is a key determinant of the quality of the outcome of the coaching venture.

The directional or strategic power of any coaching dialogue lies primarily in the nature of its questions. Questions may be asked to surface submerged issues or may be asked to help the executive to reconsider some position or proposed course of action. The executive's attitudes or opinions may become either reinforced or challenged: the person's current path will be either confirmed or probed. Even when the dialogue confirms the validity of a person's existing game plan, it adds value—boosting the executive's confidence while keeping business risks in check.

Coaching reengages with reality when good questioning is followed by inspired analysis, detailed action planning, and follow-through back in the work environment. Working together with the executive, the coach crystallizes their conversation in an action plan. The endpoint of a coaching interview invariably involves the executive planning to try out some new behavior. Most importantly, the full value of any coaching activity can only be realized when a new behavior is actually performed in the real world. At this stage—after the coaching interview has ended—the coach encourages the executive to follow up and execute the plan. In a sense, the coach now acts as both a memory and a conscience. Thus, coaching is best seen as an ongoing process or durable system, not just a single interview event.

A good coach need not be an expert in the executive's job type or industry. A good coach does not even have to possess as wide a range of social skills as the executive. With a sound appreciation of business and interpersonal dynamics, a good coach is simply a process person who can establish rapport; is informed about the executive's immediate environment; is honest and courageous in providing feedback; is a good listener; asks good questions; is visionary and analytical; and is a good planner who seeks follow-up and closure.

The sheer power unleashed in the coaching process must surely obligate the executive and coach to consider several serious questions, such as: What constitutes success in this dialogue? Who, specifically, is my client? How should confidential issues be treated? Which topics fall outside the purview of coaching, and how are those affecting work performance recognized? In the face of these ethical conundrums, the coach must strive to align dialogue in a direction punctuated by validated objectives. The coach must be brave enough to urge the executive to move forward—often by confronting some taboo topic, hitherto deliberately ignored. The dialogue will always help the executive pursue selected objectives—yet not be overly directed by the coach. After all, coaching is concerned with facilitation, not giving advice. Although the necessity remains for the executive to persevere along the most successful route that can currently be identified, there is no promise that the path will be simple to find or easy to travel.

This brings us to two crucial insights into good coaching. First, it is necessary to look behind a dialogue to realize that it will not simply "happen" without background. The most robust coaching relies on broadly informed dialogue. Quite a lot of work may have to be undertaken in the collection, validation, and analysis of information before real coaching can begin. The kind of information that is assimilated includes current facts about the markets, technology, or political environment in which the executive is working. Impressions held by colleagues, associates, and direct reports provide vital indications about the executive's personal interaction. Sometimes the only possible way forward is to begin with an executive's own anecdotal information, but coaching in a vacuum is a dangerous game.

The second insight to be gained takes us far beyond the one-to-one interview. By incorporating the ethos of the organization within the coaching dialogue, it becomes possible to relate an individual's behavior to purposeful organizational change. When the whole organization is engaged, coaching becomes strategic. Moreover, within a modern learning organization, team coaching and the development of strategic thinking may become one and the same thing.

For the coach, strategy need not reside in quarterly profit targets alone. Those committed to strategic coaching will enrich the meaning of strategy to at once embrace individual, team, and corporate actors. Strategic executive coaching is an inclusive, practical approach, incorporating the idea of a dashboard or balanced scorecard, and it is well-adapted to a complex world in which even the ground rules are in a state of change.

Transforming People

For the sponsor, a coaching initiative might be viewed as a self-contained project, rather than as part of an integrated corporate strategy. However, whenever coaching succeeds in aligning the needs of the business with the developmental needs of its people, it cannot help but be strategic in nature.

Many organizations face a situation in which an entire block of talent shifts when issues of succession and development emerge. Typically, this occurs during mergers, downsizing, or block retirement. The creation of a career path to retain top talent and a drive to expand into global markets are also examples of situations demanding a strategic coaching response. Whatever the cause, a gap opens up that has to be filled for the organization to remain strategically healthy. So at one leading automobile manufacturer, fast-track engineers are today being coached to become tomorrow's senior leaders. Elsewhere, a Fortune 500 IT innovator has implemented coaching within a program that has integrated five separate operating countries into a cohesive and highly successful business region.

For the person being coached, the experience is invariably strategic. Coaching offers the executive a golden opportunity to step back and reflect on personal development. By expressly allocating precious work time, the coaching interview momentarily suspends the immediate pressures of the day and encourages the individual to think about "just me." From this viewpoint, the coaching intervention is able to break the pedestrian logic of mere reaction and repetition. For once, the executive has time to look dispassionately and proactively at more broadbrush issues in a far wider context. The individual may well start to consider the interface between work and life. Work is within life; work is a part of life. In order that executives may learn and develop at work, they must first understand where they are in their career and in their life. Often, reflection on one's purpose will validate or challenge one's current position. Such consideration may encourage an individual to move forward or to move on to something new. To the extent that coaching sensitizes people to reflect and act in a more purposeful way, it is again strategic in nature, helping to align the organization with the people who are in it.

In times of major organizational change, coaching often provides the necessary impetus for building and motivating teams. Team coaching helps establish and then build a collection of individuals into a fully functioning business network. The resulting team unites people across functions and divisions, often including members outside the formal organization. Time and again, we have seen a team-coaching process motivate people to coalesce. Provided that the group contains that critical mass of people needed for the business to move forward, a nascent transition team starts to emerge. Many team members will have recently taken part in individual coaching sessions, and so will be ready to think strategically at the moment the team starts to form. When a foundation of trust has been established, the conditions for cohesion are in place and the team spontaneously ignites in a dialogue of business improvement. Such teams are enthusiastic; such teams have solutions that will work; such teams are unstoppable. A well-designed team-coaching process brings together the right people and raises the broadest challenge, in an environment in which failure is not an option.

Coaching also plays a special role at the most senior level in an organization (that is, with the board of directors or senior management team). At this level, issues are often motivational rather than technical. Technically, the coach will play a unique role as interpreter by insisting that jargon gets transformed into business concepts that are commonly understood. Motivationally, members may differ significantly in their beliefs about the purpose of the business and may hold conflicting expectations about what success means and how to measure it. Then again, business owners may hold wildly different views about asset valuation and a preferred exit or merger strategy. Located at an intermediate level in large companies, divisional and regional boards often grapple with a particularly perplexing question: How can we find ways to add value from our unique vantage point in the overall structure? In all these cases, coaching offers yet another framework for dialogue. Coaching provides a climate within which vital, although seemingly intransigent, issues may be brought to the surface, confronted, and then dealt with. Coaching offers the senior team a practical tool to break any logjams that are in the way of progress.

In all of these cases—for individuals, teams, and boards—coaching offers a structured dialogue of emerging purpose, directed toward success. As Figure 2.1 shows, with the right conditions in place coaching is organizational transformation; coaching is team development; coaching is strategy in motion.

FIGURE 2.1. THE STRATEGIC COACHING MODEL

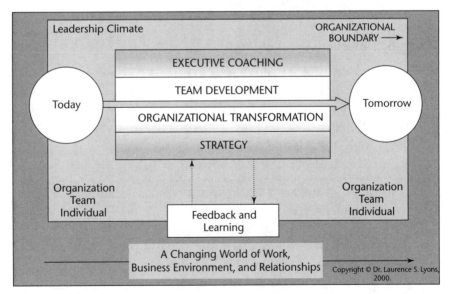

Strategic Coaching gets people, teams, and organizations from where they are today to where they want to be tomorrow. The leader is committed to ensuring the existence and maintenance of the coaching process and its alignment with business results.

Leadership

In an era when leadership is replacing management and learning is replacing instruction, coaching is surfacing as the accessible face of strategy. Business strategy no longer commands an exclusive domain secreted within the impersonal body of an abstract "organization." Today, as demands on everyone's time intensify, strategy is manifest in the flesh and blood of each executive. Coaching is not simply a passing fad: it offers a pragmatic supporting context in which modern strategy flourishes. In today's turbulent world, strategy has developed into something that emerges, always tracking a moving target. And the preferred vehicle—responsive enough to reduce the risk in successfully traveling toward that ever-changing destination—is to be found in the dialogue of coaching.

Any dialogue that brings an executive closer to goal achievement in the real world truly succeeds at a strategic level. Achievement-oriented dialogue reaches outside the immediate interview to make real things happen. Coaching has the power to let strategy come alive and therefore to work in practice. Executive coaching has become current simply because it has become relevant. Coaching facilitates success and is congruent with the way we want to work and the way we have to work. It is relevant to the modern world of business because it is holistic and adaptive. Coaching is also a method that respects people as individuals, not merely as cogs in the business machine. Rooted in conversation, coaching is evolving as a natural vehicle of leadership.

A Radically Different World of Work

As knowledge work relentlessly replaces manual work, we are witness to the dawn of perhaps the most meritocratic workplace environment in history. Management is no longer perceived in terms of maintaining the business machine, but is seen as the motivator and leader of men and women. Our understanding of the essence of management is reeling from radical change.

The management metaphor has, until now, been extremely useful in helping executives become more systematic and better organized in order to plan, motivate, and control. But the word "management" has come to represent an attitudinal straitjacket that can stifle, and often excuse the need for, that kind of truly innovative thinking that has become a prerequisite for success. As markets become more efficient and intensively competitive, ideas of coercion and control—together with a reliance on rigid rules—hinder, rather than help, businesses succeed.

Noticeably, the adjectives used to describe management work have already started to change. Terms once borrowed from engineering and finance are being replaced with descriptions from the social and humanist vocabulary. Thus the "efficient company" has become a "learning organization." Language is not the only thing changing. The perspective is shifting steadily and surely from labor to knowledge; from management to leadership; from product to consumers and service; from routine operation to inspired creativity; and from task repetition to marketing innovation. As technology and automation shift the boredom of work from people to machines, the human world of work that remains challenges our intellect, not our muscle.

Fast-paced competition means that businesses can no longer afford to reward the routine repetition embedded in the all-too-rigid "management" model. A new culture, one that prizes sensible action and appropriate adaptability, is challenging as well as complementing written strategic plans. These vast tomes were invariably out of date on the day they were published and contained too many untested or generalized assumptions to be workable in practice. Long delays in the planning cycle allowed the organization to meander aimlessly while waiting for the control loop to close. It is not easy to enter into dialogue with a written plan. These days, competitive advantage is not to be found in written plans alone. Corporate success is now intimately related to the way in which individual executives think, act, and interact on a daily basis. To win and receive reward, executives must now do the right thing, not simply the written thing. It is not enough to take problems to others and await a response. The competition simply will not stand back and wait. Today's successful executives do not "need the meetings," instead they "meet the needs."

The change in the nature of work is not only radical, it is also deeply pervasive as leaders continue to shift operations into the global arena. Worldwide, a realization that a key source of competitive advantage is to be found rooted in the social fabric of the company is opening up new vistas of opportunity. Whereas the technical business process was only recently seen as the dominant lever of change, we have come to recognize the human "etiquette" of the organization as a potent value driver. If we get the formula right, the currently emerging leadership culture offers leaders a genuine opportunity to make the world a better place.

Coaching offers us a unique response to help address that challenge at every level.

The Learning Executive

A complete overhaul is taking place in the way we see the relationship between education and work. In the traditional model, predicated on executing a single professional function over an entire lifetime, learning was confined to a single burst of training followed by years of practice. This sequence has now become less relevant for many. Today, "Education for Life" is rapidly replacing "A Job for Life" as the dominant career model. No longer does a specific job last for a lifetime; several jobs fragment a career, while learning has become continuous, rather than a one-time affair.

Executive skills must match the situation. Modern business is too dynamic to allow executives to succeed with the old rigid and simplistic assumptions. On a personal level, all executives face a recurring challenge in pragmatically responding to revolutionary trends and pressures in the world of work. A fresh dexterity is now demanded. Simply "painting by the numbers" no longer works in a world that demands so much more than a single prescribed answer. Thus, today's successful executives must embrace self-development and learning. At a time when organizations can no longer guarantee work for life, individuals have taken on "Learning for Life" as the paradigm model.

Fortunately, such an approach also helps to meet pressing organizational needs. Everywhere we find cycles becoming shorter, with businesses in a never-ending race to find a quicker way to reach a globally expanding market. The trend is also for work to make increasing demands on employees' time. In such a frenetic climate, executives cannot undertake learning as a separate activity. To keep technical knowledge up to date, an executive may have no alternative but to spend time off-site, but leadership skills are best learned in the workplace and on the job. Learning must be applied immediately, responding to issues of the moment. This "just-in-time" teaching of skills is another form of executive coaching.

Executives need knowledge and skills to cope with situations as they come up. Often the circumstances are ambiguous. An executive may need to deal with a troublesome colleague; start a new assignment; present a difficult business argument; become more "visible"; or communicate more effectively with direct reports. The coach fits into the new learning model perfectly by allowing the executive to learn, modify, and apply a suitable approach in a particular business situation. Coaching allows executives to learn while at work, while keeping up the pace.

Striving for Success

Executives are invariably concerned with issues of corporate, team, and individual success. Because they face new rules of competition and new definitions of success, modern executives must find ways to align and balance these components. They must choose activities that truly add value over efforts that merely appear effective. This may seem little more than common sense, yet it reflects a genuine attitudinal shift in the workplace. It is another important area in which a coach can challenge and validate the client's perspective. This can also engender a sense of empowerment in that the executive wants to "do the right thing."

Within the broad category of "knowledge work," mundane and passive stewardship continues to lose ground to creativity and innovation. In addition, the basis of reward is shifting from an emphasis on effort to a focus on results. Arriving at the office well before the official start time and regularly working late into the night and on weekends are no longer automatically seen as characteristics of an effective executive.

Technology has allowed working styles to be more open and flexible, while at the same time allowing work and life to impinge on each other, making both more stressful. Coaches can help executives to negotiate this delicate interface without being intrusive. Once again, the coach needs an ethical position and rules of engagement or terms of reference within which to operate. As we embrace information technology, giving ourselves more freedom in choice of lifestyle, we usually prefer—and even insist—that the value of our work contribution be measured in terms of outcomes or results. For knowledge workers in particular, the time of day or the geographic location of their efforts has become irrelevant. Outcome, not input, now attracts reward.

In yesterday's business world, the "numbers" and the routine mechanics of operations lulled organizations and their executives into believing that they were fulfilling a purpose simply by repeating traditional formulas. Certainly, repetition worked well in the factory model, but repetition is no longer a guarantee for success in a service and knowledge economy. A new style of leadership is called for. This shift from management to leadership is primarily one of outlook and attitude. Leadership moves us from rigidity to flexibility; leadership allows us to adapt in a more uncertain environment; leadership urges people to take responsibility, to take the initiative, to do the right thing, and thereby to excel.

It is not surprising to find that dynamic leadership is overthrowing the familiar and traditional "social norms" established in the era of stable hierarchical management. The successful executive today must follow this trend in order to achieve desired outcomes in a business world that is becoming more volatile.

Leadership has become crucial in creating value and achieving competitive advantage in the modern work organization. Leadership is not exclusive to a few "top executives"; it is class-free and pervasive. A leader treats people as responsible adults and encourages all to act in the interest of mutual success. A leader promotes a sense of individual worth and community and diligently directs activity toward the business ambitions of the organization. The "culture" and leadership style of an organization are not a consequence of doing work in a certain way. Instead, they are a healthy context within which excellent work is done. Managers motivate, whereas leaders inspire. Inspired companies are winners. Corporations need far fewer managers and far more leaders, and coaching offers a direct and practical way to instill this new culture into corporate life.

Coaching provides a route to leadership. Coaching can unlock the latent leadership potential in managers and reinforce leadership where it already exists. A culture of coaching can nurture leadership. And when coaching aligns the development of the individual, the team, and the organization toward a mutual definition of success, then coaching becomes leadership. Leadership through coaching offers a strategic and practical direction for all.

Coaching in Practice

It can be as lonely at the periphery of a modern networked organization as it is at the top of a traditional pyramid. Problems can come from talking too freely inside an organization, however flat or virtual it may be. Work colleagues become tomorrow's interested parties. Truly innovative concepts can sound like crazy ideas in the early stages, and few executives want to take the risk of appearing foolish. Even private discussions can contain political topics that, when touched on, even tentatively, can establish a position from which it is difficult to reverse. Leaders need a safe and supportive theater or laboratory in which to rehearse and refine their ideas. Coaching meets this need.

Coaches present executives with an opportunity to engage in a dialogue of development. Where there is no coach, the chance for this reflective dialogue may be missed. When executives have no one to talk to, there is no tested or evolved dialogue, there is no attitude formation, and so an important part of executive thinking—thinking through—is missing. In all these ways, coaching is supportive of executive and organizational learning. Coaching provides a platform for practical action directed toward intelligent and strategic intent.

Every organization is different; each has its unique definition of success. In whatever way the dimensions of success are articulated by each board, team, or individual executive, coaches are charged with finding a developmental path to progress. In striving for success, leaders must find ways to advance the business, while respecting core organizational values and fundamental beliefs. These must be understood by coaches at a visceral level. To deliver quality, a coach needs to see far beyond the superficial level, at which all corporate value statements look similar, and discover in detail the actual values in play. And then again, as the world progresses to continuously repaint an ever-emerging strategic organizational context, these values are destined to develop and change over time.

External and Internal Agents

Most leaders acknowledge that in order to remain healthy an organization must reach out to its stakeholders and into the environment. Indeed, a modern organization will actively extend its social fabric through dialogue with coaches, consultants, and others. Yet, it is a source of astonishment to many that an organization's maintenance functions require any interaction from outside.

The traditional or legal definition of a corporation can fool us into believing that it will remain forever self-sufficient. The need for external nurturing agents may seem to fly in the face of this belief. However, the "outside" or external aspect of the organization has been long recognized in "systems theory" as extremely important. In today's organizations, interaction with the environment is being rediscovered as a vital activity required to reduce business risk. Here again, the coaching opportunity supports another crucial facet of leadership—the need to be in touch with the reality beyond the formal boundary of the organization.

Yet, an organization that regards executive coaching as a service provided entirely by external suppliers can never attain a true climate of leadership. Modern corporations must be capable of maintaining cohesion in the newly evolving, flatter, and networked workplaces. Today's leaders do not seek to set themselves apart, but instead are determined to replicate their best leadership behaviors in those around them. They are also open to absorbing, as well as propagating, such exemplary behaviors. Thus, internal coaching—or internalized coaching—is vital to working in the modern, cross-functional network in which all participants find it natural to coach.

However flat an organization may be, executives will always need to interact with their direct reports. Here again, coaching provides the executive with a foundation for dialogue that is well-suited to leading "free agents," who are less likely to respect positional power as a legitimate motivator.

The term "mentoring" is widely used to describe an activity closely related to coaching. A mentor is likely to have had a successful personal track record in a role similar to that of the client. Thus, the nature of this relationship may tend to contain relatively more content than process. Reputation and trust toward the mentor are powerful determinants in making the chemistry work. A senior mentor can be a great asset who is likely to be able to tap into an otherwise inaccessible range of useful business contacts.

When working in the same organization, a mentor requires no learning curve to absorb culture. Steps should be taken—and periodic checks should be made—to ensure the internal mentor does not inadvertently become a compromised interested party in the day-to-day operations of the person being mentored. There is only one other essential qualification: a good mentor simply needs to be a good coach.

The coaching approach is also spilling into all kinds of work relationships. For example, some organizations have instituted an informal "buddy" system, which can be little more that sharing contact information at training events. Some larger divisions of Fortune 500 companies are now putting coaches on the payroll as full-time employees. It is not uncommon for senior executives to take their coaches with them when switching companies. This becomes part of the hiring negotiation process, along with share options and other benefits. The sheer pervasiveness of the coaching relationship in organizations today—whether inside, outside, or between organizations—confirms that coaching is seen as an effective style of working with the blurring boundaries in and around organizations.

A Blueprint for Success

Coaching has been able to draw practitioners from many established fields, including consultancy and counseling. An important challenge facing them all is to link personal development of individual clients to attainment of solid business results. Only when this can be achieved consistently can a coaching program hope to fully justify the investment that it demands.

The formula for success in achieving this will display a number of characteristics. Coaches must address issues that are individual, team, and organization-wide; they must act in a way congruent with the organization's style of leadership; they must promote and facilitate positive organizational development; they must be practical; and they must help in the achievement of business results.

In combining these elements, the Strategic Coaching Model (see Figure 2.1) provides a modern blueprint for business success. Couched in a culture of modern leadership and based on the powerful dynamics of human interaction, the model simply asserts that coaching is at its best when located at the heart of strategy.

Laurence S. Lyons (www.lslyons.com) is an accomplished coach, consultant, public speaker, and author. A former technical director at Digital Equipment Corporation, he has been described as a "leading authority on business transformation" by Henley Management College, where he is a member of associate faculty and Founding Research Director of the Future Work Forum.

Dr. Lyons is regarded as a pioneer in the field of executive coaching; he has coached hundreds of senior and high-potential executives in organizations in the United States and across Europe. Many of his personal coaching clients are to be found in *Who's Who*.

Dr. Lyons holds a Ph.D. and MSc from Brunel University and the CIM (Diploma in Marketing). He is an invited member of the Leader to Leader Institute Thought Leaders Forum (formerly Drucker Foundation).

Larry Lyons is author of the companion volume *The Coaching for Leadership Case Study Workbook: Featuring Dr. Fink's Leadership Casebook*. Contact lslyons@lslyons .com.

CHAPTER THREE

SITUATIONAL LEADERSHIP AND EXECUTIVE COACHING

By Paul Hersey and Roger Chevalier

Executive coaching requires exceptional leadership and questioning skills to be effective. At no point is leadership more important than in assisting clients in defining their performance issues and identifying the underlying causes.

In this chapter, we will show how Situational Leadership® provides the needed structure to guide executive coaches in working with their clients. We will add an Executive Coaching Guide© to further elaborate on the process. A model for gap and cause analysis will then be added, followed by sample questions that can be used to assist executive coaches as they guide their clients as they work together to improve organizational performance.

Situational Leadership

Situational Leadership gives executive coaches the guidance they need as they work with their clients. The underlying principle in Situational Leadership is that executive coaches should adjust their leadership styles to their client's readiness level (ability and willingness) to perform a given task. Leadership is the amount of task behavior (direction) and relationship behavior (support) given by a leader. (See Figure 3.1.)

To be effective, executive coaches must adjust the way in which they lead their clients based on their level of readiness for each task that they are expected to perform. Executive coaching is a unique application of the principles of Situational Leadership that guides executive coaches as they work with their clients.

The lowest readiness level (R1) for an individual or group is described as not willing and not able to do a given task. The appropriate leadership style (S1) is

FIGURE 3.1. SITUATIONAL LEADERSHIP

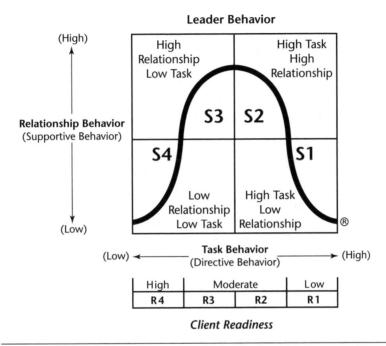

that of providing high amounts of task behavior (direction) and low amounts of relationship behavior (support). The next readiness level (R2) is described as willing but not able. The appropriate leadership style (S2) is that of high amounts of both task and relationship behavior.

The next readiness level (R3) is described as able but unwilling in that the individual lacks confidence or commitment. The appropriate leadership style (S3) is that of high amounts of relationship behavior and low amounts of task behavior. The highest readiness level for a group or individual to do a given task is willing and able (R4). The appropriate leadership style is that of low amounts of both relationship and task behavior.

The Situational Leadership model provides a framework from which to diagnose different situations and prescribes which leadership style will have the highest probability of success in a particular situation. Use of the model will make executive coaches more effective in that it illustrates the connection between their choice of leadership styles and the readiness of their clients.

As such, Situational Leadership is a powerful tool for executive coaches to use in working with their clients.

The Executive Coaching Guide

The Executive Coaching Guide is a performance aid that describes a process that is used in formal interviewing, counseling, and coaching situations. The guide is divided into two phases that focus on assessing the client's readiness and then choosing an appropriate leadership style. The first phase uses Situational Leadership Styles 4, 3, and 2 to prepare, open the lines of communication, and diagnose the client's readiness level for the tasks necessary to be successful.

When the executive coach is not working with the client, the client perceives a Style 4. The client continues to perceive low amounts of direction and support as the executive coach prepares for the coaching session by reviewing relevant materials, such as records from their previous meeting and setting goals for the session.

At the beginning of the meeting, the executive coach moves to a Style 3, increasing support by building rapport, by opening up the lines of communication, and by reinforcing positive performance or potential. In this step the executive coach works to assess how the client sees the overall situation by asking open-ended questions.

The executive coach then moves to Style 2 to focus the discussion with direct questions to gain further insight into the client's current problem areas. For each task that is critical for the client's success, the executive coach must assist the client in defining performance gaps and identifying underlying causes. The executive coach must also assess the client's readiness (ability and willingness) level for dealing with each performance issue so that the coach can choose the best style with which to intervene.

The assessment phase is described in Figure 3.2.

After assessing the client's readiness for each issue, the executive coach selects the appropriate leadership style based on the client's readiness level for each performance issue from the diagram in Figure 3.3. As is the case with the Situational Leadership Model, the performance issue must be clearly defined before a readiness level can be determined.

Clients can be at several different task-relevant readiness levels for the different issues. Once the readiness level is decided, the corresponding high probability leadership style is chosen to begin the intervention. After the initial intervention, if the client responds appropriately, the executive coach then moves to the next style to further develop the client. The selection of the high probability intervention style is shown in the diagram that follows.

FIGURE 3.2. ASSESSMENT PHASE

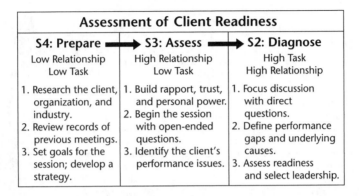

Assessment of Client Readiness		
S4: Prepare ➡	**S3: Assess** ➡	**S2: Diagnose**
Low Relationship Low Task	High Relationship Low Task	High Task High Relationship
1. Research the client, organization, and industry. 2. Review records of previous meetings. 3. Set goals for the session; develop a strategy.	1. Build rapport, trust, and personal power. 2. Begin the session with open-ended questions. 3. Identify the client's performance issues.	1. Focus discussion with direct questions. 2. Define performance gaps and underlying causes. 3. Assess readiness and select leadership.

FIGURE 3.3. HIGH PROBABILITY INTERVENTION

S4: Follow-Up ⬅	**S3: Reinforce** ⬅	**S2: Develop** ⬅	**S1: Prescribe**
Low Relationship Low Task	High Relationship Low Task	High Task High Relationship	High Task Low Relationship
1. Document session in client's record. 2. Follow through on all commitments. 3. Monitor progress and prepare for next session.	1. Reinforce the process used and the progress made. 2. Reinforce self-worth and self-esteem. 3. Encourage, support, motivate, and empower.	1. Discuss ways to improve performance. 2. Reach agreement on best course of action. 3. Guide, persuade, explain, and train.	1. Present alternative courses of action. 2. Identify the best course of action. 3. Inform, describe, instruct, and direct.
Selection of Leader's Style Matched to Client			
Able and Willing or Confident	Able but Unwilling or Not Confident	Unable but Willing or Confident	Unable and Unwilling or Not Confident
R4	R3	R2	R1

If the client is unable and unwilling or insecure (R1), initially use a Style 1 (Prescribe) to inform, describe, instruct, and direct. If the client is unable but willing or confident (R2), initially use a Style 2 (Develop) to explain, persuade, guide, and train. If the client is able but unwilling or insecure, initially use a Style 3 (Reinforce) to encourage support, motivate, and empower. After making the initial intervention, move through the remaining styles to Style 4 (Follow-Up) to monitor progress and prepare for the next session.

FIGURE 3.4. EXECUTIVE COACHING GUIDE

Assessment of Client Readiness		
S4: Prepare ➡	**S3: Assess** ➡	**S2: Diagnose** ➡
Low Relationship Low Task	High Relationship Low Task	High Task High Relationship
1. Research the client, organization, and industry. 2. Review records of previous meetings. 3. Set goals for the session; develop a strategy.	1. Build rapport, trust, and personal power. 2. Begin the session with open-ended questions. 3. Identify the client's performance issues.	1. Focus discussion with direct questions. 2. Define performance gaps and underlying causes. 3. Assess readiness and select leadership.
S4: Follow-Up ⬅	**S3: Reinforce** ⬅	**S2: Develop** ⬅	**S1: Prescribe**
Low Relationship Low Task	High Relationship Low Task	High Task High Relationship	High Task Low Relationship
1. Document session in client's record. 2. Follow through on all commitments. 3. Monitor progress and prepare for next session.	1. Reinforce the process used and the progress made. 2. Reinforce self-worth and self-esteem. 3. Encourage, support, motivate, and empower.	1. Discuss ways to improve performance. 2. Reach agreement on best course of action. 3. Guide, persuade, explain, and train.	1. Present alternative courses of action. 2. Identify the best course of action. 3. Inform, describe, instruct, and direct.
Selection of Leader's Style Matched to Client			
Able and Willing or Confident	Able but Unwilling or Not Confident	Unable but Willing or Confident	Unable and Unwilling or Not Confident
R4	R3	R2	R1

The Executive Coaching Guide in Figure 3.4 is a performance aid derived from the Situational Leadership Model and describes the process used to develop people. The executive coaching process follows a pattern that typically includes varying the amount of direction and support given clients as the executive coach prepares, assesses, diagnoses, prescribes, develops, reinforces, and follows up.

The assessment phase is critical to the coaching process in that the executive coach must prepare, assess, and diagnose prior to making the actual intervention. In effect, the executive coach must "earn the right" to intervene. All too often executive coaches intervene without taking the time to truly assess the client's readiness. While the initial intervention style is chosen based on the client's readiness for a given task, the goal is to develop the client by using successive leadership styles as the executive coach moves from prescribe to develop, to reinforce, and then to follow-up.

Performance Gap and Cause Analysis

The key to the executive coaching process is in asking the right questions in the right order to assist clients in identifying their overall situation, specific performance gaps, and the underlying causes. The executive coaching process is an application of leadership in which the consultant becomes a trusted resource for the client.

The starting point in assisting clients in analyzing performance shortfalls is called gap analysis. The executive coach must lead the client in identifying an individual's or group's present level of performance (where they are) and their desired level of performance (where they'd like to be). The difference between where they are and where they want to be is the performance gap. Another useful step is to identify a reasonable goal, something that can be accomplished in a short time that moves the organization in the direction toward where it wants to be. This should be defined clearly with measures of quality, quantity, time, and cost delineated for the goal.

Once the performance gap has been defined, the next step is to identify the causes. The Behavior Engineering Model (BEM), developed by Thomas Gilbert and presented in his landmark book, *Human Competence: Engineering Worthy Performance*,[1] provided a way to systematically and systemically identify barriers to individual and organizational performance. This model has been recently updated to better assist executive coaches in assisting their clients in identifying causes for performance gaps.[2]

The updated model (Figure 3.5) focuses attention on the distinction between environmental and individual factors that have an impact on performance. Environmental factors are the starting point for analysis because they pose the greatest barriers to exemplary performance. When the environmental supports are strong, individuals are better able to do what is expected of them.

The support given by the work environment is divided into three factors that influence performance: information, resources, and incentives. Information includes communicating clear expectations, providing the necessary guides to do the work, and giving timely, behaviorally specific feedback. Resources include ensuring that the proper materials, tools, time, and processes are present to accomplish the task. Incentives ensure that the appropriate financial and nonfinancial incentives are present to encourage performance. These apply to the worker, the work, and the workplace.

What the individuals bring to the job include their motives, capacity, knowledge, and skills. Individual motives should be aligned with the work environment so that employees have a desire to work and excel. Capacity refers to whether the worker is able to learn and do what is necessary to be successful on the job. The final factor refers to whether the individual has the necessary knowledge and skills to do a specific task needed to accomplish a project or goal.

FIGURE 3.5. UPDATED BEHAVIOR ENGINEERING MODEL

	Information	Resources	Incentives
Individual	1. Roles and performance expectations are clearly defined; employees are given relevant and frequent feedback about the adequacy of performance. 2. Clear and relevant guides are used to describe the work process. 3. The performance management system guides employee performance and development.	1. Materials, tools, and time needed to do the job are present. 2. Processes and procedures are clearly defined and enhance individual performance if followed. 3. Overall physical and psychological work environment contributes to improved performance; work conditions are safe, clean, organized, and conducive to performance.	1. Financial and non-financial incentives are present; measurement and reward systems reinforce positive performance. 2. Jobs are enriched to allow for fulfillment of employee needs. 3. Overall work environment is positive, where employees believe they have an opportunity to succeed; career development opportunities are present.
	Knowledge/Skills	**Capacity**	**Motives**
Environment	1. Employees have the necessary knowledge, experience, and skills to do the desired behaviors. 2. Employees with the necessary knowledge, experience, and skills are properly placed to use and share what they know. 3. Employees are cross-trained to understand one another's roles.	1. Employees have the capacity to learn and do what is needed to perform successfully. 2. Employees are recruited and selected to match the realities of the work situation. 3. Employees are free of emotional limitations that would interfere with their performance.	1. Motives of employees are aligned with the work and the work environment. 2. Employees desire to perform the required jobs. 3. Employees are recruited and selected to match the realities of the work situation.

The model gives the structure needed to assess each of the six factors: *information, resources, incentives, motives, capacity, and knowledge and skills* that affect individual and group performance on the job. These factors should be reviewed in this order since the environmental factors are easier to improve and have a greater impact on individual and group performance. It would also be difficult to assess whether the individual had the right motives, capacity, and knowledge and skills to do the job if the environmental factors of information, resources, and incentives are not sufficiently present.

Leading with Questions

The executive coach can lead the client with questions to identify the causes of performance shortfalls. Thomas Gilbert published a collection of questions used to assess the state of the six cells in his Behavior Engineering Model. He called these questions The PROBE Model, a contraction of "PROfiling Behavior."[3] The PROBE model consisted of forty-two questions to be used to assess the accomplishment of any job in any work situation.

Following Gilbert's lead, updated PROBE questions were developed to support the Updated Behavior Engineering Model. In addition to the direct questions that reflect the original PROBE questions, open-ended questions have been added to start the discussion with the client. It is important to start the discussion with an open-ended question so as to keep the client from getting defensive from a series of direct questions.

Updated PROBE Questions

A. Information

Open-ended, exploratory question: How are performance expectations communicated to employees?

Direct, follow-up questions:

Have clear performance expectations been communicated to employees?

Do employees understand the various aspects of their roles and the priorities for doing them?

Are there clear and relevant performance aids to guide the employees?

Are employees given sufficient, timely, behaviorally specific feedback regarding their performance?

Does the performance management system assist the supervisor in describing expectations for both activities and results for the employee?

B. Resources

Open-ended, exploratory question: What do your employees need in order to perform successfully?

Direct, follow-up questions:

Do employees have the materials needed to do their jobs?

Do employees have the equipment to do their jobs?

Do employees have the time they need to do their jobs?

Are the processes and procedures defined in such a way as to enhance employee performance?

Is the work environment safe, clean, organized, and conducive to excellent performance?

C. Incentives

Open-ended, exploratory question: How are employees rewarded for successful performance?

Direct, follow-up questions:

1. Are there sufficient financial incentives present to encourage excellent performance?
2. Are there sufficient nonfinancial incentives present to encourage excellent performance?
3. Do measurement and reporting systems track appropriate activities and results?
4. Are jobs enriched to allow for fulfillment of higher-level needs?
5. Are there opportunities for career development?

D. Motives

Open-ended, exploratory question: How do your employees respond to the performance incentives you have in place?

Direct, follow-up questions:

1. Are the motives of the employees aligned with the incentives in the environment?
2. Do employees desire to do the job to the best of their abilities?
3. Are employees recruited and selected to match the realities of the work environment?
4. Do employees view the work environment as positive?

    5. Are there any rewards that reinforce poor performance or negative consequences for good performance?

E. Capacity

Open-ended, exploratory question: How are employees selected for their jobs?

Direct, follow-up questions:

1. Do the employees have the necessary strength to do the job?
2. Do the employees have the necessary dexterity to do the job?
3. Do employees have the ability to learn what is expected for them to do to be successful on the job?
4. Are employees free from any emotional limitations that impede performance?
5. Are employees recruited, selected, and matched to the realities of the work situation?

F. Knowledge and skills

Open-ended, exploratory question: How do employees learn what they need to be successful on the job?

Direct, follow-up questions:

1. Do the employees have the necessary knowledge to be successful at their jobs?
2. Do the employees have the needed skills to be successful at their jobs?
3. Do the employees have the needed experience to be successful at their jobs?
4. Do employees have a systematic training program to enhance their knowledge and skills?
5. Do employees understand how their roles affect organizational performance?

Summary

Situational Leadership is a powerful tool for guiding executive coaches in interacting with their clients. The Executive Coaching Guide was derived from the Situational Leadership Model and adds more structure to the leadership process. As the key interaction between executive coaches and their clients is to identify performance shortfalls and their causes, the Updated Behavior Engineering Model provides the basis for identifying causes by using the Updated PROBE Questions. This group of performance aid provides the needed structure for the executive coaching process.

Paul Hersey is chairman of the Center for Leadership Studies, Inc., providers of leadership, coaching, sales, and customer service training. He is one of the creators of Situational Leadership®, the performance tool of over ten million managers worldwide and has personally presented Situational Leadership in 117 countries, influencing the leadership skills of four million managers in over a thousand organizations worldwide. He is the coauthor of the most successful organizational behavior textbook of all time, *Management of Organizational Behavior*, now in its seventh edition, with over one million copies in print. Contact: www. situational.com; ron.campbell@situational.com.

Roger Chevalier, CPT is the author of the 2008 ISPI Award of Excellence recipient, **A Manager's Guide to Improving Workplace Performance**, published by the American Management Association (AMACOM Books, 2007). He is an independent consultant who specializes in imbedding training into comprehensive performance improvement solutions. He has personally trained more than 30,000 managers, supervisors, and sales people in performance improvement, leadership, coaching, change management, and sales programs in hundreds of workshops. Contact: www.aboutiwp.com.

CHAPTER FOUR

COACHING AND CONSULTATION REVISITED

Are They the Same?

By Edgar H. Schein

Before addressing the question in this title, it is important to note that coaching in various forms reached epidemic proportions in the 1990s and continues to flourish. I rarely run into a trainer or consultant nowadays who does not claim that most of his or her business is coaching, most typically "executive coaching." As this trend continues, if coaching becomes a mainstream activity of all kinds of helpers, it becomes all the more important to understand the sociopsychological dynamics of this complex process. In my forty-five or so years of consulting with various kinds of organizations, I have often found myself in a coaching role, sometimes with the explicit request to play that role, sometimes inadvertently or by default. I never thought of coaching as such a discrete activity with such unique dynamics, but it is now time to confront and describe those dynamics.

"Coaching" as an option arises under one of two conditions: (1) When a client defines the situation as one in which he or she wants individual help to work on a personal issue, in which case the resulting process can be likened to counseling or therapy, or (2) When a manager asks someone to take on a coaching role to work with an individual to improve job performance or to overcome some developmental deficiencies, in which case the resulting process can be likened to indoctrination or coercive persuasion.[1] Both of these situations can also arise with groups or larger organizational units, as when a process consultant helps a group to solve some problem defined by the group, or when a consultant is asked to "help" a group to learn some new processes or adopt some new values that the larger organization has imposed. As a consultant I have found myself working simultaneously with several members of the client system in an individual counseling role while, at the same time, working with broader group and organizational issues that would not be described as coaching per se but that involve elements of indoctrination along with elements of education. From this point of view the consultant's job is at times much broader than the coach's in that the client system is defined as more than the sum of the individual coaching projects that members may engage in.[2]

Although coaching is often defined as working with an individual based on the athletic analogy, one can imagine coaching a group, or an organizational unit, or perhaps even a whole organization. In sports, the coach is usually in a direct supervisory role, whereas in organizational coaching the coach is typically a staff member or outsider. If the CEO is being coached on how to improve her relationship to the board or on matters of company strategy, one could argue that any behavior change on her part influences the entire organization. But if a middle manager is being coached on how to make himself more effective and promotable, the connection to organizational effectiveness is more remote. What this suggests is that the degree of overlap between coaching and consulting depends on (1) who initiated the request for coaching, (2) who is being coached, (3) in what role he is being coached, and (4) on what issues he is being coached.

Before analyzing each of these issues, let us examine the interpersonal process that is involved in what we call "coaching." To begin, what is the *essential* difference between indoctrination, training, education, and coaching? All of these processes involve an agent of the society, occupation, or organization trying to change (improve?) the behavior of a target person. What is *implied* in coaching that is different from the other three types of interaction is (1) that the coach does not *necessarily* have in mind a predetermined direction or outcome, (2) that the coach does not have arbitrary power over the target person, and (3) that the target person volunteers and is motivated to learn. If the organization "imposes" a coach and a predetermined direction of learning, then by definition we are dealing with indoctrination, not coaching. It is only coaching if the coach asks the client in what areas he or she wants to improve and works strictly to help the client to help him- or herself. In other words, coaching as it is broadly used nowadays is an intrinsically ambiguous process in terms of its goals. An organization can ask a coach to help a manager perform better against certain company standards, but in that process the coach may find that the person is a real misfit and might work with the person to help him or her leave the organization (even though the company has footed the bill). As we will see, this distinction between working for the organization and working for the individual mirrors closely the distinction

I have made between expert consulting and process consulting, and the distinction between indoctrination and therapy.

In my previous analyses of consulting I have emphasized the need to distinguish three fundamentally different roles that the consultant can play in any client relationship: (1) the provider of expert information, (2) the diagnostician and prescriber of remedies, and (3) the process consultant whose focus is on helping the client to help herself.[3] In all of these roles, and that would include coaching, the overarching goal is to be *helpful* to the immediate client, and to be mindful of the impact of interventions on the larger client system and the community.

I have argued that the consultant must move among these roles constantly, but she must *always* begin in the process mode in order to find out in what way her expertise or diagnostic insight and prescription might be helpful. To gain this insight she has to build up enough of a "helping relationship" to stimulate the client to reveal what is really the problem and what kind of help is really needed. And we know from both therapeutic and consulting experience that clients are notoriously reluctant to reveal what is really bothering them until they have a feeling that the consultant is really trying to help.

In the case of organizational consulting, a further complication is that the consultant will never understand the culture of the client system well enough to make accurate diagnoses or provide workable prescriptions.[4] In organizational consulting, therefore, the consultant and client must become a team that jointly owns the consequences of all diagnostic and remedial interventions, even though it must remain clear that it is the client who owns the problem and is ultimately responsible for the solution. The consultant enters into what amounts to a therapeutic relationship with the client system to facilitate in any way possible the improvement of the situation as the client defines it.

Clearly, coaching can then be thought of as one kind of intervention that may be helpful to clients under certain circumstances. In that context I think of coaching as being a set of behaviors on the part of the coach (consultant) that helps the client to develop a new way of seeing, feeling about, and behaving in situations that are defined by the client as problematic. And in that setting, the same issue surfaces of when the coach should be an expert who simply shows the client how to do it, a diagnostician and prescriber who figures out why the client is having a given problem and suggest remedies of various sorts, or a process oriented "therapist" who helps the client to gain insight into his situation and to figure out for himself how to improve his own behavior. The balance and timing of these roles would, of course, depend on whether the coaching was requested by the client or suggested by others in the organization, what organizational role the client is in, and the nature of the problem that the client reveals.

Who Initiates the Coaching Relationship?

Coaching relationships are initiated for a variety of reasons, but who is the initiator? This can vary. Sometimes the boss will initiate the relationship, and sometimes the individual will initiate it. These two scenarios play out differently.

Initiated by the "Boss"

One major source of initiation is when someone higher in an organization "suggests" that someone lower get some coaching to overcome some deficiency that is perceived to limit the person's effectiveness or career potential. A common version of this is to mandate that a person's performance appraisal is to be done by the 360-degree method, where feedback is collected from superiors, peers, and subordinates. It is then assumed that an outside coach is needed to go over the data with the person being assessed, because the discussion would be too threatening if conducted by the boss. If the "problem" is primarily defined by the boss, the issue then arises of whether or not the coach is expected to report back to the boss on progress or whether the coaching remains an entirely private matter between coach and client.[5]

If the coach is expected to report back, we are dealing with a situation that may be called "coaching," but is really training or indoctrination. In that case, the "coach" is basically working for the boss, even though the coach may claim to be trying to help the individual. In such a situation, the coach should probably function as expert, diagnostician, and prescriber, because the desired behavioral outcome is defined by someone other than the client being coached. The client's basic choice is whether or not to enter the relationship at all and whether or not to make an effort to learn the new behavior and way of seeing things. If the new behavior and way of seeing things happen to fit the client's own developmental potentials, the outcome could be beneficial for both the organization and the individual. All too often, however, what the client is expected to learn does not fit his or her personality, so either failure or short-run adaptations without long-run changes are the result. From a consulting point of view this whole scenario is risky, because there are too many ways it can fail—the boss not seeing the initial situation accurately, the boss not communicating the need clearly or the consultant not understanding what is really wanted, the individual not willing or able to be "trained," or the individual making a surface adaptation without any real change.

However, there is an alternative way that the boss can initiate the process that is more likely to be successful. The boss can outline to the coach (consultant) what the problem is as she sees it, but not expect to have reports back and to license the coach to be therapeutic if that seems appropriate. In other words, in this scenario, the boss should be prepared for the coaching to result in an outcome that might not be organizationally expected but might be good for the individual client's development. The coaching may even lead the individual client to recognize a mismatch and subsequently to leave the organization. If that is an acceptable outcome from the point of view of the boss, then the coach can try to focus entirely on helping the individual to help herself and to make truly developmental interventions. In that instance, the boss is in effect playing a consulting role as well in trying to be helpful to the individual. As we will see below, this issue interacts with that of what the coaching is about—whether the boss wants to help the individual develop in a broad sense or wants the individual to learn a particular point of view or set of competencies that are organizationally relevant, for example, to learn how to use a new computerized budgeting system.

Initiated by the Individual

Any time a member of an organization goes to an outsider or staff insider for some kind of help there is the potential in the relationship for coaching or individual counseling/therapy. Helping the individual becomes the primary agenda. In that situation, the outcome is not prescribed by the organization in any way and the issues may have very little to do with organizational problems. This kind of coaching/consulting then merges with what any of us face when someone seeks our help—do we tell them what to do, do we privately diagnose the situation and come up with prescriptions, or do we engage in a period of building the relationship in order to find out how best to be helpful?[6] This issue occurs within the family all the time, between friends, between parents and children, teachers and students and is, therefore, a generic human process that needs to be learned by all of us. The ability to do this kind of individual coaching/consulting should be part of any adult's repertory of skills. The basic principle that governs this process is to establish a relationship first through process consultation and only when the client's needs are clear shift to an expert or diagnostic role.

Who Is Being Coached?

How the coaching/consulting relationship evolves will depend on the rank and organizational position of the person being coached. Sociologically, the higher a person's status, the more sacred he or she is as a social object, and the more care the person must take in maintaining appearances. If coaching the CEO or a high-ranking executive, the coach must be able to be in a peer or even superior relationship or the client may simply not listen or may even be offended by the idea of engaging in the relationship. Given the potential sensitivities of high-ranking executives, it becomes especially important for the coaching to begin in the process mode to ensure that a helping relationship is built before any guidance, advice, or prescriptions are offered.

If the coach is clearly superior in rank or status, a different dynamic will be active—the client may actively seek and expect expert advice. The risk in giving it is that it will not fit the personality or total situation of the client and will therefore be ignored or unconsciously subverted. The subordinate cannot really say to the higher ranking or higher status coach that she does not understand or agree with what is offered, or that she has already tried that and it did not work, and so on. So even though the temptation to become the instant expert coach is tremendous in this situation, it must be sternly resisted. The coach, to be effective, must engage in open-ended inquiry to establish an equilibrated helping relationship before he or she can determine what kind of help is needed.

If the coach is a status peer, there still remains the problem that the client may feel "one down" for having a problem, for having been singled out for coaching. In Western cultures it is not OK to need help; it implies some lack, some inability to help oneself, to solve one's own problems. Here too the helper coach must build the relationship first, especially if the coaching involves fairly face-threatening personal issues.

In What Role Is the Client Being Coached?

The key distinction here is whether the client is dealing with a problem that is personal or is seeking help in his or her role as an executive. A personal issue might be how to learn some new skills, such as becoming computer competent or developing a more strategic outlook in order to be promotable to a higher level; an organizational issue might be how to learn to manage the executive team better in order to improve the organization's strategy process, how to learn to think more like a marketer, because the future of the organization lies in better marketing, or how to learn the new computerized budgeting and accounting system on which the future of the organization depends.

If the person is in an individual development role, the same ideas apply as those mentioned above. A helping relationship must be built first, and then the coaching can proceed as appropriate. If the person is in an organizational role, the issue is more complex because the client is now the organization, not just the individual being coached. Suppose, for example, that the CEO wants to be coached on how to get more out of his team, how to get them to compete more for his job, and how to drive their own subordinates harder. How does the coach/consultant decide whether this is an appropriate goal, given that it might hurt others lower down in the organization? How does the coach/consultant deal with the situation if she feels that this would be the wrong strategy for the organization to pursue? If the coach is outside the organization, he can walk away from such conflicts, but if he is part of an internal staff or HR organization he cannot. It is at points such as these that coaching and consulting part ways. As a coach the person might have to go along with what the client wants and become a trainer/indoctrinator; as a consultant, even as an internal consultant, he must consider the needs of the larger client system and, if necessary, challenge the CEO's goals.

One might suppose that a similar issue can come up with personal coaching in that the coach might disagree with the learning goals that the client articulates. The goals can then be negotiated between client and coach. However, if those goals have been set by others in the organization, then the coach is bound to them even if the client is not. That is again the indoctrination or "coercive persuasion" scenario in which many coaches de facto find themselves. As a consultant, the helper can "push back," but as a coach the implication is that the organization decides what is needed and the coach's job is to help individuals get there.

What Is the Actual Goal of the Coaching?

Coaching as training or indoctrination covers everything from helping people to learn a new computer system to helping people broaden their whole outlook on what the company is doing. Our most familiar version is, of course, athletics, where the coach helps a person to improve his golf or tennis stroke by observing, diagnosing, providing feedback, demonstrating, and setting training routines and targets. The goal is chosen by the client, but the coach functions as an expert and trainer, often being quite coercive in that process. Such coaching can also involve broader goals, as in the previously cited case of having a coach go over the results of a 360-degree feedback process with the client who has been assessed. In a case that Flaherty cites throughout his book, the goal is how to broaden an executive's outlook so that he can become promotable to a higher level in his company.[7]

My own assumption is that, for any of these goals, from the most concrete skill development to the most abstract reshaping of basic mental models, one will not succeed without establishing a *helping relationship* first. This is relatively obvious in the more abstract personal arenas, but it is often overlooked in skill development coaching. I notice, especially in coaching people on the use of computers, that the coach quickly falls into the expert or doctor mode and "instructs" without any sensitivity to the problems the learner is experiencing. No such coach has ever asked me what my problems were in dealing with the computer or what my learning style is. We jump in with instructions and I find myself struggling, resisting, and not learning.

On the organizational side, this distinction has an important counterpart. Are we talking about coaching on mission, strategy, and goals, or are we talking about coaching on the means, measurement, and remedial processes the organization uses to accomplish its goals?[8] I think coaches are much more sensitive to the needs of the client in the mission and goals area because those are more abstract. When it comes to coaching on the means and processes, coaches quickly become "trainers" and forget to build helping relationships. This tendency to become experts may account for the poor implementation of many programs, such as new computer systems, reengineering, quality circles, total quality programs, and 360-degree feedback programs. If the learners are not involved in designing their own learning and if they do not have a relationship with the coach in which they are comfortable, they will not learn to the level that the organization expects and needs. To avoid this, coaches must become skilled process consultants as well.

Conclusion

Coaching is a subset of consultation. If coaching is to be successful, the coach must be able, like a consultant, to create a helping relationship with his or her client. To create such a helping relationship, it is necessary to start in a process mode, which involves the learner/client, which identifies what the real problems are that need to be worked on, and which builds a team where both the coach and the client take responsibility for outcomes. How the coaching relationship develops then varies according to who initiated the process, the status differential between coach and client, whether the client is working on an individual or organization problem, and whether the content of the coaching concerns organizational mission and goals or organizational process and means. In each of these situations, the coach should have the ability to move easily between the roles of process consultant, content expert, and diagnostician/prescriber. The ultimate skill of the coach, then, is to assess the moment-to-moment reality that will enable him or her to be in the appropriate role.

Paradoxically, indoctrination and coercive persuasion do not work when the target person or group does not have a relationship with the coach, but can work very well if such a relationship has been created by involving the learner at least in the process of learning. Whether or not one wants to call this process "coaching" depends on how broadly one defines coaching. What one calls it matters less, however, than understanding the psychological and social dimensions of the different kinds of relationships that can exist between a coach and a client.

Edgar H. Schein is Sloan Fellows Professor of Management Emeritus and continues at the Sloan School part-time as a senior lecturer. He is also the founding editor of "Reflections," the *Journal of the Society for Organizational Learning*, which is devoted to connecting academics, consultants, and practitioners around the issues of knowledge creation, dissemination, and utilization.

Professor Schein has been a prolific researcher, writer, teacher, and consultant. Besides his numerous articles in professional journals, he has authored fourteen books, including *Organizational Psychology, Career Dynamics, Organizational Culture and Leadership, and Process Consultation Vol. 1 and Vol. 2, Process Consultation Revisited,* and *The Corporate Culture Survival Guide.* He wrote a cultural analysis of the Singapore Economic Development Board entitled *Strategic Pragmatism* and has published an extended case analysis of the rise and fall of Digital Equipment Corporation entitled *DEC Is Dead; Long Live DEC: The Lasting Legacy of Digital Equipment Corporation.* He was coeditor with the late Richard Beckhard of the Addison-Wesley Series on Organization Development, which has published over thirty titles since its inception in 1969.

Professor Schein's consultation focuses on organizational culture, organization development, process consultation, and career dynamics, and among his past and current clients are major corporations both in the United States and overseas.

CHAPTER FIVE

DEMYSTIFYING THE COACHING MYSTIQUE

By Dave Ulrich and Jessica K. Johnson

Any good leader wants to get better. To improve, leaders have attended seminars, read books, shadowed colleagues, received formal (and informal) feedback, and taken on new assignments. In recent years, coaching has been the rage. So much so that it has almost become all things to all people. Coaches have ranged from being trained professionals to executives between jobs. As coaching broadens both in content (what is being coached) and process (who is doing the coaching), it becomes more difficult to help executives improve through coaching. In the complex landscape of coaching, executives have a more difficult time answering the questions: What can I expect from my coaching experience? Who do I turn to as my coach?

We want to answer both questions by starting with a simple typology of what they can expect from coaching and then discuss five coach archetypes that executives can select for coaching.

What Can I Expect from My Coaching Experience?

We suggest that there are two general coaching foci: behavior change and strategy realization (see Figure 5.1).[1] Behavior change means that the executive being coached has behavioral predispositions that get in the way of being an effective executive. Strategy realization means that the executive being coached needs help to clarify and focus the business strategy to help the business achieve financial, customer, or organizational goals. These two dimensions lead to four outcomes of coaching.

FIGURE 5.1. COACHING OUTCOMES

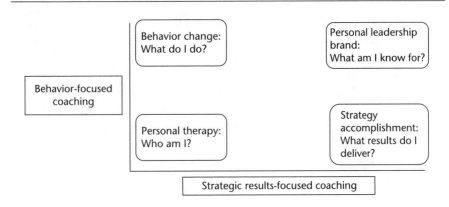

Behavior-Focused Coaching

Changing behavior is not easy. We know from research that about 50 percent of an individual's values, attitudes, and behaviors come from DNA and heritage; the other 50 percent are learned over time.[2] This split means that while we each have predispositions, we can also learn new behaviors. We also know that about 90 percent of how we behave comes from habits (either from our heritage or learned over time) and that these habits are very difficult to change.[3] When working to help leaders change behaviors, it is helpful for them to recognize their predispositions, but understand that they are not bound by them. When specific behaviors are identified, examined, and modified, coaches help executives change. The past sets conditions on our behavior, but our behavior is not preconditioned.

Strategic Results–Focused Coaching

Strategic results coaching focuses more on helping the executive gain clarity about the results he or she hopes to accomplish and how to make them happen. It is less psychological and more organizational. Strategy coaching starts with clarity about desired goals, then reviews how the coachee can spend time with key people and accomplish tasks to reach those goals.

Personal Leader Brand Coaching

Every leader has an identity, a reputation, or what we call a *leader brand*.[4] The leader brand is a combination of both behavior and results. Behavioral coaching helps a leader recognize and develop his or her style and results coaching helps the leader focus on and deliver desired results. The combination of the two results is a personal leader brand. A personal leader brand is an individual's identity, reputation, or distinctiveness as a leader; it identifies strengths and predispositions and includes provisions to mitigate the effects of weaknesses. This personal identity becomes a reputation that others respond to and reinforce. Mature executives realize that over time people will tend to forget some of the things leaders do (initiatives completed, speeches given, goals set and accomplished), but they will remember the combination of these acts and the personal style that leaders demonstrate.

Therapy-Focused Coaching

Often, coaching scratches the surface of deeper psychological and emotional issues. Professionally trained therapists will, at times, moonlight (or even masquerade) as coaches to avoid the apparent executive stigma against seeking out professional psychotherapy. At times, coaches open emotional wounds that require more intense therapeutic work. Historical relationships with parents, emotional trauma, and early childhood experiences may cause leaders to act in ways they don't fully understand. In these cases, coaches who either are, or refer to, trained therapists can help redefine cognitive patterns.

Executives who enter into coaching should be clear about what they hope to gain from the coaching experience. Are they interested in behavior change? Strategic results? A personal leader brand? Psychological discovery and healing? Each outcome requires different levels and types of executive commitment. And each can be facilitated by selecting the right coach.

To Whom Can I Turn for My Coaching?

We have identified five coaching archetypes. Each coach archetype represents an individual or type of individual where a leader can turn for coaching (see Figure 5.2):

1. *Self-coaching.* By being self-aware, leaders can change their behaviors and improve their performance.
2. *Peer coaching inside the organization.* Leaders can find allies or friends inside their organization who can advise and guide them.
3. *Peer coaching outside the organization.* Leaders may join social networks of like-minded professionals outside their organization to help them.

FIGURE 5.2. COACHING ARCHETYPES

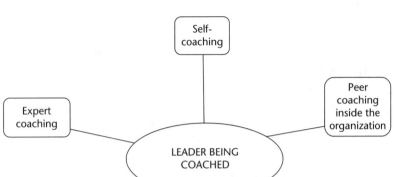

4. *Boss coaching.* A leader's direct supervisor may coach behavior and results change.

5. *Expert coaching.* A leader may turn to an expert coach who has credentials and experience to inform behavior and improve results.

We find this typology enormously helpful when we advise leaders on how to become better by selecting the coach type that works best for them. Each coaching archetype has strengths and weaknesses and may be more or less able to accomplish one of the four outcomes of coaching. These coaching types are not mutually exclusive, but can work in tandem to achieve desired outcomes.

1. Self-Coaching

In some ways, we know ourselves better than anyone else and can employ the most effective form of incentive—internal motivation. Self-coaching occurs when we self-monitor and recognize how our intentions are not aligned with our actions. At some level, self-coaching is the most ideal and efficient. If and when leaders recognize their predispositions and act on them, they are more likely to make change stick. Dave knows, for example, that he is predisposed to being an introvert. So when he teaches or gives talks, he knows he has to overcome this tendency and engage the group in conversation. Jessica knows she mentally sets expectations for herself and others. She's learned through reflection that if she doesn't recognize and communicate those expectations, others have an impossible time meeting them.

Leaders who self-coach need to be very aware of their personal predispositions and how they come across to others. We advise leaders to be mindful and "have their heads on a swivel" to see how others are responding to them. Self-coaching takes time. Leaders need to carve out space to reflect on what worked and what did not work. Ego should not be invested in what they have done or who they are, and they need to be willing to publicly acknowledge that they are changing. Leaders should solicit and listen to feedback without being defensive and employ self-discipline to change.

One leader we worked with had received some feedback that he had a tendency to let his frustrations out often and it was affecting the morale of his employees. He decided he wanted to work on the issue and examined the triggers that set him off, went public with his employees and talked about those triggers, and asked for their help as he worked to keep his frustrations in check. He now reports a much happier workplace environment and less personal stress.

Self-coaching may be more attuned to delivering results than changing behaviors. Results are more visible and public while behaviors are more private and personal. Self-coaching leaders may be able to dig into why results did or did not occur more easily than figuring out how their behaviors help or hinder a result.

However, self-monitoring is as dangerous as doctors who self-medicate. We often judge ourselves by our intentions and others judge us by our actions. An executive we coached wanted to make sure that the team made the best possible decisions. He often intervened in team decision making—advocating his recommended decision. His intent was to improve decisions, but his team members saw this as intrusive and autocratic. They withdrew and became passive observers. He was not mindful regarding how his intentions were seen by others. Marshall Goldsmith has found that 80 percent of the people rate themselves in the top 20 percent of performance because they are judging their intentions not outcomes.

2. Peer Coaching Inside the Organization

In almost every training program, one of the introductory comments is to turn off all cell phones. We have found remarkable success at the end of a training program when we ask participants to take out their cell phones and to e-mail or text a friend something that they have learned and something that they will do.

Most participants send notes to peers inside the organization whom they trust. These peers become coaches, either formally or informally, as they help leaders make change happen.

Leaders who use peer coaching often have a friend at work who cares for them. As a friend, this peer observes the behaviors of the leader and knows his or her intentions. In informal and casual settings, the peer coach can help the leader change behaviors and better deliver results. Leaders who take the personal risk of asking their work allies how they are doing will quickly learn if a friend can also be a coach. Friends who do not give honest feedback—even when asked—may stay friends, but they are not peer coaches. Smart leaders seek out insightful peers who are willing to be coaches. One leader intentionally sought out allies on her team and throughout the organization who would privately let her know how she was doing. These allies were peer coaches and an invaluable source of insight on her leadership style.

Peer coaches need not always be in the same line of business within an organization. We've seen much success when leaders from different business units of the same firm get together on a regular basis to discuss areas they're working to improve, and issues they're grappling with. The same types of issues arise around the organization, and hearing a different perspective on possible solutions and proven practices can be instructive.

Relying only on peers has limitations as peers may not see the whole picture, nor may they have a deep understanding of the leader's motives and expectations. Friends as peers may also not be as objective as they could be—not wanting to cross the line between friendship and coaching.

3. Peer Coaching Outside the Organization

Social networking has changed how strangers connect to each other. A fascinating movement exists today where older adults who want to stay in their own homes join a village network organization that connects them to others in similar circumstances. About a hundred of these "villages" exist in the United States and are growing rapidly; in these villages, independent people pay a fee to join, and then serve each other. Former strangers connect with each other:[5]

- Ferni, 25, an options trader, provides computer coaching to Susan, 73, a retired family nurse.
- Bud, 89, a retired executive, helps Bob, 66, a retired attorney, develop a preschool volunteer program.
- Susan, 32, helps Carole, 68, a retired college administrator, organize her files in her new apartment.

If social networking can help retired individuals learn and grow, it can also help leaders.

We have identified four types of networks where people come together to improve. In each of these networks, leaders can connect with those outside their organization to gain insight and become better:

1. *Relationship networks:* who we go to when we want to have fun. The Gallup organization has argued that we need to have a best friend at work. We would argue that it is equally if not more important for leaders to have a best friend (outside the family) NOT at work and who does not really tie the relationship to the work setting.

2. *Knowledge networks:* who we go to when we need information. Leaders can be encouraged to join professional associations, to create cohort groups of peers, and to attend conferences to meet and associate with peers who have ideas to solve problems.

3. *Trust networks:* who we go to with personal or confidential information. Leaders may find trusted advisors in neighborhoods, religious associations, social groups, longtime friends, or extended family to whom they turn for personal questions and insights.

4. *Purpose networks:* who we go to when we need to accomplish a task. Leaders may get insights from consultants, advisors, former faculty, or other experts about projects they need to accomplish.

Depending on the network, these peers outside of work offer insights on both behavior and strategic change. There are a lot of tools to help build your network online, but remember that they alone are not your network. Whether online or in person, all networks must be nurtured.

Peers outside the organization may offer candid insights, because they are not in a position to harm the friendship, but they may also lack the emotional sensitivity required for sustained change. The research on relationships suggests we need close friends (called *tight ties*) who emotionally support us and more casual friends (called *loose ties*) who give us innovative and fresh approaches to problems. Leaders who invest in relationship, knowledge, trust, and purpose networks develop the loose ties that help them succeed.

4. Boss Coaching

In one organization, the senior executive squashed the coaching budget, because she felt that the leader's immediate boss was the most important coach and she did not want anything to detract from that relationship. In many ways, she is right.

Leaders who coach and communicate rather than command and control have enormous opportunities for impact. In other ways, she is wrong. When we coach individuals, they need to be able to explore a range of issues—some of which may include their relationship with their boss, their future with the company, and other personal issues that will not likely be discussed in boss coaching.

Bosses who coach need to develop not only a mindset but a set of skills to coach. Instead of demanding results, they learn to ask thoughtful questions and listen to understand. We have encouraged bosses who coach to master the questions shown in Table 5.1

Bosses who can ask questions more than give answers, who seek to understand before giving direction, and who work to build trust before taking action can become excellent coaches.

However, bosses as coaches also have limitations. The Lominger group found that of the sixty-seven key skills for business leaders, "coaching" is toward the bottom.[6]

Many bosses rose to their positions of influence not by coaching but by doing. The derailment that many of them face is that although they are competent, they are not able to multiply that competence in others. Leaders wanting to improve can and should rely on their boss not only for performance reviews, but also for career counseling where the boss can point the leader in a positive direction.

TABLE 5.1: COACHING QUESTIONS FOR BOSSES

Principles of Coaching	Coaching Questions Bosses Should Be Asking
Build relationship of trust	How can I be helpful? What would you like from this conversation? Help me understand . . .
Describe current performance	What are the results you are after? How well do you think you have done? Why? What led you to this current result? What do you do that helps or hinders reaching your goal?
Articulate desired results	What would you like to accomplish? How do you feel about the outcome you are after? How will you know when you have succeeded?
Build action plan for change	What are the alternative actions you can take to reach your goal? What are pros and cons of each? What are the first steps you need to take? What can I do to help you be successful? How will you learn from things that don't go well? To whom will you be accountable for progress?

5. Expert Coaching

Expert coaching may take a variety of forms. The expert may be inside the company as a trained coach who can work with someone generally not in the same department or function. The expert may be a licensed psychologist who may help a leader explore some of the more emotional issues underlying his or her behavior. Most often, the coaching expert has training in personal and organization change, has experience with multiple executives in multiple companies, and can tailor and bring to bear their previous experiences to the leader being coached. Coaching certifications, like all certifications, ensure that the coach has basic knowledge, not that the coach can be successful. For example, an attorney, architect, or psychologist who is licensed has certified that they know the basics of their profession, but the license does not mean that they can practice well.

Experts with face validity need to be selected for the individuals being coached. Leaders being coached need to have personal and professional chemistry with the expert, and need to be willing to share personal issues that may be difficult to share with those inside the company. Leaders need to be willing to face reality and commit to making changes.

Expert coaches may help leaders make both behavior and results changes. They may explore candid and, at times, brutal information about the leader's behavior and performance. They may make suggestions about how to improve and challenge the status quo. They may also help the leader create a personal leadership brand by combining behavior and results into a leadership identity. One senior leader we coached said that he enjoyed our sessions because, "When you come into my office, I am your primary agenda. Everyone else who sees me has an agenda of what they want to get from me, either explicitly or implicitly. Your agenda is giving to me." Experts give leaders coaching help when their insights turn into actions.

However, expert coaches also have limitations. They do not live inside the organization and see the day-to-day operations. They may be used as sounding boards without real accountability for action. As expert coaches, we have found it most useful to meet with the leader's HR head before and after the coaching session. The HR head can alert us to current political issues in the organization and on the leader's mind before the coaching session. After the session, while maintaining confidentiality, the leader's HR head may ensure that the follow-up is institutionalized and sustained.

Conclusion

Increasingly, coaching is a valued part of leaders wanting to improve. But, when it is nebulous—both in terms of content (what we accomplish) and process (who is the coach)—it is superficial window dressing, not sustainable leadership. We encourage leaders who desire the assistance of a coach to be clear about what they want from the coaching experience and who they want to help them as coaches.

Dave Ulrich is a professor at the Ross School of Business, University of Michigan, and a partner at the RBL Group, a consulting firm focused on helping organizations and leaders deliver value. He studies how organizations build capabilities of leadership, speed, learning, accountability, and talent through leveraging human resources. He has helped generate award-winning databases that assess alignment between strategies, organization capabilities, HR practices, HR competencies, and customer and investor results.

Jessica K. Johnson is a principal consultant at The RBL Group. Prior to joining RBL, Jessica worked with Cisco where she created Cisco's first global results-based strategy for their external events. Prior to that she worked at the McLean, Virginia–based consulting firm BearingPoint. While there she managed the operations for BearingPoint's Global Delivery Centers in India and China. She started her consulting career working on a variety of federal client projects.

PART II

PORTRAIT OF A LEADER

What do leaders look like? What do they do? What is expected of a leader of the future? The articles in **Part II, Portrait of a Leader,** answer these questions as well as some that in the days of management past were not even a consideration. Laurence S. Lyons opens this section with his piece, "The Accomplished Leader." An important work, this article not only gives invaluable insight into executive coaching and its value in organizations, it is also the precursor in content and style to the "management novelette," which is *Dr. Fink's Leadership Casebook.* In Chapter Seven, "Writing for Leadership: Penning Your Leadership Voice," Sarah McArthur takes a complex and vast subject and distills it down to its very essence. In her article, Sarah provides a road map for both novice and experienced writers on how to start (or continue) their respective treatises on leadership. Nathan Lyons, a young high-potential leader himself, has written a description of what it is to be a high-potential forging a path to "success" in today's trying times in Chapter Eight, "Seeking Value in a Shattered World of Work." John Baldoni believes that leaders have "earned authority" and that they also possess qualities that allow them to empathize and relate to their employees. Read John's article "The Right Stuff of Leadership" and find out where you stand. Richard J. Leider, a huge proponent of what he calls "the power of purpose," both in leadership and in life, makes the case that purpose is "connected to caring, and caring is essential to engagement." Providing a relatively unusual checkup list for readers of his chapter, "The Purposeful Leader," Richard's expressed view on the pursuit and accomplishment is refreshing and profound. Rounding out this section on the portrayal of leaders and leadership today is the classic article, "When Leaders Are Coaches," by James M. Kouzes and Barry Z. Posner. In this foundational article, Jim and Barry define leadership as a relationship.

CHAPTER SIX

THE ACCOMPLISHED LEADER[1]

By Laurence S. Lyons

Personal success merely brings achievement. Helping others succeed confers genuine accomplishment. Passion for "success through others"—the common aspiration of the consultant, counselor, and coach—is a source of synergy and a hallmark of leadership.

Only an accomplished leader leaves a social legacy. Having "made his mark" on the organization, he leaves behind talented people who will in turn make their mark into the future. For this to come about, the accomplished leader will have made time to pass on learning to others.

This idea was taught by Dick Beckhard whose motto—"we have a duty to pass on our learning"—was a deep source of inspiration for this book. The practice of leadership coaching has much to offer the person being coached. Inescapably, it offers the coach an opportunity to become accomplished as a leader.

A leader becomes complete only after giving something back.

The Sheraton Hotel at Brussels airport is a short walk from the terminal building, making it a popular meeting place for the affluent traveler. Those adventurous enough to explore beyond the spacious restaurant level will find a secluded café frequented by the business jet-set. Chuck, a dapper fifty-something, confidently saunters in, immediately searching out a quiet corner. The plush atmosphere evokes a feeling of opulence and a sense of power. This is the life.

Chuck has arrived early, so finds time to reflect. Surely twenty-five years' experience in the corporate world amply qualifies him for this imminent encounter.

---

[1] Laurence S. Lyons © 2005.

Chuck has worked in small businesses and in huge corporations. He was once a line manager responsible for a department of six-hundred people. He has done major tours of duty in operations, finance, and customer service. In one posting, Chuck served as a deputy regional manager. Chuck has experienced the thrills and spills of mergers from both sides. Chuck has lived the corporate life, and Chuck has survived.

In his time, Chuck has come across many difficult situations and plenty of challenging people, each providing some new learning experience. An alumnus of the "hard knocks" school of management, he has acquired a sharp taste for reality. Chuck knows how much damage is done daily by organizational politics and mindless rules. He has seen great ideas get quashed, and underspent budgets wastefully squandered at year-end. Chuck is mature now, and has learned how to play the corporate game. Chuck understands—and often correctly predicts—organizational outcomes that are completely counterintuitive to the man in the street. Chuck speaks the language of management. Chuck is able to think as a leader. Chuck has much to offer; today he is ready to give something back, to pass on his learning.

Remembering that this will be his very first face-to-face meeting in his new role as an independent business coach, he opens his briefcase and again reads his notes. . .

Soon, Chuck is to meet Susan, a fast-track executive currently running the marketing department at a blue chip. In her early thirties, Susan has ambitions to work in public relations before moving to some more senior position, maybe one day to join the board. In their phone conversation last week, Susan told Chuck that she does not get on well with her boss and has recently been passed by for promotion. Susan suspects she is hitting a "glass ceiling." Susan directs the work of fourteen marketing communications and program people, and seems to have only a vague idea about the work or personality of her peers.

A careful observer sitting in the lobby might notice Chuck lightly biting his bottom lip while contorting his eyebrows. He is now deep in thought: *How do I start to make sense of Susan's story? What do I really know about marketing or glass ceilings? What should we talk about? Where should I take this? What good can I do?* And, more acutely: *What damage might I do?* As Chuck ponders these grave matters, he realizes that deep down he is just a tiny bit worried.

We'll leave Chuck in suspended animation, anticipating Susan's arrival at the hotel. *Painting by numbers* won't effectively guide their conversation because Chuck does not know what gambit Susan might bring. Chuck's strength lies in his ability to be responsive to Susan, to follow the needs of his client. To help him in this, Chuck needs general orientation, not specific advice. How should Chuck define the area of his work? How should he deal with his own lack of familiarity with some of Susan's situations? How can Chuck play to his strengths? He does not realize it yet, but Chuck is in great shape. What he badly needs right now is a good theory.

A Clear Focus on Coaching

Now would make an excellent time for Chuck to focus his thoughts on what he is meant to be doing. In the conversation yet to take place, Chuck will follow Susan into many and varied topics. As coach, Chuck will at times touch on career planning; he may borrow techniques from personal counseling; he will sometimes process-consult. He will always bring his own experience and knowledge into the room. Yet at all times it is *executive coaching* that must remain at the forefront of his efforts. A commitment to *coaching* places Chuck's work squarely within a learning context. The client is always an *executive*, so Chuck works exclusively within an organizational setting.

Executive coaching is about helping clients gain benefit from learning in an organizational setting. Ranging from the development of general personal skills, to helping Susan figure her way out of a tight corner, all that Chuck does as coach is in pursuit of that end. Chuck's impact will be determined by his ability to transform organizational situations into realistic learning challenges matching the immediate needs of his client. Supremely important, *How the client now thinks* and *How the client might think differently* will be key components of that project.

Requisite Variety

Different people prefer different learning styles. This makes it extremely important for Chuck to offer Susan a choice of learning approach. As manager, Chuck himself may be able to get easily from *A* to *C* via *B*. As coach, his task is not to escort Susan to *his* intermediate comfort point *B*; rather he should help Susan find her own path to *C*. Or, indeed, find an even better destination.

At work here is the systems concept of *equifinality* permitting a variety of personal styles, any of which may be applied to a given situation, to meet the same learning or business objective. Such choice is vital to ensure that each and every step in Susan's learning program respects her personal values. It is only freedom of choice that allows Susan to remain true to herself. She must never feel that her quest to become a leader is forcing her to mimic a style that is distasteful to her, or make her adopt noxious behavior that she would recoil from seeing in others. Her ability to design her own authentic "Susan" style will bolster Susan's feeling of comfort with herself and with her coaching program. She may at times test an unfamiliar tactic; while doing so she must never be asked to compromise her integrity of action.

At the root of designing such a learning strategy lies the coach's ability to deeply understand "the organization," how it works, and the different ways in which a client may survive, win, and prosper within it. Fortunately, this is an area where Chuck can claim to be something of an expert. Good coaches do more than point out an executive's faults. They best help their clients by encouraging them to play to strengths. It is no different for Chuck, one of whose strengths is his expert understanding of *organizational dynamics* absorbed from his exposure to the corporate world. This is a skill he must leverage when making the transition from manager to executive coach.

Thinking Like a Theorist

An effective manager-turned-coach thinks like a theorist; acts like a researcher; never gives advice.

Theory can be that dry stuff found in textbooks. Alternatively a good theory inspires and stimulates action. Theory is capable of doing many useful things. It helps focus our attention on what is important when it encapsulates useful ways we have found in which to view our world. Theory can help get us quickly to the point. Theory helps us discover hidden connections; it helps us remember what we might otherwise forget. Theory may be the only thing we can cling to when we have little reliable data at hand. For coaches, who are behavioral practitioners in an imperfect world, a good theory is simply shorthand for good practice.

Theory truly comes alive when it helps practitioners tackle practical problems. While waiting for Susan in the freeze-frame action at the hotel, it is this more vibrant type of theory that Chuck definitely needs. Chuck may believe he is simply looking for some tested theory to help guide him along his new coaching path. Theories and models abound; simply collecting them is largely a sterile activity. Chuck adds value only when he helps his client. He will only start to do that and make real progress as a coach when he comes to understand that in his new job he has *become* a theorist. A theorist is someone who admits to not knowing and who is prepared to begin by making an informed guess as to cause and effect in a problem situation.

Learning by Theory

There are many parallels between Chuck's work and that of a scientist. Both pick up the theorist's work and conduct experiments in the real world from which learning results.

As a coach, Chuck must be clear about his role and know the boundaries of his work. He must be able to crystallize what he already knows and have the ability to transfer his insight. His deliverable will always be a learning opportunity. Of course, this is far from saying that Chuck will always have the right answers. Chuck's perspective on a situation will never constitute more than a candidate hypothesis which may have to share the stage with several competitors. As always, the client must herself select between approaches and choose an appropriate way to learn. The best Chuck can hope to do is question and inform Susan based on his experience.

Chuck is concerned that some of Susan's presenting issues seem to be outside his immediate experience. For one thing, he has never personally encountered a glass ceiling. The good news for Chuck in his conversations with Susan is that although he may come across subject matter with which he is totally unfamiliar, as a former manager he is well qualified to analyze what counts—the patterns of situations and relationships he is likely to find. Even better news for Chuck is that as he is now a coach not a manager, his role is all about learning systems: this positively prohibits him from giving any content advice. Shifting a gear into the theoretical level is just what Chuck needs to help keep him honest.

Chuck knows that very soon he will hear Susan's story. He is preparing himself to draw out and organize Susan's ideas. He considers for a moment the far-ranging scope that this conversation will likely have. During today's little chat, Chuck must expect to exert considerable influence over the lives of Susan, those close to her, and others in and around the organization for which she works.

Chuck feels it important to shed any prejudices and false assumptions that may be in play—in his own mind, as well as in Susan's. He feels a deep sense of listener responsibility and realizes that he will need to discipline himself in the way he chooses to receive Susan's story. Chuck does not want to contaminate or judge that story. He will succeed by assuming a research style, or, in more familiar management terms—by conducting a friendly audit. Today, Chuck will say little, and instead concentrate his efforts on building rapport while simply *listening to the music.*

Susan's Story

Susan has proven herself to be an exceptional marketing professional. Susan has the experience of growing and leading an excellent team. She has reached a career stage where perceptions of her by peers in other functions have become critical to her advancement in the company. To be credible at her present level, it is important for Susan to express herself in terms of broader business ideas.

To remain strong, Susan must demonstrate that she can think strategically and orchestrate the political dimensions of her role.

Susan's regional boss wants to combine the marketing and public relations departments locally, and can see economies in doing so. But Susan works in a matrix organization in which her marketing boss wants to keep these functions separate. His logic for this is that PR audiences and market sectors need very different handling, different skill sets, and different kinds of people to engage them. It also happens to be the case that the alternative would mean a smaller marketing empire.

Susan remains loyal to both camps and therefore has pursued only timid policies that are controversial to neither manager. This has caused her some personal frustration. For as long as this issue remains unresolved, it also harms the business. While Susan treads water, the business remains suboptimal: resources are duplicated; motivation stays low; productivity inevitably suffers. For as long as such ambiguity in her position persists, Susan's long-term future as a leader is at risk.

The political situation causing this stress is a form of organizational madness, even though it is constructed solely out of rational positions taken by interested parties. Susan needs to succeed in the face of and despite this madness. As is often the case, many of the tools she needs are closer at hand than she realizes. Susan needs to become more politically astute, to play to her strengths, and capitalize on her proven knowledge of marketing. She needs a coach to help her see how easily she could apply her existing know-how to promote *herself* in the company—in the same way her marketing team promotes the company.

Systems Change Agent

At any time the coach may appear to be talking to one individual person but in reality he is always—in some sense—in dialogue with the entire client system. Shortly, Susan will tell Chuck about her situation. We do not yet know what they will say. But we know it is likely that, as a result, Susan will be doing some things differently tomorrow. Susan may ask her bosses new questions; she may try out new responses in familiar situations; she may even create totally new situations in which to initiate new dialogue. Susan may start to investigate the feasibility of integrating two departments by floating a few probing questions.

Today's conversation is going to extend far beyond the hotel walls. Its ripples will be felt by Susan's bosses and others. With thoughtful preparation and presentation, Susan has an opportunity to impress her peers and inspire her direct reports along the way, as she makes progress in learning how to address the structural dilemma she faces.

Chuck will speak to Susan yet engage her whole organization. And Chuck will do even more than that. He will influence Susan's career beyond this corporation. He will expand the skills Susan employs in her personal life too. Chuck has become an agent of change in a set of complex systems, and he carries a heavy burden of responsibility.

Theoretical Foundations

Thinking in a Corporate Setting

The most basic concept in executive coaching is how a person thinks in a corporate setting. It is the degree to which this concept is developed by the coach that makes any coaching intervention impactful. A good theory distinguishes itself by offering a working model that captures a sufficiently rich corporate description for the job at hand.

Depending on circumstances, Chuck or Susan might use this model in different ways. Chuck reflects on his own thought processes to better understand how he thinks as a manager; in this case Chuck becomes the model's subject. In another application, Chuck employs this model with Susan as the subject, the aim here to unravel Susan's thinking toward the supposed glass ceiling. Then again, in their conversation the pair considers how Susan's work colleagues regard Susan, now placing her managers, direct reports, peers, or customers under the lens at the center of the model. Chuck and Susan have the option to collect *feedback*, to populate their current model with data, to ignite a more public learning process. When a coach is present, some model for *thinking in a corporate setting* is at work whether we are aware of it or not.

No single discipline holds a monopoly on thinking about thinking. Sharing our common interest in the topic of thinking, psychology and philosophy each has something to offer for coaching theory. Both contribute insights to help us understand *how the client thinks*. These contributions only become valuable to executive coaching clients, however, when they are set in a management context that directs practical action toward business results. It is primarily the job of the coach to help the client translate insight into action within their specific corporate setting.

We might observe that a certain executive thinks fast. Indeed, this may be very important where the objectives of coaching are purely behavioral: there is a potential danger that colleagues who think at only the normal rate may get left behind. This situation is grist for the mill for the middle-manager behavioral coach who may suggest trying out new techniques for "bringing the audience along."

Thinking Deeply

At senior levels in the organization the application of coaching tends to shift focus into the strategic and political arenas. Here, these same words *how the client thinks* should be understood to extend their meaning to include whatever rational, social, attitudinal, emotional, interest-centered, planning, goal-directed, or any other aspects of *thinking* may be relevant so that useful coaching work can get done.

Suppose Susan tells Chuck she has "engaged" participants in her new marketing project by writing them a memo. Chuck has seen this memo and agrees it contains logical, impressive, compelling, and elegant arguments, the correctness of which seems indisputable. Susan is surprised that none of the recipients has taken any notice whatsoever.

The problem here is that Susan thinks about engagement in purely rational terms. Her *thinking* about engagement does not yet extend to recognize the importance of her personal presence or the power of an appeal to her colleague's own interests. To usefully engage she must articulate the link between her pet project and the greater good of the business; rewards to shareholders, benefits to customers, contribution toward a better life on the planet. For her, *engagement* means giving a rational explanation: this is how Susan now thinks.

The challenge for Chuck is to explore how Susan might think differently. Modeling Susan's thinking, Chuck will extend the idea of *thinking* to include any important attitudinal components in play. Susan lacks confidence in inspiring her peers. She harbors feelings of restraint when there is a need for her to stand up to her line manager. Then again, Susan may have some genuine blind spots of which she is totally unaware. She may have a phantom obstacle she needs to expunge: a glass ceiling, perhaps.

Chuck finds it useful to say that all of this has to do with how Susan "thinks" in a corporate setting. Insight into Susan's thinking provides Chuck with an essential building block for designing her learning program.

Rich Description

Sometimes we use words such as *think* to include other factors that are more commonly described by separate words. Another example is *process*, which may simply mean a mechanistic repetitive set of actions. Equally, we may use the word to denote a complete system that has knowledge of its purpose, the structure, and culture in which it operates, and even has the ability to adapt itself to change. In one sense, a whole business could be described simply as a process.

When theorists choose to extend the meaning of a word in this way, far beyond the regular face-value dictionary definition, they are using *rich description*. Rich description can open new horizons to expand the extent of a coach's impact.

For the client, too, it offers a useful choice about how to think in a given situation. If Susan were to use a rich description of the word *audiences* in her conversations with her managers, she would have at her disposal a vocabulary highly conducive to integrating the work of marketing and PR in her region.

Acting Like a Researcher

As a coach, Chuck will spend a lot of time involved in research. A researcher is someone who, when presented with a tangle of information, will first sift out what is important and then go on to formulate new questions. These research questions seek to uncover what might be important yet currently unknown. With its focus on learning in an organizational setting, the research aspect of executive coaching will often have as its objective the discovery of perspectives to assist the client's personal development. Susan benefits from finding out the extent to which her credibility as a leader will improve were she to properly engage her peers and inspire her bosses.

Chuck needs to be more than just a regular researcher; he must be forensic and meticulous when looking at evidence. In today's conversations with Susan, all data comes from a single source—Susan. Quality data will likely be scarce, especially as Susan has some blind spots. Though it may be safe for Chuck to assume Susan's reporting of her own experience is totally genuine, any data describing Susan's environment—including any perceptions held about her by work colleagues—will be largely unsubstantiated. In truth, from today's exchange alone, Chuck may have little verifiable information to work with.

Tentative Solutions

Given the high degree of risk in Chuck's raw material—reliable information—we might allow him to pause for a moment and rejoice that he has become a theorist. With a paucity of data, any coach is in real danger of making a serious mistake through incorrect inference. It is in such a situation that theory excels. Chuck's insight into real-world organizations contains exactly the theory he needs to help bridge gaps in data and make his intervention more robust. Chuck brings to the conversation a large number of theories and research questions grounded in the experience of real organizational life. Chuck uses storytelling to bring proto-type models into his conversation with Susan.

Client Learning

The research that Chuck will engage in will always be of the *pure* kind. This again keeps him at the theoretical end of his partnership with Susan, whose role is to do all the hard work. It is Susan as client who will be interacting with her work system by raising new questions with peers and bosses. After all, the learning must be experienced by Susan, not Chuck.

Reaching Out

Chuck may find he does not have access to Susan's stakeholders. Susan will periodically return to future coaching sessions with stories that relate interactions with work colleagues from which theories will get built and refined. This coaching approach can be extremely effective in highly charged political situations; when the executive is new in post and so is "unknown" to colleagues; and in other cases where supporting data cannot reasonably be collected. This does not mean that involving more people in data gathering is necessarily better. Triangulating data from multiple sources brings its own problems.

Challenge Versus Validation

Like many amateur coaches, Chuck is in danger of becoming evangelical, insisting that his client *change for the better.* Chuck zealously wants to make Susan a "better" executive, and to do this he thinks he must *challenge* her to instantly address some perceived weakness indicated by the feedback. It is possible he will feel the need to say: *"Susan, I know you think you are an excellent listener. But I have here the feedback from twelve of your direct reports who completely disagree with you. Now, should we get started on improving your listening skills?"* There are many useful techniques for achieving this, such as leaving pauses in the conversation to allow people the opportunity to seek clarification.

Chuck will not make such an elementary mistake. Chuck, who thinks like a theorist and acts like a researcher, asks: *"Susan, they say you don't listen; why might they think this?"* Susan responds that during the past six months, as well as running the marketing department in Europe, she has been representing the company in secret merger discussions, reporting directly to the CFO. These talks take place frequently, involving specialist consultants from the Big Five, together with teams of attorneys, accountants, and technical experts, all of whom take up residence across discreetly separated suites at a top Beijing hotel. The consequential volume of travel and follow-up work placed on Susan in monumental. Susan says that she is aware her team might feel alienated but insists she is not allowed to tell them why.

Instead of immediately looking for compensating behavior, a researcher first questions source and context. An expert coach will *validate* raw data. Chuck will be interested to know what was happening when Susan's feedback was being collected, and whether anything unusual might have been going on at that time. A research approach wins the day. Suggesting to Susan that she should fix her listening problem by taking long breaths between sentences would not have been helpful.

HOW CHUCK CAME ON THE SCENE

Joe is the management accountant responsible for, among other things, approving expenditure in Susan's company. A few months ago, he made his first serious mistake. Joe almost bounced Thelma's budget. Thelma is Vice President, Human Resources. Thelma is a no-nonsense executive with attitude. Joe's e-mail had asked Thelma to produce a *return on investment* justification for her coaching program. Joe reasoned that management is responsible for investing shareholders' money, and shareholders are entitled to know what they should expect in return. *Where is the bottom-line benefit?* Joe had questioned in his e-mail. The answer, *that the bottom line will be there,* was not the one he had expected, or indeed was prepared for.

Instead of replying with a curt e-mail, Thelma sensibly invited Joe to her office. Joe was prompt. As Thelma was running behind schedule that day, her personal assistant told Joe he could wait in her office, which he did.

When she eventually arrived, Thelma offered her apologies, announcing with a knowing smile that she was exactly ten minutes and twenty-two seconds late. She had unexpectedly stopped off to fit a replacement watch battery. Joe suspected that Thelma's accurate time-check was her way of making sure she was getting good value for money from her recent purchase, a quality Joe highly admires in a budget holder. Little did he know that in a very short time he would be back in his office wondering what had happened.

"You asked me to estimate the return on investment for our coaching program, so let's start there. As an investment the ROI from this program would simply be an increase in share price. In my experience, investors tend to like that. So I guess that settles *that* question. Our investor relations people tell us that share price is strongly related to analysts' confidence in the quality of management. Coaching is the method we're using here to grow our management quality and translate it into tangible business impact.

"As I remember, your standard accounting paperwork doesn't ask for the most fundamental measure of success that's relevant here—the protection and enhancement of share price. Until it does, how can I be expected to properly respond?"

Thelma beamed. Joe tried to say something, but was cut short.

"But that's not the point. By asking for ROI, you're telling me you haven't yet understood what we're dealing with here, Joe. We're not justifying our *Coaching for Leadership* program as an investment. Make no mistake, this program is an unavoidable expense; we won't safely achieve this year's plan without it. That's why your request for a return on investment figure is technically meaningless."

During the short pause that followed, Joe scribbled something on his multicolumn legal pad. To Thelma, who, admittedly was reading upside down, it seemed to resemble a cartoon character, but she could not be totally certain about that.

"Moreover, you should be aware that the relevant asset has already been acquired. It's in place right now. And this planned expenditure on it has already been implicitly justified at corporate level by the main board. Frankly, further justification seems unnecessary."

For some reason, at just that moment, Joe had unexpectedly become aware of the existence of his Adam's apple, but was unable to say why. He had so many questions; he did not know which to ask first. He did not get the chance.

"You look confused, so let me explain. The asset in question is the senior management team, our regional board. Corporate expects us to carry out a program of work, plus whatever unexpected change the world might throw at us—over the coming year. Our success in this as a business is not negotiable. Indeed, as a board we have a responsibility to do whatever is necessary to give ourselves the best chance of achieving our objectives. The coaching program resources that responsibility.

"It strengthens our bottom line by squeezing out the risk of missing it."

Joe repeated that last sentence to himself slowly inside his head. Thelma paused to give Joe time to take this in, then smiled broadly, her face now full of reasonableness. Conspiratorially, she continued:

"Look around. We have members who are new to the board, and with the recent reorganization we have people on the board who will need to work together in totally new ways this year. We also have aggressive sales targets, growth targets, and an extremely turbulent business environment which may include making a local acquisition. We are running this coaching program to make sure the people we have in place are given the best chance to be as effective as the business needs them to be in doing all this. It's simply the 'soft' part of our business plan that has already been agreed and signed-off. I am only sorry we didn't start all this earlier.

"Yes, it is true that there are some choices to be made. Of course we'll be prudent. The key to getting all this right lies in the design of our HR program which we've framed as a change initiative. We've put a lot of effort into that. Naturally only suitably qualified coaches will get anywhere near our top talent. For high potentials like Susan we've found an individual named Chuck who may fit the bill perfectly. For the senior management team, we want a heavyweight coach to work closely with the entire regional board. Given the strategic challenges and degree of change we're facing this year, we've decided to get a very experienced coach at the top end of the range. Of course, I'll copy you on the figures as soon as I have them all.

"Joe, I appreciate your taking a personal interest in this. I know that direct share price enhancement and bottom-line risk reduction may not be the typical benefits you normally recognize in our regional cost center budget. But our business has to recognize exactly that. If we've learned anything from our experience of *business process reengineering* it's that soft factors drive hard results. We have a board who strongly believes in that maxim, and in response to that, we in HR have built a robust plan to achieve those hard results today and protect our talent well into the future.

"The senior management team is a corporate asset, even though you may not see it as an accounting asset. Yet it still needs nourishment. This new approach will make us a stronger company. That's what this coaching program is really all about. This is how modern companies look at senior coaching programs.

"Well, I guess that just about covers everything. It was so good for us to talk today rather than to simply exchange paperwork. I am a great believer in cross-functional cooperation like this. Joe, I want you to know how much I value your support. Thank you so much for taking the time to see me today."

As Joe was leaving, Thelma locked his gaze, smiled, and then lovingly looked down at one of her personal assets—the diamond-studded Rolex Cellini Quartz sparkling on her wrist. "Nobody will balk about paying a fair price for a replacement battery," she said. Then, looking directly into Joe's eyes with the slightest hint of a wink: "But who'd want to propose owning an expensive watch that can't correctly tell the time?"

In an era when HR is striving to find ways to add strategic value to the business, it is leaders such as Thelma who hold out a blazing beacon to lighten up a path. And, as Joe will attest, its brilliant flame has the power to cauterize as it goes along its way.

The Hybrid Coach

We have become familiar with the consultant as an external agent of change or as someone responsible for helping managers develop the purely technical aspects of their business, such as marketing or operations. More recently, working with individuals and teams, the behavioral coach has emerged as a practitioner in the development of the social fabric of the organization. Today's executive coach is a hybrid of these prototypes and whose playground is the management of an entire socio-technical business system. As such, he or she must be adept in engaging the mesh of political-behavioral and strategic-philosophical components of the organization.

The modern corporation has awakened to realize that a business does not exist in splendid isolation. Far beyond its functions of simple economic exchange, the corporation is today regarded from those outside as having its place in society and its role in the world. Those managers who inspire coworkers by linking the immediate task at hand to their personal development and to the greater purpose of their enterprise are among the new breed of corporate leaders. And those coaches able to foster this sense of *purposeful connectedness* by inducing inspiration in the minds of leaders are truly coaching for leadership.

Back at the hotel, Susan enters the lobby. Chuck has returned the notes to his briefcase alongside his well-thumbed copy of *Practice of Leadership Coaching*. Chuck is prepared. He will succeed today and into the future. With more experience,

Chuck will go on to coach more-senior individuals; to work across an entire management team; and even to accept the hardest coaching contract of all: coaching clients across organizational levels within the same team. In that very challenging context, he will advance his capability. Chuck has the potential to one day be among those few able to offer coaching as a highly effective results-oriented conflict dissolution alternative, reaching way beyond brute confrontation and suboptimal mediation.

Chuck is focused, oriented, and ready. That's partly because Chuck is well-read in the subject of coaching. It helps a lot that Chuck brings a track record as a solid line manager. These factors go a long way in explaining how Chuck will so easily succeed in his inaugural coaching assignment. Chuck will excel, to one day become a truly great coach. For in the deep recesses of his heart and embedded within the very fabric of his approach to life, he is a leader.

In a few weeks, Susan proclaims her first success as a coaching client; she is beginning to make her mark in the organization. Only now is Chuck certain to have truly given something back: he has started to pass on his learning. Susan's breakthrough gives him an especially deep sense of achievement. He also has the feeling that something fundamental has changed. Then the awesome self-realization dawns: Chuck is an accomplished leader.

Laurence S. Lyons (www.lslyons.com) is an accomplished coach, consultant, public speaker, and author. A former technical director at Digital Equipment Corporation, he has been described as a "leading authority on business transformation" by Henley Management College, where he is a member of associate faculty and Founding Research Director of the Future Work Forum.

Dr. Lyons is regarded as a pioneer in the field of executive coaching; he has coached hundreds of senior and high-potential executives in organizations in the United States and across Europe. Many of his personal coaching clients are to be found in *Who's Who*.

Dr. Lyons holds a PhD and MSc from Brunel University and the CIM Diploma in Marketing. He is an invited member of the Leader to Leader Institute Thought Leaders Forum (formerly Drucker Foundation).

Larry Lyons is author of the companion volume *The Coaching for Leadership Case Study Workbook: Featuring Dr. Fink's Leadership Casebook*. Dr. Lyons pioneered his storytelling style in this chapter, which first appeared in *Coaching for Leadership*, second edition. Contact him at lslyons@lslyons.com.

CHAPTER SEVEN

WRITING FOR LEADERSHIP: PENNING YOUR LEADERSHIP VOICE

By Sarah McArthur

The most original thing a writer can do is write like himself. It is also his most difficult task.
—Robertson Davies (Canadian novelist, 1913–1995)

At the moment of this writing, there are 1,427,897 Business & Investing titles listed on Amazon. More than one-third of these books are in the Management & Leadership category. And yet, there are thousands more books on the subject being written at this very moment. Business runs shy of the gamut of History books (2,374,960 titles) and Literature & Fiction (2,135,181 titles), but appears to be more intriguing a subject for readers than Religion & Spirituality (with 985,484 titles). It's far more exciting to readers and possibly more engaging for writers than Arts & Photography (413,947 titles) or Entertainment (496,568 titles).[1]

What does this say about the subject of "writing for leadership"? It says that if you are one of the many, many people who want to write or are currently writing about leadership, it won't be easy to stand out—and it won't be a breeze to write from a fresh perspective. In addition, without content that reveals something new, interesting, and useful to readers that is written in a unique leadership voice, your book will be tossed aside into the massive sea of unread business books. In my experience these books often tend to end up on the authors' bookshelves, so that others will notice the title in their library. Its function is a form of intimidation. In reality, theirs is just another one of the millions of unread books ranked on Amazon with one star or less.

Where Do I Start?

The beginning is the most important part of the work.

—The Republic, Plato (Greek philosopher, 424/423 bc–348/347 bc)

First, I have to say, I feel uniquely *un*qualified to tell business leaders and coaches anything about coaching high potentials for leadership. I've never coached a leader (I've worked for them); I've never led a business (I've worked in them and run my own small editing firm). But I *have* read hundreds of books on the subject both before and after publication, written by established thought leaders, high-potential budding leaders, frontline leaders, and their coaches. And for nearly two decades I've spoken with countless aspiring and established authors about their business and leadership works to help them understand what they might offer to their readers. All this has made me somewhat of an expert in the field of business, leadership, and management writing. As a matter of fact, one of my mentors, coeditor of this book and author of the hilarious exploits of Dr. Fink,[2] Larry Lyons, once said to me, "Sarah, I believe with all of the writings of ours that you have helped us with, we should give you a PhD in Leadership Writing!"

Having worked with authors, coaches, and leaders to find their leadership voice in writing—be it book, article, or blog—I always advise people to begin by asking themselves introspective and *so-what?* questions, such as:

- What is my idea?
- What is my experience?
- Why do I want to share this idea?

Take me. My answer is simple: help people find meaning and inspiration in their own lives by contributing their ideas, experience, beliefs, and stories to the global pool of knowledge through the written word.

What Is My Idea?

Imagination has brought mankind through the dark ages to its present state of civilization. Imagination led Columbus to discover America. Imagination led Franklin to discover electricity.[3]

—L. Frank Baum (American author, 1856–1919)

You've probably heard it said that everyone has at least one work of writing in them. It's true! Everyone has a story to tell and something to teach the rest of us. However, it takes dedication, perseverance, and devotion to bring your ideas to fruition in the written word. And it takes concerted effort, hard work, and skill to put forth your idea in such a way that you connect with your reader. Deeply.

For novice authors, the first inkling of your idea is often the thought that comes right off the top of your head. It is the *given subject* about which you have always wanted to write. It is your foundation or the first layer of the onion. It is what you know. And it's always been there nagging at you and imploring you to write it down.

For experienced writers, *the idea* is often the passing thought that comes to you while writing about something else, or while you are chatting about something else. It might emerge from some challenging situation, person, or learning point. It is the thought that strikes you in a conversation, while doing a task, or attending a meeting. It is the aha! moment. This idea is so loud and impactful you want to explore it further, because you feel there is much more to be uncovered about your newfound subject and *you* want to say it. These moments are fleeting and fickle. When you have such an idea, write it down—not in another moment, but *right now*—as it may never return!

If this is your first foray into writing, do take the opportunity to run your idea past a friend or colleague to gauge their interest. Does it resonate with your confidant? Does it inspire a conversation? These are sure signs that there is more to be explored. However, if the idea dead-ends or hits a seemingly impassable roadblock, you have two options *and you can do both*: (1) massage the idea until it inspires enthusiasm; (2) find another confidant.

Experienced writers know that sharing their concept with others helps them flesh it out. This helps you answer the question: is it still worth following through on this idea? This is one of those questions about which it's good to have feedback. Also, talking with another person helps you gather energy to get started and it often provides previously unconsidered content, direction, and parameters for your piece. In other words, such discussion points out the experience you have to share about the subject and the information you'll need to gather to fill in the blank spots.

What Is My Experience?

Words empty as the wind are best left unsaid.

—HOMER (GREEK EPIC POET, 8TH CENTURY BC)

Have you ever come across a piece of writing that is empty? There are many words on the page, but there is nothing being said? In such a case, the writer likely had an interesting idea but didn't prop it up with his or her experience, thus empty, meaningless, repetitive words were thrown onto the page, which readers quickly interpret as *fluff* and *nonsense.*

So, a good question to ask yourself is: "What is my experience with this idea that I would like to share?" And, further, what stories do you have to tell about it? What have you been taught about it in life, in school, at home, on the job? How are you connected to this idea, emotionally, intellectually, personally, professionally? What tales have you heard from those who have experienced it? To whom can you talk who has knowledge of this subject? How interested are you in doing the research it will take to fill in the blind spots and empty passages that are inevitable—because no one knows everything about anything?

You can, of course, try taking the know-it-all approach, but it's unlikely to work. Know-it-alls sound arrogant and superficial even when they are not; even worse, they sound phony. One thing readers are sure to spot is a phony—someone whose words are empty, who is not invested in his or her subject or reveals no clear experience with it. This wastes the reader's precious time. Sadly, this is a common style today, rampant really; publishers used to be the guards of the *fluff* and *nonsense* floodgate, but with the advent of the Internet, self-publishing, and e-media it seems that this is now out of their hands and has become the grassroots responsibility of the hapless *reader.* So, be warned, readers do not like *fluff* and *nonsense* and they will not forgive you!

Why Do I Want to Share this Idea?

The desire to write grows with writing.

—DESIDERIUS ERASMUS ROTERODAMUS (DUTCH RENAISSANCE HUMANIST, THEOLOGIAN, 1466–1536)

Assuming that you are not taking the know-it-all approach, and you are armed with an intriguing idea about which you have experience, stories, and resources to share, why do you want to share it with readers? The answer to this question will be your saving grace. It will provide the meaning and purpose to keep on writing when you feel like giving up.

So, again, I ask, why do you want to share the idea? Are you hoping it will change something? Are you banking on it making you famous? Is it, do you think, the key to the future of humanity? Do you want to steer people in a certain direction? Why? What's the point? What exactly are you hoping to achieve and receive by sharing this idea?

Getting at the reason for sharing your idea is a process of exploration and discovery. And when you've got even an inkling of that reason, grab onto it!

Lock it into your mind when you begin work on your piece, as finding it in the middle is near impossible. As a matter of fact, without it most writers would get lost and give up. Many are the times I have seen would-be, potential, and even experienced writers, who have great ideas, lots of experience and resources, and many stories to tell reach this stage and give up. They start like gangbusters, write a paragraph or chapter, lose focus on their purpose either because life gets in the way or simply because they follow a misleading path in their writing. They get to an impasse and can't remember why they started this project in the first place. They re-read what they've written and finding no cogent meaning or purpose, toss it. The ideas—however great they may have been—are now forever lost.

If you're committed to writing your piece, holding onto the reason for sharing your idea in the midst of writing is difficult, but not impossible. Writers will sometimes put a note near their writing table to remind them of their purpose, their audience, their goal. Or they may choose to consult an editor (cheerleader) or writing partner or coach, who knows their purpose and helps them return to it when they get lost in their own words.

Music to Their Ears or Scratching Nails Across a Chalkboard?

Writing has laws of perspective, of light and shade just as painting does, or music. If you are born knowing them, fine. If not, learn them. Then rearrange the rules to suit yourself.
—TRUMAN CAPOTE (AMERICAN AUTHOR, 1924–1984)

Equipped with an idea, your experience, and a clear purpose, the final hurdle before reaching your reader is developing the skills and technique to portray your idea. Doing so in a voice with which you are comfortable speaking and to which they will receptively listen is a challenge. There are as many voices on the subject of business, coaching, and leadership as there are books on the subject. And, as mentioned previously, there is ample number of these. Some voices are smooth, gentle, kind, and compassionate. Some are abrupt, disconcerting, rude, and disheartening. Some are quick, mercurial, light, and humorous; some stately, reserved, intellectual, and calm. All are different, just like people. Which voice is *yours?*

One of the most exquisite writers I know won't put pen to paper anymore. Trained, schooled, and even published as a writer, he says it has become too excruciating for him to find the right words. So, for now, he has made the choice not to write at all, leaving it to the rest of us to contribute to the global pool of knowledge. Another writer I enjoy immensely takes such care in his writing that it is a veritable masterpiece composed of individual parts. It is like a building. If one beam (even a punctuation mark!) is removed, it can upset his entire structure. Other writers are less meticulous. They may throw words on a page that relate to their chosen subject (or even speak them into a recording device and have them transcribed), and then rely on a heavy-handed editor to make it accessible to their audience. None of these methods are right or wrong; they just are. They are what work for the writers; these are their established voices. This is how they speak in writing.

A voice is established through trial and error—through writing, sharing the work, and withstanding the inevitable critiques and responses that come from sharing. You see, a good writer may be born, but great writers are made. And, the fact is, they are made by asking for, learning from, following up, and growing from readers' feedback. Just like leaders.[4]

In my experience, writers, both novice and practiced, who ask for others' responses and opinions of their works, and who are open to integrating that feedback, find it much easier to develop an amenable leadership voice that others can hear and one from which readers desire to listen and learn. These are all leadership qualities; good leaders all have the potential to become great leadership writers.

Conclusion

Finally, a few tips of the trade for those of you interested in pursuing writing on leadership.

1. Research your subject: explore it on the Internet, at the library, in your daily life, and with friends, colleagues, and family. You cannot know too much about it.
2. Keep writing even when you feel discouraged or feel that the writing isn't going anywhere. It is probably fine; you're likely just having an insecurity attack. Write through it; ask for feedback; do some research. Don't give up.
3. Start with an outline. Otherwise, don't start with an outline. Everyone has a different approach. Find the one that works for *you*.
4. The paragraph, chapter, sentence, or thought that you labor over longest and feel most strongly about is the one that will inevitably be cut. Make peace with that. If you are so attached to it, save it and use it somewhere else.
5. Set a time to write every day; write even when you don't want to. It doesn't have to be much. It doesn't have to be astounding. It just has to keep you connected. In other words, just do it!

And if all this sounds too difficult, too arduous a task to take on at this moment, then consider Socrates:

Employ your time in improving yourself by other men's writings, so that you shall gain easily what others have labored hard for.

—Socrates (Ancient Greek philosopher, 469 BC–399 BC)

Sarah McArthur is founder of *sdedit, an editorial firm based in San Diego, California. With nearly two decades of experience in the publishing field, Sarah is an expert in the field of management, leadership, and executive coaching writing. Her expertise has furthered the successes of the best-selling management classic, *Coaching for Leadership* (1e, 2e, and 3e), as well as the best sellers *What Got You Here Won't Get You There* and *MOJO: How to Get It, How to Keep It, and How to Get It Back When You Lose It* by Marshall Goldsmith. She is coeditor, with Marshall Goldsmith and John Baldoni, of *The AMA Handbook of Leadership,* named one of the Top 10 Business, Management, and Leadership Titles of 2010 by Choice. Contact Sarah at sarahmc@sdedit.com and www.sdedit.com.

CHAPTER EIGHT

SEEKING VALUE IN A SHATTERED WORLD OF WORK

By Nathan Lyons

Generation Why

Something extraordinary is happening. At least it feels that way to me.

Youth Protest

August 2011. I'm in Tel Aviv, strolling down Rothschild Boulevard—this city's answer to New York's Park Avenue. Lined with fancy restaurants and boutique stores, the street usually throngs with well-heeled women walking their poodles, businessmen laughing over al fresco lunches, and lycra-clad joggers pounding the manicured flowerbeds.

Today is different. The boulevard has disappeared under a thousand tents; what's left of the sidewalk is literally crammed with excited young people. Some brandish placards bearing political slogans, some are playing musical instruments; most merely mill about, talking and smoking. They've been here a month, protesting against the high cost of living.

Beneath the balconies of disgruntled gray-headed residents, the campers have set up kitchens, portable toilets, lecture rooms, and makeshift cinema screens—huge canvas sheets that hang between eighty-year-old ficus trees. Every Saturday night the residents of this new Tent City march through Tel Aviv. They are joined by tens of thousands of supporters in a huge public demonstration of deep discontent.

Baby Boomer Fallout

The protesters have much to complain about. Mostly in their twenties, they somehow never got the opportunities they were promised: they feel disappointed, let down. From their slogans and banners stream global concerns: the plight of doctors, nurses, and teachers; the lack of private sector jobs; the cost, and probable uselessness, of education; the growing gap between rich and poor; the prohibitive cost of a beer; a deficit of Good Men.

The main gripe is that the older generation, the baby boomers, screwed up our chances for the good life, recklessly partying too long and too hard, leaving my generation to pick up the tab and nurse a colossal hangover. All the stability, safety, and generous institutional comforts taken for granted by our parents' generation simply vanished into recession. It's no longer clear where to turn. While it's easy for the young to protest about what we don't want, it isn't at all clear to us what we should strive for, and what is truly valuable.

Lost Graduates

These days I live in Israel, but I'm originally from the United Kingdom, where the situation is similar. Many of my bright, hard-working, and well-educated contemporaries have wound up in their late twenties staring at a brick wall, watching daytime cable. Top-class graduates from first-class schools, they were ironically first in the firing line during the economic bloodbath. Many who had left home have since moved back in with their parents. Those who were most expected to move up are moving down.

That was not the plan on graduation day.

Here is a frustrated generation. The product of an affluent global middle class, this cohort feels a strong sense of undelivered entitlement. They studied hard for degrees in industries that no longer need them; the lucky few who do find jobs collect salaries that don't pay the bills. Unable to support themselves, let alone fulfill their career dreams, these young people are at the point of losing all confidence in the future.

Now What?

What can sovereign governments be expected to do? Do they hold those structural levers that are in need of adjustment? What can business organizations be expected to do? Global corporations have omnipotent reach, but can the necessary "fixes" be expressed in terms of implementable programs? Who will foot the bill?

What sort of questions are these? They cannot be merely questions of management, for isn't it clear that management of existing systems is part of the problem? We are in a crisis situation. Isn't the remedy for a crisis the domain of leadership? Where is this leadership to come from?

A Search for Values

On the other side of the coin, we have a unique opportunity to start fresh. All the negatives, the chaos and discontent, only highlight a delicious subtext: there is no option for my generation *but* to try something new. We can't retreat to a shack in the country and complain about "the mess we're in"—at least not for another four decades!

Unsurprisingly, youthful expressions seem impossibly idealistic: Equality and opportunity for all. Universal health care. World peace. The breakdown of antiquated nation-state, open borders, and open source.

Let's clarify: we're not hippies—we may share their ambitions, but not their starting point. Now is a different world. The first task of leadership is an articulation of values.

Money Don't Talk

Until now, my generation has never been hard up. We simply don't know what that means. Even when we're technically broke, it's abstract. Sure, sometimes we'll forgo the gourmet pasta sauce in favor of the supermarket brand. Maybe I'll buy those designer jeans next month when I've cleared my bank overdraft—or on second thought, my credit card can take the hit. We grew up comfortable enough, entertained enough, cushioned by Nintendo on a rainy day. Nothing really bad happened when you overspent your pocket money.

We're just not motivated by money. We expect it—that's for sure—but the raging lust for money for its own sake seems the crass preserve of the very poor, the very rich, and shiny, grasping people in New York City.

More than money, we want you to agree we're brilliant. We're going to achieve goals, become famous, get on television, write a by-line in the papers. We're going to get photographed holding degrees and winning sports medals and clasping our life partners in wedding ceremonies. We want recognition for being uniquely and completely ourselves.

With the current dips and depressions, we're not really sure what success is. The banking crisis gave the impression that the "glittering prizes" were presented to whoever wore the Emperor's New Clothes. Financial achievement built on shadows and dust seems morally reprehensible. When I hear the sentiment "the markets will rally, we'll all go back to business," I feel a twinge—not of excitement—but of disgust.

Maybe economic conditions will improve. But if success means spotting and riding the next technology or communications bubble, pioneering in the moment, parasitic in hindsight, and I slip into my opulently manicured suburban grave, I'll be kicking all the way down, cursing that I've missed the bigger picture.

Dream Chasers

My generation was always told "be yourself." We've been encouraged to say what we think, follow our hearts, aim for our dreams. Money is portrayed as a helpful *means*, never as the reason for that journey. We know that a large part of our life will be time spent at work; we'd like that experience to be fulfilling and enriching.

Searching for meaning, we want to arrive, belong, make our mark, be appreciated and indulged. There is a strong element of self-discovery along the path to find the right workplace, to create a satisfying way of life. For those who haven't landed on both feet, it's perfectly legitimate to sling that knapsack over your shoulder, traveling off to the horizon, seeking value.

Wish List

I'm piecing together a wish list, the wants of my generation:

I want my job to help people, make the world better—and certainly not make it any worse; do something real not abstract, and good for the people I work with. I want colleagues I would have as friends outside of work; I want to be part of a team. I want, I want, I want . . .

It's unrealistic I know, but . . . *I want to get paid slightly more than—and certainly not less than—my peers; I want my work to nourish me intellectually, train me, and provide skills I can trade later on down the line; work should connect me to a network of like-minded people and fresh ideas; nonnegotiable are health care, a car, an office where everybody knows my name. I want responsibility for part of a business; I want to be trusted; I want to feel that my efforts have some effect, even minor, in a bigger picture.*

Case Study: The Triceratops

I am lucky to have Mark Levy as my mentor. When I last spoke to Mark, I confided that I felt out of my depth writing a chapter for *Coaching for Leadership*. The intention of the chapter is to provide a slant on leadership from the Generation Y viewpoint. Now, what do *I* know about Leadership? I wasn't sure what I could contribute. We were speaking on Skype, so as I talked I could see Mark nodding, questioning, and encouraging me. Then his smile gradually grew into a huge mischievous grin.

"Nathan, your readers are experts in their field," he said in a matter-of-fact manner. "Imagine they are paleontologists. They've just discovered a triceratops, a Generation Y specimen with three horns. Only a handful of people have ever encountered one, and you can't go study one in a zoo. The world knows nothing about the Triceratops apart from the fact of its discovery."

(Continued)

Honestly, in that moment I thought he'd lost it. But then he continued, "Now just stop and consider that for a moment. You're out there in the wild, their subject is your real-life experience. You are one of those young Hi-Pos they'd love to study. Nathan, they're talking about *you*!

"You, my friend, are the triceratops."

Mark is right. I am a fairly typical product of my generation. I'm twenty-nine and I don't have a mortgage. I'm proud of my allegedly useless history degree, I've worked all over the world, in various industries, traveled a fair bit and done some serious soul-searching. I hope my story can provide some insight into what starting a career looks like, down here in the murky twenty-first-century mud.

I'm a triceratops charging through the world of work, living on diet of Meaning and Fulfillment. With that thought in mind, below I have sketched a rough outline of my personal experience of work, the lowlights and highlights of an eight-year journey.

Work as a Journey

My first real job was a posting to Gurgaon, India. In other words, the first time I put on a suit and walked into an office was in forty-degree (Celsius) heat on the outskirts of New Delhi. Aged twenty-two, I found myself with two other Oxford graduates, also in suits, acting as mouthpieces for a finance start-up. The local analysts were magnificently overqualified and had fantastic ideas, which confusingly came out in garbled "Victorian" Indian English—it was our task to "translate" and "modernize" their insights into The Queens' English for consumption by American banks.

If I'm honest, I had absolutely no idea what I was doing.

One Friday, for no particular reason, I clocked off uncharacteristically early, cancelled my personal driver, and walked the five miles to my hotel. I took my sweet time, watching seemingly endless chains of manual laborers carry masonry and scaffolding between rickety construction sites. Huddled groups of women cooked stew by the roadside, cows idled on the tarmac, forcing traffic to veer around their bulky rumps and swinging tails.

Then something happened that I will never forget. A tiny man wearing a simple orange tunic appeared out of nowhere, directly in front of me. His forehead was daubed in thick white marks, in his hand he held a simple wooden cane.

I noticed this holy man walked barefoot on the hot uneven ground. I looked down at my own patent leather shoes, shirt, and striped tie, wondering what impression this Western man-child must make on the wandering mystic. He simply smiled and walked on.

I later learned that this otherworldly apparition was a religious Jain in the final years of his life: renouncing all worldly goods, leaving family life, he was making a pilgrimage of holy sites, and will end his life at a shrine by a sacred riverbank.

Our meeting lasted only a moment. Nothing was said. But the experience of meeting him has left an indelible impression. In one direction my mundane road to work lay ahead; his road to meaning went the totally opposite way.

Old Fashioned Start-Up

With a little finance experience to paper over my history degree, it was time to trade up. I applied for a job at G-corporation in London. It was attractive, a great blue-chip brand, well paid, and a thriving young company to boot. It checked all the boxes. Or so I thought.

In my first few weeks as account manager, all the new recruits, including me, were bombarded throughout intensive training days with films of the corporate founders, repeatedly congratulating us, promising creativity and opportunity. They smiled broad grins and asked us to be ourselves.

We dressed down, in jeans and funky T-shirts. Coworkers brought their dogs to work, enjoyed a biweekly massage, free lunches, snack areas with fluorescent bean bags, ski trips to St. Tropez. The office looked like a Generation Y paradise playground, full of colored bouncy balls and computer games. Perhaps here was the sense of arrival I had been craving?

Maybe the early years at G-corporation were truly zany. However, in 2006 the office was run like a Roman galleon. Hierarchically structured, heavily targeted, there was a real threat of disciplinary action if an employee left his desk for an overlong spell. Turning up five minutes after the 9 o'clock start led to a severe dressing down. Worse still was the job itself. Using clunky back-office administrative software, sales teams mechanically logged and processed payments. There was virtually zero client time. It was cripplingly boring.

Imagine this elaborate modern-day torture; forever surrounded by brilliant young people with excellent paper credentials, and even better dress sense, performing the most repetitive and unimaginative of jobs. The system was so beautifully designed, the brand impressed friends at dinner parties; the whole ambiance oozed creativity and splendor. Yet stripped of its sugar coating, here was a cold, plastic environment. I had been scammed, lured by my own petty (and misguided) understanding of value and success.

Fake Equity

Several years later I took a job with a financial events company in the City of London. Founded by former stockbrokers, the organization presented a unique seed-funding offering to employees. Initially training on the job while being paid a salary, employees would eventually establish their own conference series, and share in the equity. You'd end up with your own company, with protection and support from the bigger organization.

This sounded very exciting. Mostly under thirty, employees worked around the clock, eager to prove their creditworthiness. At highly orchestrated monthly meetings, the management echoed the promise "the dream of having your own business," highlighting and rewarding the staff who progressed along this route.

I too was lured by this promise; a sense of independence, of being my own boss. I was hardly alone; the company attracted entrepreneurial graduates who each wanted to be master of his or her destiny. Although the number of employees who actually "won" seed funding was minuscule, the fact this target was even possible electrified the office into a veritable hive of activity.

(Continued)

On the advice of a lawyer friend, I investigated the company's public records. With his help I quickly realized the "staff equity" offer was a fraud. The directors maintained complete control, and had in fact recently liquidated the "employee equity" account, now glowing red in negative numbers, to purchase a pair of yachts for their personal use.

Here was another generational scam—the scent of independence, a promise to share the pie. The company continues to perform well, attracting dedicated hard-working staff, buzzing like fireflies around the hope of owning the fruits of their labors.

I resigned immediately, forwarding the incriminating documents to another colleague, who also resigned. This fake equity promise was the total opposite of the value I seek.

Responsibility Incentive

Crashing from job to job in London, I stumbled on a gem. An eccentric finance company, at ten years old too young to be considered a start-up, employing only a handful of staff. The founders, semi-academic visionaries, were driven by the dream of a more open marketplace. I perhaps never understood the heart of their idea, yet in this small team environment I quickly felt valued and keen to make a good impression.

The thrill of responsibility pushed me to work harder than ever. Running events in London and New York, marketing trips to Europe and Canada, I enjoyed taking decisions and standing by them. After producing a successful conference for hedge funds in Manhattan, I was asked to stay in New York City, a one-man sales operation for the long summer.

Trusted to manage my own time, armed with a Skype connection, a fake Connecticut landline, and a smart new suit from Dad, I booked meetings up the length and breadth of Wall Street. I stayed in touch with London via e-mail, sharing my meetings through Google Docs and scheduled weekly calls. I wasn't earning much money, but woke up each day high on the adrenaline of independence and New York City.

For the first time, it felt like what I had to say mattered. Still, I had no idea how little any of it stacked up in the grand scheme of things.

Riding First Class on the Titanic

The little finance company was completely submerged by the financial crisis. I remember calling a Bear Stearns manager to finalize his keynote speech at our upcoming event. Vaguely aware that his company had been mentioned on the news that morning, he took me by surprise: "I'd love to speak at your conference, but I don't think I'll be able. They've called in the entire management team. We're riding on the Titanic, Nathan, and we've hit a tremendous iceberg. I can hear the violins playing."

Throughout the crisis I heard the roll-call of dozens of former clients on the evening news. Each name, each bailed-out bank, brought visions of offices visited in New York; vast mahogany rooms halfway up skyscrapers, decked out in designer furniture, gold-framed doors, and impeccably dressed secretaries, marble paperweights and magnums of champagne resting on capacious desks.

I still wonder what happened to all those offices, secretaries, and paperweights. Sometimes I imagine them floating down Park Avenue, out into the Hudson river, all that high-rise value evaporating into city smog.

Community Initiative

Back in London, the newspapers spread doom and gloom, prophesying financial meltdown. From the early morning bus I saw long lines at the unemployment office trying to shake off the rain. My friends were out of work, I was barely making ends meet as a copywriter, with the presentiment of a very drab end of the world.

I fantasized opening up the shuttered shops, using the premises as a café or wireless hotspot or soup kitchen, anything but a derelict space. By chance I came across a fledgling art project; a group of design graduates living in a council estate earmarked for demolition. Housed by the construction company, their presence acted as a deterrent to illegal "squatters," who might otherwise interfere with the site.

We came up with a bold plan, to occupy the entire site of four hundred apartments with a living arts festival named for the estate—*The Market Estate Project.* After submitting funding applications, appeals to the local council and the construction company, we amazingly won the right to occupy the site for five full months.

The project quickly took over my entire life. I slept on my teammates' floors, day by day assembling a legal and practical infrastructure. We recruited over a hundred artists to redesign the estate, offering them the blank canvas of empty apartments and total creative freedom. With one condition: artwork was to reflect on, and include, the local community.

Gradually my winter fantasy came to life. Setting up an office in a nearby building, we were soon joined by enthusiastic locals, artists, and an army of volunteers. We won enough funding to hire sound, light, and security experts, and even a few of my out-of-work friends. When the project opened to the general public, 2,500 people visited the one-day event.

Three kitchens heaved to feed hungry visitors, local school children flocked to visit a flat converted into a blue vacuum-packed bubble. Bands entertained guests from a specially constructed stage, a drama troupe performed Othello in the car park. As night fell, a laser show lit up the estate.

Gazing around during the event, having barely slept for two weeks, I was overcome with emotion. We had made something happen.

On a site of dereliction and poverty, powered by goodwill and a volunteer spirit, our small team had carried the momentum for a community project that, for one day at least, brought light to this dark corner of London. We brought creative, visionary young people, and given them space to practice their utopias.

The newspapers celebrated the festival, a week later the buildings were torn down, and everyone went home. This felt to me a truly valuable project, albeit completely unsustainable.

(Continued)

Working Community

For the past year, I've been working for an innovation company in Tel Aviv. They pioneer cultural change in large and small organizations across the globe. Experts in new product development, with a strong pedigree in problem solving, the company is commercially successful—but that's perhaps the last reason I work for them.

Before long I realized that this organization had some incredible cultural differences. For example, the CEO divulges to clients his exact profit. He spells out costs, staff time, resources, then indicates his profit margin. It is up to the client to agree or disagree. This story impressed me; breaking the façade of business as a game that's either won or lost, approaching the client as a fellow human being, and with absolute honesty.

S.I.T.—the company goes by the acronym for Systematic Inventive Thinking—is self-consciously an experiment. Privately owned by founders and staff, it is principle-led, and strongly values-oriented.

There is a sense of equality. The top level of management earns just twice the secretary's salary. Loyalty is valued above personal achievement: there is no sales commission; any bonus is shared equally by the whole company. Each person contributes as best they can to the overall team.

There is a distinct lack of ego; most assignments are in pairs; rewards are given for teamwork. The company takes an extremely flexible approach to child care; mothers bring babies to work, employees leave early to pick up kids from school. The office is overwhelmingly female.

S.I.T. is a business paradigm unlike any I've encountered. The company seeks to understand cultural differences, to accept and find space for difference. These sound like buzz words, but the reality is striking. For example, I don't speak Hebrew very well; at any meeting I attend, large or small, the entire room switches to English to accommodate me, so I don't feel left out.

My colleagues show up to work because they love the experiment, the way of life, the intellectual excitement of constantly questioning and improving the business. They feel emotionally invested, both in S.I.T. and in their work with clients. There is an office mantra: *we work with people, not clients.*

This environment thrives on mutual trust and pride in a job well done. Helping a colleague achieve his best has become the highest form of work. There are ups and downs, but for me, the excitement of being a part of this team, operating commercially but with a moral and social heart, makes me love my work.

If a company can create and sustain this working climate, surely the sky is the limit. People actually smile in this office. Surely, this shouldn't be so rare?

Talking About My Generation

There is no one-size-fits-all formula for Generation Y. Still, there are strong themes that when well understood and recognized, can make work rewarding, stimulating, and fulfilling for emerging leaders.

Quality work has to feel cocreated, responsive to personal input. My generation appears to conceive itself at the center of the universe, but really we're delighted to be on the team. Cosmopolitan, well-traveled, and globally wired, here is a generation open to hard graft, who can cope with high levels of ambiguity, and make things happen.

Learn what makes us tick, what motivates us. Find Generation Y's hot buttons; make us feel part of something, involved in something. We've been around the block a few times, so we'll quickly smell fake radical, fake opportunity, fake cool. Be honest, clear, and to-the-point. Don't tell us "it's an exciting idea"—we'll tell you.

Help us fire our passions, our sense of community, ownership, and worth, encourage us to cocreate the workplace, so our considerable energies can be focused on business achievement. Remember, we are trying to create our own value. That's no simple task. We need a guiding hand, gently emphasized experience, and a realistic overview.

What do we really want? Who knows. You may have more luck asking what we *value*, what matters to us. Keep asking the questions, listen carefully, and be prepared for some strange answers. Accept the next generation has a different starting point—but get us on board, speak our language, and will happily share a cocreated vision of success.

Nathan Lyons holds an MA in Modern History from the University of Oxford, and lives by the seaside in Israel. Contact Nathan at nathan.lyons@gmail.com.

Mark Levy is the founder of Levy Innovation (www.levyinnovation.com), a marketing strategy firm that helps thought leaders increase their fees dramatically. He's also the author of the book *Accidental Genius: Using Writing to Generate Your Best Ideas, Insight, and Content.*

CHAPTER NINE

THE RIGHT STUFF OF LEADERSHIP

By John Baldoni

One aspect of leadership development that receives relatively little focus is the topic of "presence." The topic often arises in coaching as something that is missing. Often a senior executive, or a human resource partner, will comment that a rising executive has everything necessary to succeed and perhaps make it to the highest levels of management save one thing—an inability to present him or herself as a leader.

I use the term *present* in a holistic sense, an inability to convey the right sense of authority, the necessary comportment, and sadly, an inability to get others to see this individual in a senior leadership position. What is missing can be fatal to a career, but if addressed early, a leader can acquire the bearing, the demeanor, or to quote the phrase Tom Wolfe made famous, "the right stuff."[1]

Why Presence Matters

Coaching for leadership presence is really an exploration of the leadership persona. So often the term "executive presence" is used. I reject the term as too simplistic; it relegates presence to the status of a shiny new suit. Yes, you need to look the part but leadership presence is what I have defined as "earned authority." A leader is given authority via title, but as they say in the military, trust is earned. Leadership presence then becomes a reciprocal process. It is something a leader projects but is granted by followers.

Central to presence is authenticity. Or to put it bluntly, the real deal. Authenticity is earned through example. Leaders earn it over time by being visible to their people; employees see them regularly. (This can be challenging for bosses managing employees in multiple locations, but successful ones I know do it by touching base virtually by phone and, when possible, with actual visits.)

Leaders are often heard; they communicate the meaning of work and why what employees do matters. They connect the dots, as it were, between what an employee does and how the company succeeds. They also listen frequently. Most important, leaders follow through on example by "being there."

Being present with presence is the act of leadership. When the team is down, the leader is there to lift it up. When the team needs an extra hand, the leader is there doing the heavy lifting. Or when the team succeeds, the leader is there, off stage, pushing the employees into the limelight so they can be recognized. Being there means being counted on.

Aspects of Presence

How do leaders earn their authority? Quite simply, they earn it through their example. Three factors play into the equation.

1. *Competence.* This is when you know you are doing the job. You need to be good at what you do. Not only do you have mastery of your task and your role, you are someone who goes the extra mile to get things done. You do not wait for further instructions. You do it.
2. *Credibility.* This is when others say you are doing the job. Credibility is a coin of the organizational realm. It comes to the fore when people know you are reliable and dependable. Not only do you do good work; others believe in you.
3. *Confidence.* This is when you and everyone else says you are right for this job. Confidence is crucial to leadership presence. Without a sense of your ability to do the job, you cannot inspire others to follow your lead. Why would they?

When a leader manifests competence, credibility, and confidence, he or she inspires people to follow. As James McGregor Burns has taught us, leaders succeed when the beliefs of the leader and followers become as one. People actually want to do what you ask them to do. In short, they trust their leader.[2]

This forms the context for leadership presence. As coaches, we work with specifics. What can an individual do to discover and nurture a sense of presence? I have developed an assessment for leadership presence that breaks it down into specific areas of development. A short explanation of each area will give us a means to explore the topic in ways that are transferable to the development process.

Coaching for Leadership Presence

When coaching for leadership presence, a good starting point is communications. Many executives need help in become more authentic communicators. This is understandable because as representatives of an organization, they learn early to tone down or sublimate their own ideas in service to the organization. But now as leaders, the game changes; they are expected to have a point of view and present it in ways that are credible.

A technique I use even with experienced presenters is to do at least one session on presentation skills. By working on simple activities like how to take the podium or to present from a conference room chair, the executive begins to connect with his body the way an actor does—an instrument to be utilized in support of the voice.

Vocalization is essential. It is not enough to recite words—a leader must invest himself in what the words mean. Proper vocalization with an emphasis on inflection as well as on pausing can help the executive learn how to make the important message ring true.

A leader's communication is the means by which she informs as well as persuades, and challenges as well as reassures. Communication complements a leader's presence because it is how the leader makes herself understood. And over time authentic communications build higher levels of trust between leader and followers.

For experienced leaders, there may be a tendency to overlook communications as something that, once mastered, is always there. Not true. Many veteran leaders may overlook it because they get busy with management responsibilities. The first thing to suffer is listening. As much as they realize its importance, they are so pushed by their bosses or pulled by peers and direct reports that listening, taking time to have a conversation or discussion about key issues, falls by the wayside.

Those leaders who put their presence into action are those who work hard to make certain they listen. They make the habit of walking the halls and engaging in conversations about what is going on in the workplace. The best ones make it a regular habit to visit employees where they work, even if it means flying cross-country to do it. Presence, as the word implies, is a physical manifestation; the more a leader is seen and heard, the better opportunity employees have to understand their roles.

How Leaders Can Practice Implementing Leadership Presence

Communication serves as a door opener. The other attributes of presence require thinking and planning regarding the best way to implement them in the workplace. Here are some suggestions.

Appearance—how you look. Leaders need to look the part. Dress smartly, but not extravagantly. One rule of thumb is to dress a notch of formality above those you supervise. For men, it may mean wearing a jacket and tie, for women a dress or suit. More important than dress are your facial expressions. Keep them relaxed unless you are intentional. It is appropriate to adopt a severe look when serious issues arise, but if you always look that way, people may fear to approach you.

Authority—how you exercise your power. With title comes authority. New leaders sometimes shy away from exercising their power for fear of upsetting the status quo or ruffling feathers. This undermines authority, and people will take advantage of you. On the flipside, the heavy hand, specifically failing to delegate authority to others, weakens the leader's ability to build a cohesive team. Authority reflects on presence and needs to be utilized appropriately.

Compassion—how you show concern. Leaders need not, and should not, seek to be their employees' best buddy. It is important to show concern for employees as people. Employees want to know their boss has their back, especially in tough situations affecting family members. Leaders need to keep appropriate distance emotionally, so they can make the hard decisions that being in charge brings with it. But leaders achieve results chiefly through others, so it makes good sense to treat them with dignity and respect. Adopt the attitude that says employees are valued contributors. *(Note: bosses do not pry into the personal lives of employees; they only inquire when invited.)*

Comportment—how you carry yourself. Leaders have bearing, a sense of gravitas, or seriousness of purpose. Composure is vital to comportment. Leaders who come unglued when trouble strikes demonstrate to followers that they lack what it takes to lead the team in a crisis. Leaders may feel fear, and in fact that's normal, but showing it makes people around you nervous. If the leader is not in control of himself, then things must be very bad indeed. It is okay to show emotion, even anger, but you need always to be in control. Keeping emotions on a more even keel is an aspect of presence. Again, you need not look serious all the time, but you must be of serious intention, that is, focused on the job.

Humility—how you view your limitations. Leaders make mistakes; they are human, after all. Owning up to failure is a sign of humility. It shows that you recognize your shortcomings. Good leaders surround themselves with people who compensate for their weaknesses. This too shows humility, because it is an acknowledgment that you cannot do it all, nor should you.

Passion—how you convey what you feel. Enthusiasm feeds on passion. The person in charge must care about the work and its consequences. Passion is rooted in personal belief; for leaders it emanates from the desire to make a positive difference. When the leader has passion for the work and conveys it to others, it can be contagious to the team.

Optimism—how you look at life. People are more likely to follow someone who looks primarily on the bright side rather than on the dark side. Optimism is not the same as "happy talk," the kind of "everything will be OK" babble that some managers fall into the habit of doing. No, optimistic leaders face up to adversity with a clear head; they give their people the straight dope. But in the face of trouble, they refuse to succumb to negative thoughts. They may not always succeed, but they maintain a positive outlook on life. This attitude helps them, and their team, deal with challenges with the intention that they will succeed, not succumb.

You can likely think of other attributes and behaviors that leaders use to confirm their presence and apply it for the good of the team. All these things affirm what the leader is and how she or he serves the needs of the organization. A leader who reflects on these items and seeks to put them into practice is one who knows him- or herself. Self-awareness is a cornerstone of leadership presence.

Word to the wise: Leadership presence is a lifelong activity. To hone it well, pick one or two things at a time on which to focus. For example, speaking and listening are two activities that complement one another. Think of how decisiveness complements alignment, how providing timely clarity makes the marching orders easier to follow. It is also fine to choose one thing, such as strategic thinking.

Perception of Presence

As much as a leader may focus on presence, the arbiter of whether a leader has it or not comes down to those she must lead. Think of presence as a form of a leadership brand, how you appear and present yourself to others. Consider a favorite consumer product. Likely the company has spent a good deal of time and money on honing a brand image that resonates with the attributes that reflect not simply features and benefits, but also perception. The owner of those perceptions is not the company; it is you.

This is especially true with leaders. They may think they are connecting the right way with their employees but if they are short with their messages, do not take time to listen, are inconsistent and indecisive, and worst of all, act as if others are there to serve them rather than the other way around, their presence is strong, but not in ways that are worthy of emulation.

The best way to check on perception is to ask a trusted colleague for an honest assessment of how you are coming across in the workplace. Talk about how you want others to think of you and ask if this is the reality. An executive coach, too, can be extremely helpful in this area. The coach can talk to your boss as well as others who work with you to ascertain if you are following through on your own perception of yourself.

Sometimes, especially in coaching situations, feedback can be brutal. Many an executive thinks he is an engaged leader who is present for his team only to discover that his self-assessment is no match for reality. Rather than protest, a savvy leader will know that acknowledging the feedback is the first step to becoming a self-aware leader. A good way to begin to demonstrate presence is to accept the feedback with a sense of calmness. Keep your emotions in check and maintain an even keel. This can be a good first step toward becoming the mindful and even-tempered leader you desire to be.

A Note on Gender

Let me say that leadership presence is not gender specific. While we may have an iconic image of a leader as male, the cavalry officer on a steed, there are all kinds of presence. Certainly we imbue presence with charisma—that sense of head-turning and in some cases, heart-stopping appeal—that makes people sit up and take notice whenever that person enters a room.

John Kennedy and Ronald Reagan certainly had such charisma. In fact, Reagan is famously quoted as saying that he did not know how anyone could be president without being an actor. That comment was not flippant; it was his heart-felt conviction that leaders have a stage role, that is, one that calls for them to project themselves and their cause on others. An actor knows how to modulate his voice for effect as well as how to get out and shake hands with everyone in the room.

Leaders with presence are those who have the ability to connect one-to-one with individuals and make them feel as if they are the only people in that room. In this regard, it is my opinion that women have the edge. Women are better equipped emotionally to reach out and listen to other people.

One woman who I have long admired for her presence was Mother Theresa. Consider this diminutive woman from Albania. No one would call her beautiful but few would deny her charisma. From heads of state to people in the street, many lives were touched by Mother Theresa. She cared for the "poorest of the poor," including lepers and AIDS patients. Dressed in her white nun's habit with blue trim, Mother Theresa positively glowed with a sense of mission, one that drew people to her.

So while the male image may be a default in discussions of presence, women too have presence. What matters is that sense of authenticity, the ability to convey the true self so that others sense that the leader is really who he or she says he or she is.

Presence to Purpose

A leader needs to project presence for one simple reason: a leader's job to create common cause around specific issues. Having that sense of presence enables the leader to build that cause in a way that touches the heart of followers.

Fundamental to the act of leadership is persuasion. Savvy leaders not only build their case around logic and reason, they also know that as compelling as facts and figures can be, they are cold and inert. People want to feel the passion of their leader. Passion comes through when the leader knows the needs of the people he or she must lead and can connect the purpose of the organization to them.

Case in point is Beryl Companies of Bedford, Texas. Beryl provides call service for the health care industry. Most employees are "front-liners" who spend the majority of their time with patients on the phone. This is not a well-paid position typically (although Beryl pays competitive wages), but it also does more. Under the leadership of its CEO and founder, Paul Spiegelman, Beryl connects purpose to what employees do. Everyone who works at Beryl knows how their job contributes to the mission of the organization that is providing care service with a human touch.[3]

Paul is someone who exudes leadership presence. His demeanor is quiet and reserved, but to hear him speak about what his company does, and to see the results of his company's work, is to know that purpose matters. A leader who connects purpose to what employees do and demonstrates it by living the example is one who others will follow. Proof of this is the fact that Beryl Company earns high employee engagement scores and generates lower than average turnover rates for call service employees.

Creating "Followership"

Leaders who know themselves, and can connect effectively with others, are those who others want to follow. Leadership presence is a manifestation of the leadership persona that brings people together and facilitates that sense of esprit de corps that emerges only when leader and follower are working together to achieve the same intended results.

Things to Do to Develop Your Presence[4]

- Identify someone you believe epitomizes leadership presence. Observe his or her behaviors and choose some to emulate.

- Speak in ways that demonstrate you are a person of character, that is, do you tell the truth even when it may hurt?
- Act in ways that demonstrate you are a person of character, that is, do you let your actions speak for you?
- Find inspiration in the example of others and celebrate it through the work you do.
- Consider the effect your power has on others. How will you make certain you apply it for the good?
- Identify opportunities to share power with colleagues, so that the team and the organization benefit.
- Consider ways you can balance deliberation (*thinking it over*) with decisiveness (*pulling the trigger*).
- Find ways to make it comfortable for your direct reports to ask you questions.
- Before you make an important announcement, make certain you find out what the real issues are, that is, what people have concerns about.
- When meetings drag on, remind yourself to soften your facial muscles.
- Invest in a wardrobe that reflects the leadership position you hold.
- Link what individuals do to what the organization does.
- Celebrate the meaning of work by showing how your work affects the lives of your customers.
- Find opportunities to showcase the talents of the people on your team.
- Radiate optimism in ways that affirm the self-worth and personal dignity of your people.
- Get in the habit of using the pronoun "we" when speaking about the work you and your team do.

John Baldoni is an internationally recognized leadership development consultant, executive coach, author, and speaker. John teaches men and women to achieve positive results by focusing on communication, influence, motivation, and supervision. In 2011, Leadership Gurus International ranked John number 11 on the list of the world's top leadership gurus. John is the author of ten books on leadership including: *Lead with Purpose: Give Your Organization a Reason to Believe in Itself; Lead by Example: 50 Ways Great Leaders Inspire Results;* and *Lead Your Boss: The Subtle Art of Managing Up.* Readers are welcome to visit John's website at www.johnbaldoni.com.

CHAPTER TEN

THE PURPOSEFUL LEADER

A Purpose Checkup

By Richard J. Leider

M oney, medicine, and meaning are essential to true engagement. Every person is driven, deep down inside, to discover what is truly meaningful, and we are incapable of being happy until we find it. Meaning matters.

I have not met a single leader who doesn't have a clear gut feeling for the difference between what's meaningful and not meaningful. We may get sidetracked from time to time with activities that are purely self-serving, but their very nature is that we get tired of them—their meaninglessness is unavoidable.

Meaning Matters

What does it take to engage people today? First it takes being engaged. One big difference between the success and the failure of leaders can be traced to their own engagement. Purposeful engagement usually accompanies greatness in anything, and it is largely responsible for the passion found in high-performing people.

Recently, His Holiness the Dalai Lama visited my home state of Minnesota to give a series of talks and was asked what he thought was the best way to teach your children to lead an ethical way of life. "It doesn't matter what you tell them," he responded. "They will watch and imitate you. They will do what you do, and so you are faced with the hardest task of all—to be ethical yourself."

A primary role of leaders today is to face the ultimate test of leadership— "to be purposefully engaged." We must be clear that leadership respect is earned from the inside out. Respect comes from first asking ourselves (and answering) the tough meaning questions.

Talented people instinctively seek a work environment where they know they will have a full voice in matters of consequence. They seek a workplace where they don't feel constricted, where they don't have to check themselves at the door. Such a work environment lets them breathe life into their work. If they don't find an environment that feeds their hearts and souls, all they're left with are paychecks, and that's not enough for most talented people today. Put purpose-driven talent up against people who simply work for a paycheck, and who do you think will succeed?

During my thirty-plus years as an executive coach, I have been continually impressed with the courage that purposeful leaders have for holding up the mirror to look inside themselves first. They understand that the "who" is leading is as important as the "what" is being achieved. The "who" always trumps the "what" of leading.

"What Gets You up in the Morning?"

Purpose goes by many names and descriptions, and a fair number of researchers and thought leaders have explored it. I refer to purpose as "your reason for getting up in the morning."

In his book *Servant Leadership*, Robert K. Greenleaf urged leaders to go "beyond conscious rationality" and to go into the "uncharted and unknown" to lead from within.[1] Our *purpose* is our personal mission; it is the central quality or essence that is revealed in our leadership, and it is always larger than we are. It inspires us, of course, but it is also the central quality that inspires others.

Greenleaf wrote, "Serving and leading are still mostly intuition-based concepts." He believed that self-insight is "the most dependable part of the true servant."[2] By finding and leading from the purpose deep within us, we can meet Greenleaf's criteria for servant-leaders: "Those served grow as persons."[3] To be purposeful leaders we must be willing to look inside, to understand "what gets us up in the morning" and to lead from it.

What Is Purpose?

Those of us who wrestle with understanding purpose, despite the disparity of our language, seem to agree on at least these two lines of belief:

1. Purpose is not invented; it is uncovered.

    Stephen Covey, author of the hugely popular and bestselling *The 7 Habits of Highly Effective People*, states, "I think each of us has an internal monitor or sense, a conscience, that gives us an awareness of our own uniqueness and the singular contributions that we can make."[4]

Purpose is within us. It is waiting to be uncovered. Purpose is a calling; thus, uncovering it is an act of listening rather than inventing.

Purpose directs our decisions about what to do, when we do it, and when we let go or turn away from it. Purpose is the quality we shape our leadership around.

2. Purpose is "concrete assignment."

Viktor Frankl, who might be considered a founder of modern thinking about purpose, expounds on the subject: "One should not search for an abstract meaning of life. Everyone has his own specific vocation or mission in life to carry out a concrete assignment which demands fulfillment. Therein he cannot be replaced, nor can his life be repeated. Thus, everyone's task is as unique as is his specific opportunity to implement it."[5]

Purpose is an external expression of our gifts, our talents. It infuses our work and is not solely within us or for ourselves. Our calling is our gift to the world, and our leadership is our unique and tangible way in which the gift is given.

We do not pursue our purpose because it is strictly self-fulfilling, nor because it is rewarding in the conventional terms of power or influence. We pursue it because we must.

Why Should I Care?

Today's talent doesn't blindly follow. They are educated, street smart, globally wise, and connected. Their engagement is dependent on the respect they have for us as leaders. They are yearning for purposeful leaders—leaders who care.

Most people have a keen awareness of "caring" when it is present in our leaders, and we have an uneasy feeling of engagement when it is absent. Let's assume for a few minutes that you have been asked to interview your new leader. What would *you* want to know about him or her as a leader? Assume you know the basics of the person's résumé: work history, age, family, and so forth. What would you want him or her to know about *you*?

Purpose is connected to caring, and caring is essential to engagement. Do we have a reason to get up in the morning? Do we, while also savoring our lives, have a reason larger than ourselves for leading? As renowned American author E. B. White captured it, "I arise in the morning torn between a desire to improve (or save) the world and a desire to enjoy (or savor) the world. This makes it hard to plan the day."[6]

EXHIBIT 10.1 THE PURPOSE CHECKUP

Many of us accept the necessity of regular physical checkups. We're also generally willing to review our financial situation with some regularity.

So if money, medicine, and meaning are all essential to a purposeful life, we might be wise to take guidance from the financial and medical worlds and adopt the practice of a regular checkup on that third dimension to ensure that our spirit—our sense of purpose—remains healthy.

Please read each statement carefully and take a few moments to decide on a true response for yourself. Then write the number that most nearly reflects that response. The answers offer the following range of responses:

1. Definitely disagree
2. Somewhat disagree
3. Somewhat agree
4. Definitely agree

Having (Outer Life)

_____ I derive satisfaction from what I have in my life.

_____ I express my creativity in a number of ways.

_____ I have found ways to offer my gifts and talents to the world.

_____ I have a positive vision for my future.

_____ I feel satisfied with my location.

_____ My physical energy is vital.

_____ I feel satisfied with my personal relationships.

_____ *Total Having score*

Doing (Inner Life)

_____ I follow my purpose when making major decisions.

_____ I feel content when I am alone.

_____ I focus and think clearly.

_____ I have the courage to face adversity.

_____ I offer compassion to others readily.

_____ I offer forgiveness to others easily.

_____ I am growing and developing.

_____ *Total Doing score*

Being (Spiritual Life)

_____ I sense the presence of a Higher Power.

_____ I have a regular spiritual practice.

_____ I feel a sense of the sacred when I am in the natural world.

_____ I feel a sense of gratitude for my life.

_____ I maintain a balance of saving and savoring the world.

_____ I invest time in making a difference to others or to the world.

_____ I know what I want to be remembered for.

_____ *Total Being score*

_____ **Total Purpose Checkup score**

Interpretation

Having (Outer Life)

The dimension of your external experience and activity—how effectively you relate to the "having" choices in your life.

Doing (Inner Life)

The dimension of your internal experience and inner activity—how effectively you relate to the "doing" choices in your life.

Being (Spiritual Life)

The dimension of your invisible experience and spiritual activity—how effectively you relate to the "being" choices in your life.

Scoring

Your score in each section is one measure of your development in that dimension. Your total Purpose Checkup score (out of 84) gives a measure of the power of purpose you are experiencing in your life at present.

Use this review worksheet to check in with yourself yearly, perhaps every year on your birthday!

Source: Used with permission from *The Power of Purpose* by Richard J. Leider (Berrett-Koehler, 2010).

The Ultimate Test for Leadership: Success with Fulfillment

What truly matters in life, according to Viktor Frankl, Nazi concentration camp survivor and author of the classic book *Man's Search for Meaning,* is not the meaning of life in general, but rather the specific meaning of a person's life at a given moment. To restate: "One should not search for an abstract meaning of life. Everyone has his own specific vocation or mission in life to carry out a concrete assignment which demands fulfillment."

When we lead on purpose, we aren't motivated exclusively by external wants like money or influence. We are motivated from within—and stand a far better chance of being successful in our leading and fulfilled in our work. The ultimate test for leadership is this: "Can we look back at our lives and achieve success and fulfillment from the reality that we have made a purposeful difference in people's lives?"

We know inside ourselves, if we have spent our work lives working on our "concrete assignment," we can look back with pride, for this is the real meaning of a human life. This is the ultimate wealth.

Richard J. Leider is a pioneer in executive coaching. Forbes and other media have repeatedly cited him as one of the top coaches in the world. Founder and chairman of The Inventure Group, he is a best-selling author and speaker to thousands of people worldwide each year. His clients include many of the world's leading organizations. He is the author of eight books, including three best sellers. His work has been translated into twenty-one languages. *Repacking Your Bags* and *The Power of Purpose* are considered classics in the career development field. He is a Senior Fellow in the acclaimed University of Minnesota Center for Spirituality and Healing and is an Executive Fellow in the University of Minnesota Carlson School of Management. Along with his professional pursuits, Leider leads yearly Inventure Expedition walking safaris in East Africa. Believing passionately that each of us is born with a purpose, he is dedicated to coaching executives to discover the power of purpose. Contact www.inventuregroup.com or www.richardleider.com.

CHAPTER ELEVEN

WHEN LEADERS ARE COACHES*

By James M. Kouzes and Barry Z. Posner

Leadership is a relationship. Sometimes the relationship is one-to-many, and sometimes it is one-to-one. Regardless of whether the relationship is with one or with one thousand, leadership is a relationship between those who aspire to lead and those who choose to follow. Success in leadership, success in business, and success in life have been, are now, and will always be a function of how well we work and play together. Leaders are wholly dependent on their capacity to build and sustain relationships.

Evidence abounds for this point of view. For instance, in examining the critical variables for success in the top three jobs in large organizations, Jodi Taylor and her colleagues at the Center for Creative Leadership (CCL) found that the number one success factor is "relationships with subordinates."[1] Claudio Fernandez-Araoz, a partner and a member of global search firm Egon Zehnder International's executive committee, is very direct about the importance of relationship skills. After studying success and failure in the executive ranks around the world, he concludes that "serious weaknesses in the domain of emotional intelligence predict failure at senior levels with amazing accuracy."[2] We were intrigued to find that even in this nanosecond world of e-everything, personal opinion is consistent with the facts. In an online survey, respondents were asked to indicate, among other things, "Which is more essential to business success five years from now—skills in using the Internet or social skills?"[3] Seventy-two percent selected social skills compared to 28 percent for Internet skills. Internet literati completing a poll online realize that it's not the web of technology that matters the most, it's the web of people.

---

*Portions of this chapter are excerpted by permission from: James M. Kouzes and Barry Z. Posner, *Encouraging the Heart: A Leader's Guide to Rewarding and Recognizing Others* (San Francisco: Jossey-Bass, 2003).

Similar results were found in a study by Public Allies, a nonprofit group dedicated to creating young leaders who can strengthen their communities. Public Allies sought the opinions of eighteen- to thirty-year-olds on the subject of leadership.[4] Among the items was a question about the qualities that were important in a good leader. Topping the eighteen- to-thirty-year-olds' list was: "Being able to see a situation from someone else's point of view." In second place was: "Getting along well with other people."

These days we're constantly being asked to learn new skills, take more risks, try out unfamiliar behaviors, and, like all humans, we fail a few times before we succeed. These requests can cause us great distress and create extreme discomfort. We're not likely to embrace the challenges unless we trust the person guiding and coaching us. So forever erase from your minds the image of the coach as that stern-faced, chair-throwing, dirt-kicking, ass-chewing tough guy who yells orders to the players. Maybe it makes good sports theater, but it definitely does not produce outstanding business performance. What you'll get instead is a demoralized group of disengaged constituents who'd rather quit than excel.

Success in the one-to-one leadership context is dependent on the ability of the leader to build a lasting relationship in which the talent sees the coach as a partner and a role model. In other words, you can't order others to perform at their best or improve what they do because of a position you hold. You can only get extraordinary things done because you have a heart.

Yes, heart. It turns out that the best leaders are caring leaders. We discovered this while researching for our book, *Encouraging the Heart*, and we'd like to apply some of those lessons to the role of leader as coach. Here are three essentials that contribute greatly to establishing and sustaining a successful coaching relationship:[5]

1. Set clear standards;
2. Expect the best; and
3. Set the example.

Set Clear Standards

Tony Codianni of Toshiba America explains it this way: "I have a need to be personal with my folks. To me there's no difference between work and personal life. Encouraging comes from the heart. It's heart-to-heart, not brain-to-heart. It has to be genuine."

Codianni is one of those people who loves people. He loves buying them presents; he loves inviting them out on his boat; he loves to cook for them. Codianni has nineteen first cousins, and he's taken them all to Italy. Ask anyone who works with him, and they'll all tell you they love to be around him. He makes them feel good.

But don't ever mistake Codianni's love of people for a willingness to forget about standards. Exemplary leadership is soft and demanding, caring and conscientious. As Codianni puts it, "I always tell trainers in my group that they have to master the program first, and then they're free to change it." To Codianni, having a clear set of expectations about what people will achieve is part and parcel of being caring.

The first prerequisite for encouraging the hearts of our talent is to set clear standards. By standards we mean both goals and values, because they both have to do with what's expected of us. Values serve as the enduring principles that enable us to maintain our bearings wherever we are throughout our lives. Goals are those shorter-term ambitions that provide us with the metrics for measuring progress.

Human beings just don't put their hearts into something if they don't believe in it. We won't commit with energy and intensity to something that's not a fit for us personally. It's like wearing a pair of slacks that are too tight. It's uncomfortable, we look awkward, we feel embarrassed, and we can't move around easily.

We know from the research we've been doing since the late 1970s that values make a difference in the way people behave inside organizations and how they feel about themselves, their colleagues, and their leaders. But when we take an even deeper look at the congruence between personal and organizational values we find something quite provocative.[6] We find that it's the clarity of *personal* values that drives an individual's commitment to an organization. Shared values do make a difference, but it's personal values that determine the fit between an individual and organization.

Exemplary leader-coaches also make sure that work is not pointless ambling, but purposeful action. Goal setting affirms the person, and, whether we realize it or not, contributes to what people think about themselves. As University of Chicago professor Mihaly Csikszentmihalyi points out: "It is the goals that we pursue that will shape and determine the kind of self that we are to become. Without a consistent set of goals, it is difficult to develop a coherent self. . . The goals one endorses also determine one's self-esteem."[7]

People need to know whether they're making progress or marking time. Goals help to serve that function, but goals are not enough. It's not enough to know that we want to make it to the summit. We also need to know whether we're still climbing or whether we're sliding downhill. Therefore, effective leader-coaches also provide constructive, timely, and accurate feedback. Encouragement is a form of feedback. It is positive information that tells us that we're making progress, that we're on the right track, and that we're living up to the standards.

The wonderful thing about encouragement is that it's more personal than other forms of feedback. Encouragement requires us to get close to other people, to show that we care about other people, and to demonstrate that we're really interested in other people. When leaders provide a clear set of standards and provide positive feedback on how we're meeting those standards, they encourage people to reach inside and put forth even more effort to get extraordinary things done.

Expect the Best

Successful leaders have high expectations, both of themselves and of their constituents. The belief that "I know you can do it" is a potent performance enhancer. It definitely is not some tasty pabulum that leaders dispense to help us keep a positive outlook on life. When someone else believes in us, we're much more likely to believe in ourselves. While high and low expectations influence other people's performance, only high expectations have a positive impact on both another's actions and feelings. And, most significantly, only high expectations can improve performance.

Nancy Tivol, executive director of Sunnyvale Community Services (SCS) in California, is a wonderful example of this principle in action. She believes strongly in her own ability and in those of every staff member and volunteer. When Tivol first arrived at SCS, volunteers were, in her opinion, underused. Many board members and paid staff felt that volunteers didn't have the skills to handle interactions with clients, donors, and corporate contacts. Tivol believed they did. Today, SCS has volunteers doing things previously done only by staff members. Indeed, more than seven hundred volunteers run the front office, the agency's three food programs, the Community Christmas Center, the agency's computer operations, and the Volunteer Language Bank—all under one director of volunteers. Most of the lead volunteers are over sixty-five years of age, and volunteer hours have increased from 6,000 to 20,000 annually, which enabled paid staff to be reduced through attrition from twelve to eight full-time equivalents.

Not only that, but SCS became the country's only emergency assistance agency that has not turned eligible clients away because available funds have been depleted. Under Tivol's leadership, SCS has increased its funding for the emergency assistance program for low-income families during a recession and a period in which many agencies experienced significant funding cutbacks!

Previous administrators, as well as paid staff, had made certain assumptions about volunteers. They assumed volunteers would be neither motivated enough nor skilled or experienced enough to take on the responsibility that the agency would require. As a result, volunteers were mostly employed at jobs that demanded little of them, and they were given only minimal responsibilities. The bottom line was that they weren't given the opportunity to explore or demonstrate their own capacities beyond the performance of the most menial tasks. Their beliefs held the volunteers back; Tivol's beliefs encouraged the same group of people to excel. She placed volunteers in responsible positions, gave them the training and direction they required, and encouraged them to do their best. And they did just that!

What was the motivation that drove the volunteers? Why did the SCS picture change so radically under Tivol? The key was her high expectations of the volunteers, and her expectations literally breathed new life into the people around her. She prophesied their success.

This demonstration of belief in another's abilities comes not only in organizational settings. It can show up anywhere. A moving and powerful instance came to us from Idaho businessman Don Bennett. Bennett was the first amputee to climb to the summit of Mt. Rainier. That's 14,410 feet on one leg and two crutches!

During a difficult portion of the climb, Bennett and his team had to cross an ice field. To get across the ice, the climbers had to put crampons on their boots to prevent slipping and to dig into the ice for leverage and stability. Unfortunately, with two crutches, and only one boot with a crampon, Bennett got stuck in the ice. He determined that the only way to get across the ice field was to fall face forward onto the ice, pull himself as far forward as he could, stand up, and then fall forward again. He was going to get across the ice field by falling down.

On that particular climb, his teenage daughter, Kathy, was with him, and she saw what was happening to her dad. While the team leader cut holes in the ice so Bennett could hop onto clear snow and traverse the ice field, Bennett's daughter stayed by his side through the entire four-hour struggle. As Bennett hopped, she shouted in his ear: "You can do it, Dad. You're the best dad in the world. You can do it, Dad!"

After Bennett told us this story, he added: "There was no way that I was not going to make it across that ice field with my daughter shouting that in my ear. You want to know what leadership is? What she did is leadership." Kathy's belief in her father and her verbal encouragement touched a place deep within Bennett, strengthening his resolve and commitment.

It's no wonder, then, that when people tell us about leaders who really make a difference in their lives, they frequently tell us about people who have believed in them and encouraged them to reach beyond their own self-doubts, to more fully realize their own greatest strengths. They talk about leaders who treat them in ways that buoy their self-confidence, making it possible for them to achieve more than they themselves initially believe is possible.

The thoughts and beliefs we hold in our minds are intangible. They can't be weighed and measured like raw materials or finished products. But seen or not, measurable or not, they have an enormous impact on the people around us. Exemplary leaders know this and know how to purposefully hold in their minds high expectations for themselves and for other people.

Set the Example

In research with Christy Tonge, we found that the factor most related to coaching effectiveness is "investing in the relationship." (There's that leadership-is-a-relationship finding again!) And, of all the items used to measure coaching behavior, the one most linked to success was "this person embodies character qualities and values that I admire."

In our continuing research on the qualities that people look for and admire in their leaders, time and time again we find that, more than anything else, people want leaders who are credible. Credibility is the foundation of leadership.[8]

People want to believe in their leaders. They want to believe that their leaders' words can be trusted and that their leaders will do what they say. Personal leadership credibility, we've found, makes a huge difference in performance and in commitment to organizations. A group's loyalty, commitment, energy, profitability, and productivity, among other outcomes, are directly linked to the credibility of the leader. Our findings are so consistent over such a long period of time that we've come to refer to this as the first law of leadership: *if you don't believe in the messenger, you won't believe the message.*

So exactly what is credibility? What is it behaviorally? How do you know it when you see it? When we ask people these questions their most frequent response is: "They do what they say they will do."[9]

When it comes to deciding whether a leader is believable, people first listen to the words and then watch the actions. They listen to the talk and watch the walk. Then, they measure the congruence. A judgment of "credible" is handed down when the two are consistent. If people don't see consistency, they conclude that the leader is at best not really serious about the words, and at worst is an outright hypocrite. Constituents are moved by deeds. Actions are the evidence of a leader's credibility. This observation leads to a straightforward prescription for sustaining credibility over time: DWYSYWD, Do What You Say You Will Do.

Over and over again, it's the same story. Wherever you find a strong culture built around strong values—whether the values are about superior quality, innovation, customer service, distinctiveness in design, respect for others, or just plain fun—you'll also find endless examples of leaders who personally live the values.

Personal involvement is what setting the example is all about. Terri Sarhatt, customer services manager of the Applied Biosystems Division of Perkin-Elmer, learned how important that is even in situations in which the rewards are tangible. Sarhatt was looking for a way to increase the amount of supportive communication she had with employees at the company, and as luck would have it, her decision to become more personally involved coincided with the annual distribution of stock options. At Applied Biosystems, as in many high-tech companies, people often receive stock options when they've had a good year, and because Applied Biosystems has been growing at around 20 percent for the last few years, it's been a regular occurrence.

In years past, Sarhatt would receive the options from her manager. She would then present options to her direct supervisors and request they do the same with their direct reports. In 1998, she decided to use a different tactic. She wanted to thank folks directly, so she asked her direct supervisors if they'd mind her meeting with each of their employees who were going to receive stock options. Her direct reports thought it was a terrific idea.

"I personally thanked them for the specific projects and the work they had done," said Sarhatt. "The employees were surprised that I would actually take the time out of my busy schedule to sit down with each of them separately, have a cup of coffee, and discuss their accomplishments. One of my supervisors informed me later that her employee appreciated the time I spent with her more than she appreciated the actual stock options!" As we have found so often in our research, the gift of personal time mattered most.

Sarhatt also told us that it's "the 'little' things that make such a BIG difference!" And that's the point. It doesn't take a grand plan to begin to set the example for encouraging the hearts of others. It doesn't take a huge budget, it doesn't take psychotherapy, and it doesn't take the boss's permission. What's most critical in all these examples is that the leaders took the initiative. Being a good role model is no exception. It has to become a conscious priority.

It's About Caring

Along the journey to developing yourself as an exemplary leader-coach, there is a fundamental question that you must confront: how much do you really care about the people you lead?

Now our hunch is that you care a lot. You probably wouldn't be reading this book and this chapter if you didn't. But this question must be confronted daily, because when you care deeply the methods that we've described will present themselves as genuine expressions of your caring. When you care little, they'll be perceived as nothing more than gimmicks, and you'll be thought of as a phony.

One of the oldest observations about human behavior is that we tend to mirror those around us. If we're around someone who's sad, for example, we pick it up. Even if we enter the room full of vim and vigor, we find that our energy starts to leak out when we're in the presence of negative emotions. Put yourself in the position of a person being coached. Imagine spending your days with a down-in-the-mouth, negative, and pessimistic leader. What a depressing thought.

But what happens to you when you enter a room full of upbeat, supportive, appreciative, and enthusiastic people? You tend to be uplifted yourself, don't you? We much prefer to be around positive people. And, by the way, researchers have also found that positive, hopeful, and optimistic people get more done in their lives and feel both personally and professionally more successful than do their more negative counterparts.

As the leader, you set the tone. When it comes to your role as leader-coach, the talent in your organization will grow and thrive only when you establish a clear set of high standards, display a strong belief that those standards can be achieved, and then demonstrate by your own actions that you practice what you preach.

When you integrate these three essentials into your daily practice, you will loudly and clearly communicate the message that "I care about you. I care about your future. I care about your growth. I'm here to create a climate in which you blossom and flourish." Not only will others find great joy and success in this caring climate, so, too, will you.

James M. Kouzes and **Barry Z. Posner** are the authors of the award-winning and best-selling book, *The Leadership Challenge,* with over one million copies in print. They've coauthored six other leadership books, including *Credibility: How Leaders Gain It and Lose It, Why People Demand It; Encouraging the Heart;* and *The Leadership Challenge Workbook.* Kouzes and Posner also developed the highly acclaimed *Leadership Practices Inventory* (LPI), a 360-degree questionnaire assessing leadership behavior.

They were named by the International Management Council as the 2001 recipients of the prestigious Wilbur M. McFeely Award. This honor puts them in the company of previous recipients Ken Blanchard, Stephen Covey, Peter Drucker, Edward Deming, Francis Hesselbein, Lee Iacocca, Rosabeth Moss Kanter, Norman Vincent Peale, and Tom Peters. Kouzes and Posner are frequent conference speakers, and each has conducted leadership development programs for hundreds of organizations around the world.

James M. Kouzes is an Executive Fellow at the Center for Innovation and Entrepreneurship at the Leavey School of Business, Santa Clara University. Not only is he a highly regarded leadership scholar and an experienced executive, but the *Wall Street Journal* has cited him as one of the twelve most requested non-university executive education providers to U.S. companies. A popular seminar and conference speaker, Kouzes shares his insights about the leadership practices that contribute to high performance in individuals and organizations. Contact: www.leadershipchallenge.com; jim@kouzesposner.com.

Barry Z. Posner, PhD, is dean of the Leavey School of Business, Santa Clara University, and professor of leadership. He served previously as managing partner of the Executive Development Center and has also served as associate dean with responsibility for leading the school's MBA and undergraduate programs. He has received the Dean's Award for Exemplary Service, the President's Distinguished Faculty Award, and several outstanding teaching and leadership honors. An internationally renowned scholar and educator, Posner is the author or coauthor of more than one hundred research and practitioner-focused articles. Contact: www.theleadershipchallenge.com; bposner@scu.edu.

PART III

CHALLENGES AND FORCES OF CHANGE

In **Part III, Challenges and Forces of Change,** issues veritably nonexistent in the past yet highly prevalent today are brought to light and explored by our contributors. Beginning the section with "Awareness Coaching for Men and Women," Sally Helgesen asserts that women and men can learn to work together effectively, and that coaching may be the key to harmony. R. Roosevelt Thomas, Jr. discusses the need for coaching all people by all people and discusses important factors to consider in Chapter Thirteen, "Coaching to Empower." In "Leading Across National Boundaries," Dr. Terence H. Kwai delves into the complicated, timely topic of globalization, more specifically the global company versus globalizing enterprises and the shaping of both by the policies and values of their home countries, especially China. In Chapter Fifteen, "Coaching for Governance," Anna Bateson explains how professional coaching affords business leaders and governance boards the opportunity to build "situational intelligence," which helps them more effectively gauge and respond to challenges in the context of the business and economic climate in which they operate. We end this section with "Leadership Insight: Going Beyond the Dehydrated Language of Management" by Nancy J. Adler. Here, Nancy clarifies the importance of traditionally artistic qualities being embraced by emerging, present, and future leaders, and claims that it is those companies that encourage humanity and social responsibility among their employees that will be at the forefront of innovation and will create financial success for their teams, their customers, and the greater community.

CHAPTER TWELVE

AWARENESS COACHING FOR MEN AND WOMEN

By Sally Helgesen

For twenty-five years I've worked with women leaders around the globe to develop and hone their leadership skills. My efforts have been directed at helping women articulate their best talents, claim greater visibility in their organizations, enlist and leverage strong allies, build powerful webs of support, hold themselves accountable for change, and cultivate a more powerful and authentic leadership presence. More recently, clients have asked me to offer coaching to men in senior positions who seek to work more skillfully with women—as bosses, customers, clients, board members, and partners.

My coaching methods and protocols for men and women often differ, as I will describe below. But both practices are rooted in insights I've developed in the course of researching six books, all of which examine how social, demographic, economic, and technological changes are transforming organizations. My work with both men and women is therefore focused on helping them position themselves to address the big strategic issues their organizations will face in the *future*, given how the confluence of changes is creating new conditions. Jeffrey Immelt, chair and CEO of GE, recently predicted that the ability to "see around the corners" will be *the* most important leadership capacity in the years ahead. I work to help clients develop their ability to see around the corners—to read the changing environment with subtlety, skill, and discernment.

Coaching Women

My primary goal when coaching women is to help them be more influential at the strategic level. Organizations exist to develop and allocate resources efficiently—financial resources, natural resources, human resources. Having strategic influence means having a say in the most important decisions about how these resources are produced, leveraged, deployed, distributed, and delivered. Women now actively participate in the execution of strategic decisions, but they have limited influence when it comes to making those decisions. This limits their capacity both to shape the future and to give their most authentic talents full scope.

What is the source of this limitation and how can women address it? I find three things are essential. First, women must understand, appreciate, articulate, and defend the importance of their vision—what they see, what they notice, how they connect the dots. Second, women must skillfully leverage support so that their best observations are heard and attended to. Finally, women must develop a more powerful and authentic leadership presence.

The Vision Thing

Two major international studies make clear that women have limited impact at the strategic level because they are not seen as "visionary," particularly by senior leaders. My research indicates that women in fact have significant visionary powers, rooted in their intuitive sense and capacity for empathic notice. Yet women often struggle to articulate the value of what they see because their perceptual style—their way of noticing—is different from the traditional male style.

When researching *The Female Vision: Women's Real Power at Work,* my coauthor, Julie Johnson, and I found that men's and women's attention often operates in contrasting ways. Women tend to notice many things at the same time, picking up signals as they scan the environment broadly. Men, by contrast, tend to notice one thing at a time, focusing deeply and filtering out distractions. The operative metaphor for women's ways of noticing is radar; the metaphor for male notice is the laser. Not only did our interviews indicate this difference, but functional MRI studies conducted by neuroscientific researchers documented these differences in perceptual patterns by observing how men's and women's brains process information.

Obviously women's capacity for broad-spectrum notice should constitute an asset in an environment where organizations need to "see around the corners." To achieve this, balanced notice is essential. But because focused notice has traditionally been privileged in organizations and viewed as a leadership behavior (not surprising, given its male provenance), women are often discouraged from employing their distinctive style of noticing. Women we interviewed for the book reported being told that they'd "noticed the wrong thing" when they shared an observation; they often had the sense that top leadership wouldn't listen to "anything that's not based on quantitative data—even if that data leaves a lot out."

Recognizing that intuitive or empathic observations hold a low status, women often develop the habit of suppressing their most original and potentially useful insights, thus depriving their organizations of important information while also diminishing their own capacity for authentic contribution. As one of our interviewees noted, "After six years on the job, my ability to notice things just sort of withered up. I got used to my ideas not being heard."

There are three ways to help women out of this impasse. First, the client needs to be coached to recognize, articulate, and defend the value of what she sees, what she notices, how she connects the dots. Helping her understand her own perceptual patterns, and see how these differ from what her organization expects, is a start. She also needs to develop an understanding of how what she sees connects to how the environment in which her organization must function is evolving—that is, she must frame what she notices in the context of the future. Finally, she needs to carefully calibrate a way to share what she sees in terms that senior leadership can understand by taking into account how their patterns of perception may differ. This usually requires editing scene-setting details that feel important to her but which colleagues may view as extraneous, gathering supporting data in advance of presenting ideas, and lining up a supporter or two in advance.

Leveraging Support

There are four kinds of power in organizations: the power of position, the power of personal authority, the power of expertise, and the power of connections. Of these, the power of connections is most important. Yet women often focus upon building up their content expertise, while men build the connections they need to ensure success. I see it all the time: a woman comes into a new position, keeps her head down, and devotes her efforts to mastering the details of her work. A man comes into a new position and immediately begins looking around for people who can help him get the job done.

There is a paradox here, because women are often great at *building* relationships. Yet they are not always so good at *leveraging* relationships, or using them to achieve an advantage. Leverage implies intentionality, a quid pro quo that women may be uncomfortable in asserting. Even highly placed senior women report having inhibitions about being seen as "using people" if they blur the lines between friendship and let's-make-a-deal. As a result, their personal webs remain distinct from their operational webs, and neither evolves into the kind of strategic webs that support high-level influence.

What is required to move this situation forward? First, women often need help in avoiding the trap of overvaluing expertise. Expertise is a given at the leadership level, but being expert does not secure influence. Strategic power results from having allies who support what you are trying to achieve. Women often need help in identifying potential allies (who may be but are not necessarily friends) and figuring out what it will take to cultivate them. This in turn requires knowing what to ask of allies (the quid part of the equation) and being explicit about what those allies can expect in return (the quo). A woman may also need coaching to recognize how her allies can benefit from their association with her. This moves her past the fear of feeling like a user or a beggar and positions her as a player.

Leadership Presence

Women often ask me how they can develop a more powerful leadership presence. Should they work on their voices, their clothing, their posture? Is where a woman chooses to sit in a meeting significant? These details are important, but my work has convinced me that the real key to establishing a strong leadership presence is the ability to be fully present. There's a reason the two words are linked.

Being fully present is a challenge for everyone in our 24/7 environment, where the desire to be efficient tempts us to do several things at once, to respond rather than being intentional in our actions, or to lose our centeredness as we race through our tasks. But the problem is particularly pressing for women, who often pride themselves on their multitasking ability, whose radar-like notice can diminish their capacity to remain grounded, and who routinely manage multiple responsibilities at work and at home.

What's the solution? What can help women remain mindful even in high-stress situations? I find three approaches to be useful. First, women can benefit from coaching that helps them identify and set the boundaries they must maintain in order to be present. This requires establishing policies and procedures around their use of technologies—when they will be available and how they will respond. I call it being your own HR department; only an individual woman knows what she needs to be most effective, so part of her job is ensuring the conditions that best protect her ability to be so. Creating realistic expectations, setting boundaries in advance of a project, being clear about why these are necessary—all this is essential. So is developing what I call a "rhythm of renewal," simple practices that can be incorporated daily to connect a woman to the ground of her being and enable her to be fully present in the moment rather than anticipating or feeling at the mercy of unfolding events.

Coaching Men

My coaching practice with men is relatively new. I began offering it because there are few resources available to help men navigate the new terrain in regard to women. Most of the men I work with have faced some challenges in working with female clients, customers, bosses, and colleagues. Yet they recognize that the ability to work well and productively with women has become a career imperative. They want to do a good job of it, but they need some tools. Because most organizations were developed on what might be called the male watch, male values are often assumed to be the norm. As a result, male behaviors that cause difficulty with women often take place on autopilot. Once men recognize what's happening, they know what to do.

Identifying Stumbling Blocks

In 2011 I conducted a series of wide-ranging interviews with male executives and coaches in order to identify the problems that inhibit men from working well with women. These are problems with sexual attraction, the fear of rejection, a concern that women will talk about them with other women, the perception that women have unfair advantages, and issues with trust. These problems are often rooted in strong emotions or past experiences, and they present authentic stumbling blocks. Yet they are seldom acknowledged or discussed because of the fear of political incorrectness. Coaching can provide a safe haven for addressing these inhibitions in frank and probing ways and devising solutions that address them.

For example, men often have problems trusting women because they attribute their own values to them—this is what social scientists call the "fundamental attribution error" or FAE, a concept introduced to me by Marshall Goldsmith. Whereas women often place a high degree of value on being honest when presenting their views, men may be more likely to value loyalty. When a man asks for feedback during a meeting, a woman might say: "Isn't this the kind of strategy that got us into trouble before?" By contrast, her male colleague may respond with Homer Simpson: "Great idea, boss!"

A man may interpret her caveat as evidence that she doesn't have his interests at heart and cannot be trusted to support him. Or he may decide that, since she's willing to quibble with him in public, she might do the same with important customers and so is not to be trusted around *them*. His response is understandable, yet it shows him to be blind to the fact that, *from her perspective*, what she demonstrated in the meeting was a willingness to put his interests first.

Fundamental attribution errors often cause men to trust women who are not trustworthy and *not* trust women who are. I counseled a male entrepreneur who'd gotten into trouble after he went into business with a female marketer about whom several women in his former company had warned him. He said, "I assumed those women just wanted her position so I discounted what they had to say. It didn't occur to me that they were trying to be helpful—why would they, when I was leaving them behind? I couldn't read where they where coming from. And I really couldn't read the woman I hired. She talked a great game, said all the things I wanted to hear."

This man needed a protocol for identifying and surmounting his tendency to project his own motivations on women. This required that he begin talking to women in a way designed to elicit useful information rather than short-circuiting to what he assumed spurred their behavior. Once he had a script—a template of specific questions that enabled him to develop accurate information—he became adept in talking to people with different values, and was recognized in his company for this skill. This capacity also enabled him to develop a more accurate radar when it came to knowing when to trust women and judging which women to trust.

Stepping Up

Women's personal networks are abuzz with information—especially information about relationships. Men know this: they hear their wives discussing personal issues with female friends, often sharing precise and intimate details. Such behaviors form the primary basis of female bonding, the "tend and befriend" response that evolutionary psychologists describe as the chief way women manage stress. But my interviews with male executives suggest that women's observational powers and zest for discussing details can inhibit men from speaking honestly and directly with them because they want to stay out of range of the female grapevine.

A better approach is to view the female grapevine as a potential advantage rather than a liability; a resource a man can use to build support. For just as men can stir discussion among women by exhibiting out-of-touch behaviors, so can they also generate an almost unreasonable amount of goodwill by taking simple actions that get amplified by female networks.

For example, a male consultant noticed that a female colleague's ideas were routinely given short shrift during meetings. He wondered why she didn't push back, then decided to speak up himself. The next time he observed her being overlooked, he made a point of noting that she seemed to be contributing the best ideas.

Several of his male colleagues seemed startled; they had barely registered that she was in the room. But *she* noticed, and she and the other women present were quick to spread the word. The consultant soon found that he was perceived as a champion of women throughout the organization, even in its overseas offices. This halo effect turned out to be extremely useful when a woman was appointed to head up his division. He had credibility with her from the day she walked in the office.

The Vision Thing

Differences in male and female perceptual patterns—such as I outlined earlier—can make it difficult for men to understand and appreciate women's potential for strategic contribution. Women know this and are sensitive to it. Men—often acting on FAEs—are less apt to register when this occurs. Not only does this dynamic have a negative impact on a man's ability to gain a woman's trust, it also results in the loss of potentially vital insights. The journalist Tom Friedman likes to quote a senior engineer at Siemens who lamented, "If Siemens only knew what Siemens really knows, we'd be the greatest company on earth." A prime reason that organizations have trouble knowing what they really know is that women's observations and insights get filtered out.

What to do in this situation? I find three approaches effective. First, men need to be aware of the nature of perceptual differences, so they can avoid being unconsciously dismissive of ideas rooted in a way of seeing the world that is different from their own. It helps if men understand why information arrived at by what seem to be unorthodox methods can be important. For example, a recent study published in the *Harvard Business Review* found that, contrary to conventional wisdom, big picture strategic insights occur in those areas of the brain associated with empathy and intuition rather than logical thinking. As a result, observations framed in the language of "I feel" or "It occurred to me"—language that sounds thoroughly subjective—are often highly relevant, especially when it comes to understanding and planning for the future.

Finally, men need to know what questions to ask in order to get a better feel for the context of women's ideas. "Tell me the steps you went through to arrive at that insight" is a far more effective initial response than "Sounds good, but where's your data?" Supporting evidence is, of course, necessary for deciding on whether to act on information, but asking for it prematurely cuts off the kind of discussion required to see the big picture. By taming the desire to "cut to the chase" or to "bottom-line it," men can dramatically improve their ability to work productively and well with women while also expanding their own ability to see around the corners.

Sally Helgesen is an author, speaker, and coach, cited by the Athena Group as number fifteen in its survey of the world's most influential leadership experts. Her books include *The Female Vision: Women's Real Power at Work*; *The Web of Inclusion: A New Architecture for Building Great Organizations*, cited in *The Wall Street Journal* as one of the best books on leadership of all time; and *The Female Advantage: Women's Ways of Leadership*.

CHAPTER THIRTEEN

COACHING TO EMPOWER

By R. Roosevelt Thomas, Jr.

I believe that Empowerment Management is critical to creating an organizational environment that enables a diverse group of employees to contribute to their full potential. I believe further that Empowerment Coaching is critical to achieving Empowerment Management. This chapter explores the concept of coaching to empower, as opposed to coaching for execution.

By way of analogy, the chapter begins by looking briefly at the differences between these two modalities in the context of sports. It then explores what coaching for empowerment looks like in the field of diversity. It next examines the conditions that make Empowerment Coaching a viable choice. The objective is to enhance understanding about Empowerment Coaching and to make it more accessible to those coaching in the midst of diversity.

Coaching in the Sports Arena

Execution Coaching[1]

While the Execution Coach prepares for a sporting contest by prescribing game plays and stressing execution, he does much of his coaching during the actual game. He directs and problem solves. He gives prescriptions for winning and expects execution. In a real sense, it is as if the players are extensions of him. The players look to their coach for a game plan, and then they execute.

One often sees this model in college, where coaches perceive—rightly or wrongly—that players typically lack the experience and judgment necessary for doing more than focusing on execution. As a result, the competition often boils down to which team executes best. If players deviate from the game plan, or fail to execute, they displease their coach.

Once, in an NCAA basketball championship game, the coach called a last-minute play that, if executed properly, could win the game. The player who was to get the ball to the designated shooter did not see a passing lane that would work for him, so he took the shot and made an incredible basket.

As his teammates mobbed him and the crowd went wild, the television cameras focused on a sullen coach. One announcer noted, "Coach is not happy because [the player] did not stick with the called play." At no point did this Execution Coach compliment the player for making the winning shot. The hero was guilty of thinking and adapting—that was the coach's job. Indeed, the hero's demeanor reflected regret for not following the coach's orders, as opposed to celebration over winning the championship.

For Execution Coaches, "success" is great execution. Great game plans plus excellent execution equals winning. This formula often results in coaches receiving a disproportionate amount of credit for the team's wins.

Empowerment Coaching

The Empowerment Coach seeks to empower players with a **capability** to think through game situations and to react and adapt as necessary. This coach focuses less on coming up with a winning game plan, and more on a winning preparation that embeds "a way of thinking"—a capability—into the players. Although the word "execution" might be used in these situations, "application of" or "utilization of" the embedded capability is more descriptive of what the Empowerment Coach expects. Through the capability, players are expected to think, behave proactively and reactively, and to adjust as necessary—all on the fly.

Empowerment Coaches perform their most critical work away from the actual game as they embed the desired capability. During the game, they cheerlead for application, more so than problem solve. This approach is markedly different from that of the Execution Coach.

The Execution Coach believes that "execution" of the game plan is the key to winning. The Empowerment Coach believes that effective application of the embedded capability is central to winning, so he shies away from extensive problem solving and directing during the game. The more this execution-like coaching behavior is necessary, the more likely the Empowerment Coach has done a poor job in embedding the capability.

A good example of when Empowerment Coaching is necessary is that of the Triangle Offense.[2] Phil Jackson, former head coach of the Chicago Bulls and the Los Angeles Lakers, popularized this approach.

Most say that his offense is complex and requires players capable of mastering it. Attention to detail is critical, as are spacing specifics. Reportedly, no set plays exist, only possibilities. For most of the players, roles are interchangeable. Players must read the defense and take opportunities that become available.

Because of this complexity, players must commit fully. They also must be able to focus intensely on the offense and its requirements. It literally must become a mindset—a capability—that they apply unconsciously in a game.

To embed this offense in the mental maps of players, the coach must understand it fully himself and then must explain it effectively to the players. But, beyond the technicalities of the offense, the Empowerment Coach must foster complete commitment to the team, and also must facilitate the clarity of mind required for the sharp focusing needed to make the Triangle Offense work.

Phil Jackson proved very skillful at securing commitment and focus with the Bulls and the Lakers. This commitment to team is especially critical when superstars are on the squad. Essentially, the Triangle Offense seeks balance between the team as a whole and its best players. Phil Jackson reportedly went to the Triangle Offense to make it difficult for opposing players to hone in disproportionately on his superstar Michael Jordan.

Once he embedded the offense into his team, Jackson coached relatively unobtrusively during games. On one occasion, as matters deteriorated on the floor, Jackson's assistant hollered for him to call time-out and earn his pay. Jackson responded, "Ah, let them work it out."[3]

That is what you would expect from an Empowerment Coach who fostered capability before games, and saw self-management during games as steps toward further mastery of the offense. He sought excellence in application of the Triangle Offense in pursuit of solutions for defenses presented by opposing teams. Phil Jackson offered a stark contrast to the Execution Coach.

Coaching in the Diversity Arena

Execution Coaching

In the diversity field, Execution Coaching appears to dominate. Individuals desire the "five to-dos" with respect to a given diversity issue. This is true whether in a one-on-one coaching session or in a workshop. Workshop participants desire takeaways they can execute the next day.

Practitioners end up with "to-dos" for different types of diversity issues; such as gender, generational, ethnic, functional, acquisition/merger, and customer diversity. As issues surface, chief diversity officers (CDOs) and other organizational leaders routinely seek prescriptions they can execute.

Sometimes this Execution Coaching manifests itself through the practice of benchmarking. "Best practices" leaders in the field provide coaching through one-on-one presentations and participation in benchmarking workshops. Success for participants is the acquisition of some execution prescriptions that can be used immediately.

Four circumstances make Execution Coaching problematic for CDOs and their organizations.

One, CDOs can become experts on "best practices" without a corresponding growth in understanding about diversity and diversity management.

Two, the continued accumulation of lists of execution prescriptions as different diversity issues become priorities can become problematic. CDOs can find themselves running around asking, "What are the best practices with respect to such-and-such diversity issues?" Keeping track of these lists and their implications can become challenging.

Three, unempowered CDOs likely will not empower their organizations. Here, CDOs practice diversity management for their enterprises, much as affirmative action officers carry out affirmative action efforts. The difficulty here is that diversity management cannot be limited to the collective organization. Individual executives, managers, and individual contributors must participate as well. This is a major distinction between affirmative action and diversity management, and it is this difference that makes centralized diversity management unacceptable.

Four, "best practices" may not be optimal for a given enterprise. The conditions that make a best practice suitable for one organization may not be present in another. Without the larger context of diversity management, the CDO can be in a poor position to customize solutions.

Empowerment Coaching

These challenges account for my belief that CDOs who are serious about diversity management will benefit most by practicing Empowerment Coaching within the context of the Strategic Diversity Management Process™ (SDMP™).[4]

SDMP is a universal capability. It offers the wherewithal to think through diversity issues of *any* kind in pursuit of quality decisions that support an entity's overarching objectives. Individuals as leaders, managers, and individual contributors can apply this capability to traditional diversity issues like race, gender, ethnicity, and sexual orientation, as well as to those not usually thought of as diversity issues; such as decentralization/centralization, acquisitions/mergers, functional integration, change, innovation, and thought.

One can think of SDMP as a craft, which once mastered results in capability. The premise is that the craft can be applied to *any* diversity issue in *any* setting in *any* geographic location. As a craft, SDMP has concepts, principles, and requirements for practice, mastery, and continuous improvement, performance standards, characteristics of art, and specific discrete subskills. Most people and organizations cannot pick up the craft easily, nor excel with it immediately. It cannot be learned in a three-day workshop. Instead, it requires understanding, work, and determination over a period of time.

Three basic elements comprise the process: (1) universal concepts, (2) universal principles, and (3) a universal decision-making framework.

The universal concepts are as follows:

- **Diversity** is the differences and similarities, and related tensions and complexities that can characterize mixtures of any kind. When you speak of diversity, you are describing a characteristic of a collection or mixture of some kind; such as employees, customers, vendors, functions, organizations participating in an acquisition or a merger, citizens, family members, or congregants in a religious setting.
- **Diversity management** is the ability to make quality decisions in the midst of any set of differences and similarities, and related tensions and complexities.
- **Diversity tension** is the stress and strain that comes from the interaction and clashing of differences and similarities.
- **Diversity-challenged** describes the degree to which one has difficulty making quality decisions in the midst of any set of differences and similarities, and related tensions and complexities.
- **Diversity-capable** describes the extent to which one possesses the capability to make quality decisions in the midst of any set of differences and similarities, and related tensions and complexities.

The **universal principles** are the following:

- Conceptual clarity and operationalization are necessities.
- Context is important.
- Being requirements-driven (as opposed to being driven by traditions, preferences, or conveniences) is a must.
- Individuals *and* organizations need diversity-management capability.
- A readiness and capability for universal application is an imperative.

The **universal decision-making process** combines SDMP's universal concepts and principles into a convenient application framework with six steps:

Step 1: Specify context and overall "requirements"
Step 2: Recognize the nature and context of the mixture in question

Step 3: Assess the mixture's tensions and complexities

Step 4: Identify the mixture's requirements

Step 5: Identify the organizational culture and systemic factors that must be considered as actions are planned

Step 6: Plan actions

SDMP mastery requires acquisition of three basic diversity-management skills:

1. The ability to recognize diversity mixtures. Individuals can only use SDMP where they have identified diversity mixtures. This skill therefore is critical.
2. The ability to determine whether action is required with respect to a particular diversity mixture. An infinite number of mixtures exist. Therefore, it is imperative to be able to determine which are of such significant *strategic* importance personally or organizationally to merit priority, or indeed, so relatively insignificant to merit no attention.
3. The ability to select appropriate responses once you are sure action is required. This means that the individual has the ability to generate and explore solution alternatives.

Diversity maturity refers to the degree to which an individual or organization understands and can utilize SDMP universal concepts and principles. The characteristics of the **diversity mature individual** are:

- Acknowledges being diversity challenged
- Recognizes cost of being diversity challenged
- Accepts diversity management responsibility
- Demonstrates contextual knowledge
  - Personal objectives (knows himself or herself)
  - Organizational objectives (knows his or her organization)
  - Conceptual clarity (understands key diversity concepts and definitions)
- Acts on the basis of requirements
  - Differentiates among preferences, traditions, conveniences and requirements
  - Places differences and similarities in context when making diversity management decisions
- Challenges conventional wisdom
- Engages in continuous learning

- Copes with diversity dynamics
  - Utilizes a process framework in addressing diversity
  - Has a comfort level with diversity tension
- Utilizes the elements of SDMP effectively

A corresponding set of characteristics exists for the **diversity mature organization**:

- Collectively acknowledges being diversity challenged
- Recognizes the cost of being diversity challenged
- Provides conceptual clarity for all employees
- Ensures planning and implementation of organizational initiatives with respect to managing all critical diversity mixtures
- Pursues cultural change where appropriate
- Strives to be "**Requirements Driven**"
- Ensures everyone is comfortable with the dynamics of diversity
- Avoids "**Feel Good**" traps
- Fosters mastery of the SDMP decision-making framework by everyone in the organization at *all* levels

My job as an Empowerment Coach is to assist the individual and organization in acquiring the basic diversity management skills, and in moving into diversity maturity. I literally can do this without ever specifying how any particular diversity issue should be addressed. Success comes for me when the individual and organization, as a result of understanding and practicing, effectively apply SDMP to *any* diversity issue in *any* setting in *any* geographical location. My job as an Empowerment Coach would be done.

Challenges

Several significant challenges deserve mention. One is that people and organizations do not necessarily wish to be empowered in the diversity arena. Sometimes, they believe diversity and diversity management are simple to achieve, and should not be overcomplicated. Or, they may possess a narrow view of diversity and thus do not see the need for a universal capability. Another possibility might be that they have a strong bias toward action and an aversion to concepts and principles.

Even where awareness of diversity and diversity management exists in a universal sense, leaders may not wish to make the necessary investment of resources.

Relatively speaking, it is less expensive to go out and find a prescriptive list than to undergo the transition that likely will be required for organizations and individuals to master SDMP.

For others, the magnitude of the change possibly needed in organizational culture, systems, policies, and practices may be discouraging, even when the enterprise has the necessary resources. Leaders simply may not consider the benefits of enhanced diversity management worth the inconvenience of the necessary modifications.

Finally, some leaders may not want progress with diversity. For whatever reason, they may be content with defensive strategies such as effective public relations campaigns and annual training programs that can give the appearance of progress. These efforts could convey "commitment" without the costs and inconvenience of transitioning to SDMP mastery.

Benefits

Despite the challenges the benefits can be impressive. Mastery of SDMP brings a capability to generate and self-customize approaches for diversity issues as necessary, thus reducing the need for accumulating prescriptive lists.

This capability can be dispersed throughout the organization down to where the requisite information for a given decision resides. When this happens, individuals with issues are empowered to develop appropriate action plans, and do not have to push everything up to the CDO and other leaders.

All of this would bring greater ownership of diversity and diversity management and also momentum, thereby setting the stage for greater sustainable progress. This would facilitate the work of CDOs immensely.

The Viability of Empowerment Coaching

As one might expect, Empowerment Coaching is not for all coaching situations, although many coaches utilize it. The discussions about the Triangle Offense and SDMP can reveal conditions that are favorable for empowerment coaching.

Whenever the situation for which coaching is being offered has multiple permutations—like diversity or the defensive schemes of opposing teams, Empowerment Coaching can be beneficial. In these circumstances, the ability to generate and customize action options as needed can be a big plus, and negate the necessity of gathering prescriptive lists.

Similarly, whenever success requires the contributions of all players, Empowerment Coaching can be useful. With Phil Jackson, the Triangle Offense involved all players extensively and meaningfully, thereby making it difficult for opposing teams to hone in on super stars without paying a price. Similarly, with Diversity and Diversity Management, CDOs require buy-in, ownership and commitment by executives, managers and individual contributors, as they seek to develop an environment that works for all. SDMP can foster the necessary empowerment throughout the organization.

Further, whenever the issue under consideration is so complex that more than the coach's wisdom is needed, Empowerment Coaching can be a plus. Stated differently, in basketball the Triangle Offense can put the play selection in the hands of the players who might be better positioned to make the call than the coach—especially, if the decision-making framework has been embedded in them. Also, with SDMP, individuals down in the organization might have the necessary perspective and information to be in a better position to make decisions on an issue more effectively and efficiently than CDOs and other senior leaders.

Also, Empowerment Coaching is practiced often where development is important. In a previously cited example where Phil Jackson refused to call timeout to rescue his players from a deteriorating game situation, but elected to let them work it out, he placed a priority on development that could serve the team well in future games. Similarly, in organizational circumstances, managers can employ empowerment as a developmental strategy.

Finally, Empowerment Coaching works to connect diverse "players" through an embedded framework. If that framework is like the Triangle Offense and the SDMP, where room is left for individual differences within the context of requirements, the results can be inclusiveness without unnecessary conformity.

Initial Steps

CDOs and other executives and managers might be wondering where to begin with implementation of Empowerment Coaching. A good first step is to check the type of coaching you are providing in the midst of diversity. If you routinely give "to-dos," you probably are an Execution Coach.

A second step would be to identify a Diversity and Diversity Management model that you can use to embed capability. At a minimum, the model you adopt should offer concepts, principles, and a decision-making framework. SDMP works for me in this regard.

Next, you should make certain that your organization's culture and people management systems and practices will support Empowerment Coaching. Otherwise, you will have difficulty sustaining progress.

Finally, be prepared to pioneer. As I noted earlier, I do not perceive Empowerment Coaching to be prevalent in the Diversity and Diversity Management arena. You will be charting new territory.

For the past twenty-five years, **R. Roosevelt Thomas, Jr.,** D.B.A., has been at the forefront of developing and implementing innovative concepts and strategies for maximizing organizational and individual potential through diversity management. He currently serves as CEO of Roosevelt Thomas Consulting & Training, Inc., and as Founder/Trustee Emeritus of The American Institute for Managing Diversity (AIMD). Dr. Thomas is the author of seven published books; his most recent is *World Class Diversity Management: A Strategic Approach.* Dr. Thomas has been active for more than twenty-five years as a consultant to numerous Fortune 500 companies, corporation, professional firms, government entities, nonprofit organizations, and academic institutions, and he has served as a frequent speaker at national conferences and industry seminars. He has also served as secretary of Morehouse College, dean of the Graduate School of Business Administration at Atlanta University, assistant professor at the Harvard Business School, and instructor at Morehouse College. Further, Dr. Thomas has been recognized by *The Wall Street Journal* as one of the top ten consultants in the country, elected as a Fellow in the National Academy of Human Resources, and cited by *Human Resource Executive* as one of HR's Most Influential People. Contact: www.rthomasconsulting.com; rthomas@rthomasconsulting.com.

CHAPTER FOURTEEN

LEADING ACROSS NATIONAL BOUNDARIES

By Dr. Terence H. Kwai

There are those who argue that our age is an age of finance; others, including Alan Webber, founder of *Fast Company* magazine, says it is an age of innovation, while still others, Deepak Chopra among them, assert that we are living in an age of consciousness. In my view, it is a combination of all three. In the twenty-first century, major wars are unlikely to occur because any massive nuclear attacks will lead to a nuclear winter, which will essentially herald the end of the world.

In his book, *Money and Power: How Goldman Sachs Came to Rule the World,* William D. Cohan asserted that the age of finance had arrived. As a result of the financial meltdown in 2008, much of the Western world is in deep trouble. America's federal debt has exceeded $15 trillion, and including private sector debt and household debt, America's debt reaches $55 trillion. This does not even take into account the American government's "implicit" liabilities to fund Social Security and Medicare benefits. Social Security is sometimes referred to as the third rail by American politicians, because those politicians who touch it by suggesting any cut in benefits tend to receive a violent political shock from the American Association of Retired Persons (AARP). The shortfall in meeting these liabilities had been calculated to amount to $45 trillion. In other words, America is technically broke. The QE2, a policy pursued by the Federal Reserve by buying $600 billion of Treasury securities by June 30, 2011, has amounted to monetizing the federal debt, a polite way of saying "printing money." Certainly, America is inflating away its debt. But the consequence is, of course, the depreciation of the greenback and American real assets, or the fact that real assets denominated in American dollars could become cheap to buy. Thus far, there has been political resistance to sell off such assets to would-be buyers. But the day will come when people starved of cash will be desperate to sell.

Europe is in a debt crisis: the PIGS problem. PIGS stands for Portugal, Italy, Greece, and Spain. Currently, the Greek people have to accept austerity measures. As of June 24, 2011, European Union leaders agreed to give Greece another 120 billion euros of support. The money would come from 17 Eurozone countries and the International Monetary Fund (IMF). It is likely that Greece would not exit from the Eurozone, and the euro as a currency would not break apart.

Nearing the end of his eight-year term, Jean-Claude Trichet, head of the European Central Bank, suggested a European finance ministry that would over-see spending by national governments. There are already daily protests in Greece against austerity measures that many see as being imposed from outside. The suggestion that European officials might essentially dictate policies would be seen as a fundamental challenge to Greek democracy. Although Britain is not a member of the Eurozone, Prime Minister David Cameron faces formidable opposition as he tries to instill austerity measures too. As we've seen, there is a fundamental antagonism between finance and democracy in the West.

China is now the second largest economy in the world and holds a foreign exchange reserve exceeding $3 trillion, of which $1.15 trillion is held in U.S. Treasury securities. China is investing in European bonds in a move to diversify away from the falling greenback. In China, the antagonism is between finance and corruption. Rapid social and economic changes have made China prone to corruption, and the ruling Communist Party faces a major challenge stamping out deep-rooted official graft. In 2010, the Communist Party investigated more than 139,000 cases of "disciplinary violations"—a phrase that refers to official wrongdoing—and punished more than 146,000 party members. Of those punished, only 5,373 cases were handed over to the state judiciary for criminal proceedings.

According to a report released by China's central bank, between 16,000 and 18,000 officials and employees of state-owned companies have stolen more than $120 billion and fled overseas, mainly to the United States between the mid-1990s and 2008. The study said corruption inside China was severe enough to threaten the nation's economic and political stability.

This is certainly an age of finance because major conquests by war would be ruled out, but how finance can perform its proper function remains to be seen. Broadly speaking, financial services are to cater to people's fear and anxiety by providing a sense of peace and security. But by appropriating economic rent instead of providing a sense of peace and security, modern finance has failed in its function and role in society.

C. K. Prahalad and M. S. Krishnan have written a book, *The New Age of Innovation: Driving Co-Created Value through Global Networks* (2008). The authors expound on the proposition that the focus is on the centrality of the individual by designating this pillar as N=1 (one customer experience at a time), and another focus is on access to resources, not ownership of resources by designating this pillar as R=G (resources from multiple vendors and often around the globe). While this sounds appealing, it is questionable on the grounds of having too much faith in the omnipotence of ICT (information and communications technologies).

Those of us who are native to China, as I am, do believe in the wonderful world of technology and innovation. In fact, China has a long tradition of science, discovery, and invention that stretches over 3,000 years. Some of this is recorded in Joseph Needham's monumental work, *Science and Civilization in China*. China's Education Ministry says that there are now some 1.27 million students attending foreign universities. In 2010 alone, more than 284,000 Chinese went abroad to study, most of them privately funded. Chinese officials say the country has the largest number of overseas students in the world. While Chinese students have brought money to foreign colleges and universities hard hit by the global financial crisis, China is acquiring the knowledge and skills needed to drive the country's rapid growth. In the past thirty years or so, more than 630,000 Western-trained students and scholars have returned home, about one-fifth of that number in 2010 alone. Many of them are now engaged in research and development that is boosting China's global competitive position.

William E. Halal, Professor Emeritus of Science, Technology & Innovation at George Washington University, wrote a remarkable book, *Technology's Promise: Expert Knowledge on the Transformation of Business and Society* (Palgrave MacMillan, 2008). In this fascinating forecast of science and technology, Halal shows that relentless technological progress is driving the creative transformation of business, society, the world, and even what it means to be human. In his words,

> Both evidence and knowledgeable opinion confirm we are moving to a more populous world that is largely industrialized and intelligent, but that also poses unprecedented risks of environmental damage, energy shortages, climate change, weapons of mass destruction, and other threats that require sophisticated responses unimaginable by present standards. These crises seem insurmountable because the present world system is not sustainable, and a shift to a more sophisticated system is unavoidable to avert disaster. Some of these dilemmas may be ameliorated by advances in economics and technology, but they can only be resolved through the logic of evolution, which is now moving beyond knowledge. At about 2020, the very time when the planet is likely to teeter between calamity and salvation, routine human thought should be automated by far more sophisticated IT networks, a second generation of more powerful computers, and good AI (artificial intelligence). As various forms of

machine intelligence take over common mental tasks, we will simply move up another level on the evolutionary hierarchy to address these global challenges. It's impossible to really grasp the reality of a different era, but I think an 'age of consciousness' is likely to emerge, focusing on higher level understanding and on working together to make the tough existential choices needed to survive.

At a time of revolutionary scientific and technical mastery, it is ironic that the central role played by consciousness in this drama of the high-tech future leads back to the teachings of ancient prophets, who all saw that a domain of 'spirit' pervades life. Moses, Christ, Mohammed, Buddha, and other founding religious leaders may have missed a lot, but they all pointed toward this great unseen force that puzzles us still. Our challenge is to understand the mystery of consciousness in modern scientific terms, and use that understanding to shape awareness. The fate of the world hinges on our ability to harness the human spirit so we may guide ourselves more wisely. (Halal, 2008, xxii)

What does all this have to do with leading across national boundaries? Quite frankly, a lot. In the late 1980s, I taught an MBA course on international management at the University of Hong Kong. To prepare, I read many textbooks on the management of multinational enterprises. I followed my interests after I left the university post and came across a remarkable book, *The Myth of the Global Corporation* (Princeton University Press, 1998).

Critics and defenders of multinational corporations often agree on at least one thing: that the activities of multinationals are creating an overwhelmingly powerful global market that is quickly rendering national borders obsolete. The authors of *The Myth of the Global Corporation*, however, argue that such expectations commonly rest on a falsehood. They examine key activities of multinational corporations in the United States, Japan, and Europe and explore the relationship between corporate behavior and national institutions and cultures. They demonstrate that the world's leading multinationals continue to be shaped decisively by the policies and values of their home countries, and that their core operations are not converging to create a seamless global market. With a wealth of fresh evidence, the authors show that Japanese and German multinationals, in particular, remain only weakly committed to laissez-faire policy orientations and continue to exhibit strong allegiance to national goals in such areas as investment and employment. They also bring to light the consequences of enduring differences in government policies on, for example, industrial cartels, capital markets, and research and development. The authors agree that the world economy is becoming more complex and integrated as overt barriers to trade and investment fall away.

They conclude, however, that the extent of this integration is decisively limited by structural divergence at the level of the firm. The book will be essential reading for those seeking to understand the growing interdependence of still-distinctive industrial societies and the wellsprings of the true global economy.

In my book, *War and Peace Between America and China: How Solving the Taiwan Problem Can Lead to A Pacific Century* (BookSurge, 2006), I wrote:

> The greatest problem is that we are living in a highly uncertain world. In the scientific language, an entire system can collapse because of a perturbation to a specific part of the system. What is truly alarming is that we cannot predict how and when such a perturbation will arise, and what can constitute this perturbation. (Kwai, 2006, 113)

Truly, a perturbation can arise all of a sudden to cause a system to collapse, be it a political, economic, social, technological, or ecological system.

Leading across national boundaries is a very broad topic and one that I can only approach from a Hong Kong perspective. Under Deng Xiaoping's "One Country, Two Systems" concept, Hong Kong is a Special Administrative Region (HKSAR) within China.

The HKSAR serves the following five purposes:

1. It is one of the three major international financial centers in the world. For two centuries, global finance has been much dominated by Anglo-Saxon countries. New York, London, and Hong Kong are conveniently located in three separate time zones. There is the English common law tradition in Hong Kong, which Shanghai does not have. According to a new report, Shanghai is on track to becoming the world's largest financial center in a decade. KPMG and index compiler FTSE say that Shanghai will become increasingly important as China develops its stock, currency, bond, and derivative market. Shanghai will essentially serve the domestic Chinese market, and the Chinese economy will become the largest in the world in the next fifteen years.

2. Hong Kong, as the offshore RMB financial center, will become the RMB center for the world, and the size of the RMB bond market will be at least an order of magnitude higher than that of the equity market. Singapore will complement Hong Kong as an offshore financial center for RMB and will be connected to South Asia, particularly India.

3. Speaking of international trade and investment, there are three flows to be considered: physical flow, capital flow, and information flow. Because China's financial markets and institutions have not been well developed and because

rapid economic growth can cause social instability, for the sake of sustained economic growth and much desired social cohesiveness, the capital flow and information flow into and out of China may be somewhat restricted in the foreseeable future. Physical flow does not have to pass entirely through Hong Kong, but the Hong Kong SAR has a certain advantage in freer capital flow and information flow. Of course, the three flows, physical flow, capital flow, and information flow, have to be coordinated together.

4. Many multinationals have their regional offices in Hong Kong and many Chinese banks and corporations also have their representative offices in Hong Kong. Thus there can be convenient face-to-face contacts which somehow remove the fear of the unknown.

5. There is the anxiety of success. Although Hong Kong has been a successful story on the world stage, it needs to be integrated with the political economy of Mainland China in order to serve itself better and to serve China, East Asia, and the world more effectively. Hong Kong has often been referred to as a meeting place between the East and the West; there is no reason why Hong Kong should belittle itself in a rapidly changing world. Hong Kong has to keep on learning. When there are rapid changes, it is not the learned but the learners who inherit the earth.

Those who are leading across national boundaries have to recognize the following fundamental challenges and opportunities.

1. There is much uncertainty in the world. A perturbation can arise suddenly to cause a system to collapse, whether it's a political, economic, social, technological or ecological system;

2. The rise of Asian financial power;

3. The rise of Asian technology and innovation;

4. The rise of Asian consumption;

5. East Asian integration; and

6. The myth of the global corporation.

As a matter of fact, there are few truly global corporations as of today, no matter how you define or classify them. Most are really *globalizing* enterprises. For them, they need a presence in China. And to have a presence in China, they need to have a presence, in whatever form, in the Hong Kong Special Administrative Region.

If one insists on the belief of a flat world or that of a borderless world, one may find oneself totally absorbed in revised editions of textbooks of management of multinational enterprises or transnational corporations, written from the Western perspective. Such a view and exposition are hopelessly outdated.

Dr. Terence H. Kwai was educated at Caltech and Harvard Business School. He worked at Union Carbide Corporation and Pfizer Corporation in the United States and at Citicorp, Cap Gemini Ernst & Young, and Egon Zehnder International in Hong Kong before founding China Specialists, a research and consulting firm, which was transformed in 2010 into East Asia Research Institute.

CHAPTER FIFTEEN

COACHING FOR GOVERNANCE

By Anna Bateson

This chapter focuses on the specific context in which business coaching is delivered to those who are responsible for the governance of organizations. Motivated by the desire to improve business performance whilst recognizing business risk, "coaching for governance" focuses on an agenda for change through the deployment and leverage of board members' strengths.

The Stormy Seas of Business Leadership

Picture the captain at the wheel of his fishing trawler, scanning the horizon, watching the sonar, walking the deck, and talking to his crew. Where should they drop their nets? The familiar fishing grounds are exhausted. New grounds are protected by conventions which favor fleets from specific countries. They must range farther across the seas, but where? The choice is critical given the price of fuel.

This is not the only critical decision facing the captain. Traditional trawling methods have been replaced by new ones. Net gauges have grown smaller, trapping everything in their path. Bottom clearing has devastated the seabed, leaving only those species which no one will eat or process. Flotillas of fishing craft have been replaced by factory ships served by a host of satellite trawlers, feeding their hungry maws. Locals are furious about the damage to their environment and the livelihoods of the leisure fishing industry. The trawler captain tries to balance the need to remain commercially viable with a need to recognize and accommodate the different perceptions of the community in which he lives. We can empathize with his position.

Now picture the captains of industry, facing many of the same challenges. They are often isolated high above the organization in their boardrooms, reliant on the information which filters through the corridors of power to inform their decision making.

The position of these modern business leaders is a diverse and challenging one. Urged to scan the horizon to spot trends that might have an impact on their strategic plans; tasked with establishing risk appetite and innovative direction; expected to instigate reporting processes which indicate where the rich fishing grounds exist and where the wrecks and reefs lie, which might hole their organization below the water line; encouraged to lead by example, be visible, walk the deck, and listen to the insights shared by internal and external stakeholders—particularly the disenfranchised, whose perceptions might challenge complacent thinking.

New business models have to align capability with continually evolving strategic direction. Just as the trawler captain has to understand cool chain technology and integrity in order to get his cargo to market fresh, so the twenty-first-century business leader must understand his reliance on a web of other organizations that choose to collaborate in supply chains in order to deliver value to end customers. Without delivering value to these customers, the business is unable to deliver value to any of its other stakeholders.

All this must be achieved in an increasingly regulated environment, with multiple definitions of what "good organizational behavior" looks like. The common message seems to be that a clear focus on the tone and leadership of the governance agenda is required. This is a sea change from the historic focus on board architecture and processes. Nowadays, business leaders are required to demonstrate that the strategic decisions they take balance commercial imperatives with corporate responsibility.

Tough at the Top

Leading an organization can be a lonely business. Each strategic decision has the potential to significantly impact the whole system which the leader is responsible for nurturing. Collective board responsibility for those decisions does not preclude individual liability. The roles of directors, whether executive or nonexecutive, are clearly defined at law and include statutory, fiduciary, and moral responsibility to deliver governance and stewardship, having taken account of an extensive range of stakeholder interests.

While an increasing number of business leaders are describing their organizations as having "learning cultures," much of the actual learning takes place below board level. It is still relatively uncommon for boards to routinely assess the impacts of their strategic decisions or reflect on their collective and individual performance. To complicate matters, there is little security of tenure for the captains of industry, and their time in post can be limited by factors outside their own control.

The Governance Context

Business coaching at board level enables good governance by recognizing the regulatory environment, the multiple roles which individuals are required to balance, and the complex dynamics involved at that level. The potential impact that changes to decision making and behavior can have to whole organizational systems is significant. The principles and approaches that define good governance vary globally from the rules to the principles based and the locus of power varies across unitary and two-tier boards, with all the attendant complexities this brings to strategic decision making. It is therefore naïve to assume that the approach which has been successfully adopted in one situation can be automatically translated to another.

Rather than a remedial activity, coaching for governance focuses on enabling individuals and boards to build "situational intelligence," developing their ability to read the "rich picture" of the situations they need to address. Being "savvy" involves recognizing the context in which the individual and the business operates.

FIGURE 15.1. THE SITUATIONAL INTELLIGENCE TETRAD™: THE LYONS-BATESON REFERENCE MODEL

Source: The Situational Intelligence Tetrad™: The Lyons-Bateson Reference Model ©2012 Laurence S. Lyons and Anna Bateson. Reproduced with permission. All rights reserved.

Successful business leaders couple "situational intelligence" with a real understanding of their individual strengths and those of their boardroom colleagues. This enables them to use judgment in the way they deploy their strengths.

Figure 15.1 shows the business coaching model used. Strategy is defined as the aspirational trajectory of the organization; situation consists of the policy to be enacted in order to realise strategy and the community of motivated stakeholders who must be considered; strengths are the natural talent which could be deployed by the individual; situational intelligence creates the "rich picture" and develops the wisdom to intervene in a manner most likely to achieve individual objectives.

The "rich picture" is formed by identifying all interested and impacted stakeholders, their aspirations and motivations, and the context in which these are likely to change. At a governance level, the organization, as a separate legal entity, is a critical stakeholder. Business leaders with governance responsibility are required to take into account the perceptions and expectations of this wide range of stakeholders when making and implementing strategic decisions. Stakeholder maps are complex, going far beyond those with a direct exchange relationship. Regulatory requirements include reporting on commercial, environmental, and societal impacts, and this drives a need to consider impacts on stakeholders from across this spectrum.

The emergence of new supply-and-demand dynamics, an increasingly competitive world, and complex value chains all require business leaders to engage across geographical, gender, and generational boundaries. Diversity of insights is directly correlated with high-performance boards. The logical case is clearly made. Diverse boards are more likely to recognize and understand the diverse needs of their customers and the communities they operate in. By structuring boards to be diverse and creating an environment in which alternative insights are expressed and listened to, these boards are more likely to make better strategic decisions. Better strategic decisions well executed are more likely to lead to improved business performance and deliver the value which the board is responsible for creating.

Given the compelling argument for creating more diverse boards, why is the reality often different? Diverse boards mean having to listen to people who don't think like you, which may be exciting but is also challenging and often uncomfortable. Brave business leaders are inviting the new "Generation Y" into the boardroom. Raised in the digital era, Gen Y can help them to navigate and interrogate the rich and living library. The insights shared provide value to all parties. Boards are challenged to think in different ways, and their young talent is provided with real insights into the way in which strategic decision making and implementation happen. Whether these opportunities are called "internships," "reverse mentoring," or "shadow boards," the benefits are significant.

Coaching for Governance

Coaching for governance provides a challenging, yet supportive service for highly talented business leaders seeking to enhance board effectiveness. The service is discreet, addressing the potential reputational damage for business leaders of appearing "not to know" or "not to have thought about" the answers to the significant questions facing the business. The service is timely and flexible, recognizing the reality of most business leader's schedules. The expectation that they will be available at all times, coupled with the challenges of global and instant connectivity, have increased the "noise" which each individual has to filter in order to generate the key insights necessary to guide their strategic decision making.

Providing both a physical and virtual service, the business coach enables the business leader to "filter noise" and focus on the specific challenge they wish to address, the critical questions which require answering, and the alternative strategic paths available. Just as a nonexecutive director provides independent and constructive challenge to their executive board colleagues, so the business coach provides a robust thinking framework in a nondirective manner. The relationship provides time for reflection and review of alternatives and avoids the adoption of an unconsidered drive to action.

By clearly establishing and continuously reviewing the business leader's coaching objective, a living agenda is created to deliver value to both the individual and the organization they lead. When asked to describe the value they have derived from coaching for governance, business leaders frequently identify direct links between specific decisions and actions they have taken and business performance improvements.

Identifying Need

The events that trigger requests for coaching for governance are often associated with organizational step changes. These include changes to the composition of the board, the transition of key individuals into new posts, alterations in ownership structures, and changes in strategic direction for the organizations being governed. Most growth strategies generate these events, whether through organic or acquisitive activities. They can also generate a desire to invest in the development of strategic capability in the boardroom.

Annual board reviews can prompt the request for governance coaching for whole boards, specific committees, or individual members. Organizations often ask for a service which integrates a combination of coaching audiences over a period of time, generally between three and six months in duration. Although there are occasions where a longer relationship is desirable and effective, the frequency of structured sessions is likely to reduce to periodic reflective sessions to review strategic performance and aspirations.

The professional business coach will avoid creating mutually dependent, long-term relationships and ensure that the issue of transition is transparently discussed. Like board succession planning, this approach ensures that the client receives the service from those best placed to provide the constructive challenge required as time progresses and avoids the cozy dangers of "groupthink."

The development agendas arising from annual board reviews generally cover the structure, composition, processes, and dynamics of those boards. Changes in structure and composition often lead to a need to reestablish common purpose across the board and explore the roles and effectiveness of all members, particularly the chairman. Coaching for governance also enables business leaders to reflect on the effectiveness of various board processes, including policy formulation, strategic decision making, and the establishment and leadership of risk appetite.

Identifying Providers

Whereas other forms of business coaching are often procured through HR departments, the need and providers of coaching for governance are often identified by board members themselves, with support from the company secretariat. The latter are uniquely placed to provide insights to the chairman on the specific governance coaching objectives which form part of the board's development agenda. These insights inform the choice of suitable providers of this tailored service.

In order to be successful, coaching for governance relies on creating business relationships that are based on mutual trust and respect but not mutual dependence. The service is not one to be successfully brokered by experts in transactions, seeking to "sell on," or those providers with the one model to fit all circumstances. Rigid and blind process providers are to be avoided.

Effective providers have experience of complex, real-world business and organizational issues, and interpersonal dynamics. They combine an appropriate mix of coaching, facilitation, and consultancy capability and are likely to engage in a joint due diligence process to establish that they can create real value for their clients before agreeing on the most effective approach. It is easy to underestimate the time and effort required to create a common understanding between client and provider, and also to build the trust required to engage in an effective coaching for governance relationship.

Coaching for Governance in Practice—Case Study

The Company

Ten years ago, two entrepreneurs set out on an exciting voyage. They each brought different strengths to their partnership and a clear determination to create a technical advisory business around the rail industry. Focused on providing high-level strategic advice to key decision makers across the supply chain, they forecast and achieved double-digit growth to £1m turnover within the first five years.

The Characters

John is decisive and brings drive, determination, and a commercial focus. Andy is reflective and brings a marketing focus and a concern for stakeholder interests. Together they complement each other in their ability to assess the upside and downside risks of the strategic options they develop. They visibly share a clear set of values, which guide their decision making and behavior: being open to new ideas and sharing them; being flexible and adapting to the situations they confront; being diligent and applying honest endeavor; and, finally, being principled and guided by the human ideals of fairness, honesty, loyalty, mutual respect, and a concern for people.

The Journey

Their company, CDL, prospered and achieved double-digit growth of 11 percent per annum over the first seven years. After eight years, the business consolidated its operations from York, in the northeast of England, to the London-based office. The workforce expanded to eighty. As the company grew, John and Andy recognized the need to invite others to join them in the leadership of their business and to have a share in the ownership. They invested in the professionalization of their board and also appointed a nonexecutive chairman.

Following a business growth strategy which involved extending their global operations, in 2009 they set up a wholly owned subsidiary in Sydney, Australia. Working hard to align their business model to their strategy, CDL focused on developing a reputation for high-quality, strategic advice and distinctive competitive advantage based on service excellence and relationships. As the business grew and the global recession impacted and changed their markets, John and Andy recognized that the business and governance models needed to evolve to make them fit for the future.

Both John and Andy were aware of the challenges and tensions they faced as founders, in determining their future involvement in the business they had cocreated. John identified that a business coaching process would enable him to think through the business situation; the opportunities, challenges, and options available; and also his own aspirations and motivations. He invited Andy to participate and, after some discussion, a common agenda and objective were agreed. They shared this intention with all board members, highlighting their need to realign their own thinking as founders, major shareholders, and directors of the business. All their business coaching discussions recognized the governance challenges of balancing these different and conflicting roles. The discussions also highlighted the requirements to engage with a wide range of stakeholders during the process.

The Process

Over a period of seven months, Andy and John met together regularly for formal business coaching sessions with the author. These meetings were held away from the pressures of the office and the schedule was largely protected from operational change and national and international travel requirements. Their commitment to the value of the process was evident, and they were active in sustaining momentum. A living business coaching record also sustained momentum and created focus by capturing their decisions and their commitments throughout the process. Between the formal sessions, the author provided virtual support and John and Andy met together informally and as part of their strategic and operational business roles. A midterm evaluation of the process established the value being realized and made some modifications to the documentation that had been developed up to that point in the process.

The business coaching sessions provided a safe environment in which to have difficult conversations. The governance context provided a constructive way of challenging perceptions and ensuring that strategic options were explored in a robust and rigorous fashion.

The Results

Among the strategic options being explored by the board of CDL were a number of approaches by businesses interested in acquiring them. One of these approaches was from global consultancy, GHD (Gutteridge, Haskins, and Davey), who intend growing a UK/European transportation business, to build on their global network of regional offices. That deal was completed on July 1, 2011.

The business coaching undertaken by John and Andy contributed to the careful evaluation of all strategic options against the board's governance agenda and their own aspirations as founders and major shareholders. The deal recognizes the right cultural fit between the two businesses and GHD's values of teamwork, respect, and integrity. Future roles have been devised for the founders and other directors of CDL to ensure that value will be preserved and enhanced in the business during the transitional period.

The Value

John and Andy are clear about the value that they and the business have derived from engaging together in the business coaching process, commenting that, "For the investment, we got a big return. The return you get is extremely powerful."

By asking critical questions at key points in the process, the author enabled John and Andy to understand and evidence the real value of the business as well as more clearly

(Continued)

articulating their own aspirations in preserving and realizing that value. "It gave us time to discuss and think about important issues and align ourselves. Once we were aligned, we could talk together, with one voice."

The business coaching process was based on mutual trust and respect. "It took us on an emotional and mental journey. We had to be brave and very open. It gave us perspective and reminded us of our different strengths and roles. You need to be open minded when you do this. There is no clear route. Timing is the only issue, I wish we had started this much sooner."

Anna Bateson (www.cttg.org) works globally with boards and business leaders, addressing the challenges of leading strategic change and delivering good governance. Described by the business press as "a skilled alchemist," she shares pragmatic insights gained over four decades in leadership and consultancy roles with international businesses including Price Waterhouse and British Airways.

As a business writer and columnist for *Chartered Secretary* and through her strategic alliance with The Institute of Directors, Anna is closely involved in the design, development, and delivery of a range of initiatives to address governance challenges and professionalize boards.

Through her business consultancy, Cutting Through The Grey, and jointly with global thought leader Dr. Laurence Lyons, Anna researches, coaches, and consults on the development and deployment of *"Situational Intelligence."* Anna has an MBA from Brunel University and was a founder corporate member of The Henley Future Work Forum.

Further Reading

Bain, Neville, and Barker, Roger. 2010. *The Effective Board*. London: Kogan Page.

Bateson, Anna. 2011. "A Clearer Focus." *Chartered Secretary*. www.charteredsecretary.net and www.cttg.org.

Bateson, Anna. 2008. *Another Board Bites the Dust*. Institute of Directors (IOD) www.cttg.org.

Bateson, Anna. 2005. *Leading the Advanced Organisation*. Institute of Directors (IOD) www.cttg.org.

Burkan, Wayne. 1996. *Wide Angle Vision*. New York: Wiley.

ecoDa and Institute of Directors. 2010. *Corporate Governance Guidance and Principles for Unlisted Companies in the UK*. www.iod.com.

Financial Reporting Council. 2011. *Guidance on Board Effectiveness*. www.frc.org.uk.

Financial Reporting Council. 2010. *The UK Corporate Governance Code*. www.frc.org.uk.

Garratt, Bob. 2011. *The Fish Rots from the Head* (3rd ed.). London: Profile Books.

Institute of Directors. 2009. *The Handbook of International Corporate Governance* (2nd ed.). London: Kogan Page.

Lewis, Richard. 2008. *When Cultures Collide*. London: Nicholas Brealey International.

Lyons, Laurence S., and Bateson, Anna. 2006. *Leadership—A Principled Approach*. www.cttg.org; www.lslyons.com.

Lyons, Laurence S., and Bateson, Anna. 2009. "How to Crack the Toughest Leadership Challenge of All." A Lyons-Bateson Summit Paper. www.cttg.org; www.lslyons.com.

Lyons, Laurence S. 2012. "The Tetrad (Lyons-Bateson Situational Intelligence Reference Model)," in *The Coaching for Leadership Case Study Workbook: Featuring Dr. Fink's Leadership Casebook*. San Francisco: Jossey-Bass.

PSCI. 2007. *Pharmaceutical Industry Principles for Responsible Supply Chain Management and Implementation Guidelines*. www.pharmaceuticalsupplychain.org.

Sull, Donald N. 2009. *The Upside of Turbulence: Seizing Opportunity in an Uncertain World*. New York: Harper Collins.

CHAPTER SIXTEEN

LEADERSHIP INSIGHT[1]

Going Beyond the Dehydrated Language of Management

By Nancy J. Adler

The soul . . . never thinks without a picture.

—ARISTOTLE, 384–322 BCE

Eight-hundred million people go to bed hungry every night, including more than 300 million children. Every 3.6 seconds, a person dies of starvation. Most companies consider such poverty-related tragedies to be society's problem, not the primary concern of business. They not only fail to see the more than three billion people who live on less than $2 a day as an opportunity, but they remain completely blind to the possibility that they might constitute a lucrative market (Prahalad, 2006). Belief in the great trade-off illusion (see Figures 16.1 and 16.2) has insidiously blinded most managers into assuming that the choice to do good precludes the ability of corporations, along with the executives who lead them, to do well. Most managers falsely assume that the more they focus on enhancing societal well-being, the worse their companies will perform financially. At the close of the twentieth century, business widely embraced the illusion that generosity and compassion were bad for business.

---

[1]An earlier version of this article was published in Adler, Nancy J. (2010a) "Going Beyond the Dehydrated Language of Management: Leadership Insight," *Journal of Business Strategy,* vol. 31 (no. 4): pp. 90–99.

FIGURE 16.1. STRATEGY VERSUS PHILANTHROPY: THE GREAT TRADE-OFF ILLUSION

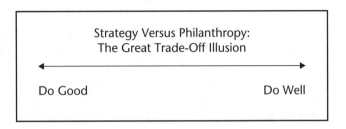

Strategy Versus Philanthropy:
The Great Trade-Off Illusion

Do Good   Do Well

FIGURE 16.2. DOING WELL BY DOING GOOD: 21ST CENTURY STRATEGIC SUCCESS

Do Good   Philanthropy   Strategic Initiative

Ostrich   Let`er rip free market Capitalism

Do Well

But by the beginning of the twenty-first century, global business strategist Gary Hamel articulated what a small but growing number of executives were beginning not only to recognize, but to act on:

What we need is not an economy of hands or heads, but an economy of hearts. Every employee should feel that he or she is contributing to something that will actually make a genuine and positive difference in the lives of customers and colleagues. For too many employees, the return on emotional equity is close to zero. They have nothing to commit to other than the success of their own career. Why is it that the very essence of our humanity, our desire to reach beyond ourselves, to touch others, to do something that matters, to leave the world just a little bit better, is often denied at work? . . . To succeed in the [twenty-first century] . . ., a company must give its members a reason to bring all of their humanity to work. (Hamel, 2000, 249)

Reflecting the same human desire to leave the world a better place, the Rev. Rick Warren's 2002 book, *The Purpose-Driven Life*, became one of the world's all-time best sellers. Nowhere in *The Purpose-Driven Life* does it say that managers and executives are exempt from the human craving for purpose and meaning. Hamel (2000, 24), a business strategist, not a theologian, reminds business people that God commanded the nomadic Israelites to rest one day out of seven—but that God did not ". . . decree that the other six had to be empty of meaning." Hamel (2000, 248) coaches executives to embrace "a cause, not a business . . . Without a transcendent purpose, individuals will lack the courage" they need to innovate beyond the ordinary. "Courage . . . comes not from some banal assurance that 'change is good' but from devotion to a wholly worthwhile cause" (Hamel, 2000, 249).

A Leadership of Possibility

When you cease to dream, you cease to live
—*Malcolm Forbes,* Forbes *magazine (as cited in Bryan et al., 1998, p.25)*

Twenty-first-century society yearns for a leadership of possibility, a leadership based more on hope, aspiration, wisdom, and innovation than on the replication of historical patterns of constrained pragmatism.[2] Luckily, such a leadership is now possible, although unfortunately still rare. For the first time in history, leaders can work backward from their aspirations and imagination rather than forward from the past. The gap between what leaders can imagine and what they can accomplish has never been smaller (Hamel, 2000, p. 10).

Designing options worthy of implementation calls for levels of inspiration, perception, and innovation that, until recently, have been more the province of artists and artistic processes than the domain of most managers. To meet the challenges of the twenty-first century, we increasingly need artistic imagination to co-create the planet's best approaches and most influential solutions:

There is a good practical reason for encouraging our artistic powers within organizations that up to now might have been unwelcoming or afraid of those qualities. The artist must paint or sculpt or write, not only for the present generation but for those who have yet to be born. A good artist, it is often said, is fifty to a hundred years ahead of . . . [his or her] time . . . The artist . . . must . . . depict this new world before all the evidence is in. They must rely on . . . their imagination to intuit and describe what is yet a germinating seed in the present time, something that will only flower after they have written the line or painted the canvas. [Leaders] . . . must learn the same artistic discipline, they must learn to respond or conceive of something that will move in the same direction in which the world is moving, without waiting for all the evidence to appear on their desks. To wait for all the evidence is to finally recognize it through a competitor's product. (Whyte, 1994, 241–242)

Leading in the twenty-first century calls not just for creativity, but for approaches based more on anticipation, imagination, and personal sense-making than on conventional entrepreneurial experimentation, no matter how creatively conceived (Botkin et al., 1979). The potential for irreversible, catastrophic outcomes caused by companies' and governments' experiments gone awry—from global economic collapse and mass famine to nuclear holocaust and species extinction—renders such traditional approaches as no longer acceptable. To embrace the type of leadership the twenty-first century most needs, managers must return to their most profound personal perspective, imagination, and wisdom.

Leadership Insight: Seeking Wisdom Through Reflection

[W]hen we are in the buzzing-worker-bee mode . . . [w]e do not even have time to find out if our momentum is taking us over the nearest cliff. If we are serious about [who we are as leaders] . . ., all of us must confront the question of quiet and contemplation in the workplace. (Whyte, 1994, 98)

More than 2,500 years ago, Confucius admonished leaders to seek perspective and wisdom through reflection, rather than simply attempting to learn through experience and imitation (Sharma, 2008). Confirming Confucius's understanding, Harvard professor Howard Gardner's (1995) contemporary research identified daily reflection as one of only three core competencies (along with leveraging and framing) that distinguish leaders who make an extraordinary difference in the world from their more ordinary counterparts. Management guru Peter Drucker (1999) similarly advocated daily reflection, as have many of the most prominent leadership experts (see, for example, Loehr and Schwartz's *Harvard Business Review* article [2001] and Palmer's 2000 article "Leading from Within"). Even with such admonitions to regularly engage in personal reflection and sensemaking, management and leadership, both as taught and as practiced, have focused almost exclusively on action rather than reflection. Most managers guard little or no time for reflective silence. They all too frequently recognize themselves in the words of poet and global management consultant David Whyte that opened this section.

Aspiring to Leadership That Matters

To be truly radical is to make hope possible

—Lovins, 2007

What do managers need to do to strengthen their capacity to lead wisely and creatively in the twenty-first century? How can executives best envision and implement initiatives that matter? Building on Confucius's wisdom and Gardner's research, along with the yearnings and experience of hundreds of managers from around the world, it is clear that today's leaders need to:

- *Reflect*—to return to the quiet and contemplation it takes to be wise;
- *Gain perspective*—to acquire the courage needed to see reality as it actually is, rather than continuing to rely on illusions perpetuated by colleagues, the media, and the broader culture;
- *Aspire to exceptionally exciting possibilities*—to envision extraordinary possibilities by drawing on the depths of their own and others' hopes, aspirations, and creativity; and
- *Inspire others*—to inspire people to move beyond current reality back to possibility.

Based on these four fundamental leadership capacities and drawing from a range of artistic traditions, we created a journal that can be of significant practical value and serve as a prototype for other journals. The *Leadership Insight* journal (Adler, 2010b) supports managers' and their companies' capacity to craft and implement strategies that produce outstanding financial results by making a positive difference in the world (see Figure 16.2). Combining paintings, insights from world leaders, reflective questions, and, most important, blank pages, the journal is designed to draw managers away from their often frenzied lives and to return them to a deeper dialectic with their influence, and potential influence, on the world. By reintroducing a daily practice of reflection, the journal offers leaders the quiet and contemplation it takes to be wise.

Reflection: Coming Back to Your Unique Perspective

To be human is to find ourselves behind our names.
—David Krieger (as cited in Franck et al., 1998, 272)[3]

All true leadership starts with coming home to oneself. The blank pages are the journal's most direct invitation to spend time quietly recollecting (literally recollecting) one's personal perspective. They challenge us to take ourselves as seriously as we take the people whom we most admire. Do not simply listen, read, and repeat what others say. Grant your own perceptions, ideas, images, feelings, and dreams the same respect that you give to the world's most respected leaders. True leaders, whether in the arts, business, government, science, or the military, view the world through their own eyes, their own values, and their own dreams.

The journal acts as an antidote to society's pervasive collusion. It acts as a barrier against the persistent attempts by the media, politicians, and every organization's culture to pressure us into seeing the world as others see it. The blank pages symbolically admonish each of us not to collude with illusion, but rather to make sense of the world for ourselves. Prior to the last election in which the predominantly French-speaking province of Quebec was deciding if it would separate from the rest of Canada, management guru Henry Mintzberg spoke out, urging his fellow citizens: "Turn off your radio and TV, and open your window. Look outside and see Quebec with your own eyes. Do our French- and English-speaking children play together? Do we invite each other into our homes? Do we work together? Yes! It is an illusion that the Anglophone and Francophone people from Quebec do not get along with each other; an illusion that serves the needs of politicians who want to break Canada apart, but it is not reality." Don't collude with illusion!

Some of the imagery in the *Leadership Insight* journal is more obvious, while other imagery is more subtle. Whereas the blank pages directly invite managers to come back to themselves, the symbolism of the cover design is less evident. The design was created from a pattern of names (they are literally the names of my friends, family, and colleagues). In the same way that each name is personal, each journal is personal. Like the blank pages, the individual names invite you to record your own point of view, not that of others. Regaining the courage to express, when appropriate, one's own perspective is essential for meaningful leadership. To support leaders in reclaiming their unique perspective, one of the questions we ask each person to ponder is: "If you spoke up right now, in your own voice, what would be most important for you to say? To whom? In what tone of voice?" (Whyte, 1994).

While inviting each person to acknowledge his or her own unique voice, the journal never presents any one person as the leader. The names on the cover are from every region of the world. As you pick up the journal, you are being invited to join a global community of leaders, not to aspire to become the leader. As a leader, your voice is unique, but always embedded in a global network of influence. While your perspective is rooted in its distinct cultural, national, ethnic, geographic, and professional experience, and is therefore unique, specific, and local, the collection of perspectives from around the world is global. Leadership in the twenty-first century is created by a global network of leaders, never by a single person, no matter how competent or powerful (Adler, 2011a & b).

Sources of Wisdom

We stand on the shoulders of giants

—*Sir Isaac Newton, 1676*[4]

No person ever contributes significantly to the world without profoundly knowing his or her roots (see, for example, U.S. President Barack Obama's 1995 memoir, *Dreams from My Father*). As a leader, it is difficult to offer a vision or a new idea without having developed the type of courage that comes from appreciating the depth of one's personal and cultural history. When Newton declares that "We stand on the shoulders of giants," he is acknowledging that past generations of leaders support each of us in learning to see the truth, hear the truth, and speak the truth. There is no such thing as leadership with shallow roots.

In addition to the names on the cover, scattered throughout the journal are handwritten insights from women and men, representing an array of countries, professions, and eras, who have given all of us our collective roots as leaders. Examples include Berkshire Hathaway CEO Warren Buffet (as cited by Bryan et al., 1998, ix):

I am not a businessman, I am an artist.

Former United Nations Secretary General Kofi Annan, who states:

Let us choose to unite the power of markets with the authority of universal ideals. Let us choose to reconcile the creative forces of private enterprise with the needs of the disadvantaged and the requirements of future generations.[5]

Founder and CEO Emeritus of VISA Dee Hock (1998), who states:

. . . it is no failure if you fall short of realizing all that you might dream, the failure is to fall short of dreaming all that you might realize.

Also, the reflection of Ryuzaburo Kabu (as cited in Sbarcea, 2007, 3), the Honorary Chairman of Canon, Inc:

To put it simply, global companies have no future if the earth has no future

Each leader's reflection challenges us to think more broadly about the circumstances we face. That the leaders' handwritten reflections are in your journal, next to your own handwritten reflections, represents the invitation from these extraordinary individuals to join the community of leaders who are shaping our economy and society. As former U.S. Secretary of State Madeleine Albright (1997) eloquently stated in her Harvard commencement address: "We have a responsibility in our time, as others have had in theirs, not to be prisoners of history, but to shape history." Albright did not exempt any of us from the invitation or responsibility to shape history. And in the quietness of our own personal reflection, we know that there is no wiser, smarter, or more committed group somewhere else in the world who will take care of everything for us.

Painting Leadership: Going Beyond the Dehydrated Language of Management

Let the beauty we love be what we do.

—Rumi, thirteenth-century Persian poet[6]

In addition to blank pages, leaders' insights, and the names on the cover, the *Leadership Insight* journal presents a collection of paintings, each of which is an invitation to think visually and thus to reflect on the world from a new lens. Experiment with your own visual thinking. Think for a moment about the most compelling visual images from the last hundred years—the images you clearly remember of the most significant moments in the world's history. You might recall an image of the moon landing, or the fall of the Berlin Wall, or the mushroom cloud rising over Hiroshima, or the birth of your first child. What can you learn about your overall perspective from the particular images you chose?

Now think about the last ten years of your organization's history. What are the images of distinctive moments that stand out for you in that history? What role did leadership play in helping to create each defining moment?

Now think back over the last year. Which two or three images capture your personal best moments of leadership? What can you learn about your strengths from these distinctive moments of contribution (Roberts et al., 2005)? How could there be more moments similar to these personal high points in the coming year? Whether or not we are aware of the process, we all think visually. The images we remember give meaning to our understanding of the world and our role within the world. Similar to our own memories of important events, some of the paintings in the journal present whole images while others reveal only fragmented details—the global and the local, the universal and the particular.

Artists do not always aspire to craft works of beauty. The paintings included in the journal, however, were purposely chosen to evoke beauty. Even during one of the most challenging periods of world history, former first lady Eleanor Roosevelt repeatedly reminded people, "The future belongs to those who believe in the beauty of their dreams." The paintings offer a way to return to the beauty we each aspire to in our leadership, in our lives, and in our dreams.

In attempting to transform organizations and society, two seemingly opposite philosophies guide leaders. In the more common problem-focused approach, companies and organizations attempt to improve by finding what is not working and then on solving the problems they have found. Instead of concentrating on weaknesses and problems, the alternative approach focuses on magnifying and leveraging strengths. Beauty is not "a problem to be solved." By reflecting beauty, the paintings in the journal evoke people's (and organizations') strengths and dreams. The paintings thus support leaders in striving to be their best—to use their strengths and leverage their aspirations to guide their organization and their contributions to the broader society. Beauty is neither about fixing problems nor about being satisfied with "good enough"; rather, it is about reaching for the very best that we and society can be (Adler, 2008). Bringing the two approaches together, futurist Buckminster Fuller reflected that:

When I am working on a problem, I never think about beauty. I think of only how to solve the problem. But when I have finished, if the solution is not beautiful, I know it is wrong.[7]

The order of the paintings in the journal was carefully selected to support leadership reflection. As you open the journal, the first painting you encounter is a joyful sunflower painted in bright reds, yellows, and oranges. Its vibrant energy evokes the busy activity of most managers' everyday life. Echoing the transition from high-energy action to reflective calm, each successive painting becomes quieter and softer. When you reach the final painting, it presents an ephemeral moon in a peaceful blue-green landscape—a landscape that is only reachable once you leave the frantic busyness of action and return to the peaceful calm of reflection.

Each painting invites the viewer to go beyond the dehydrated language of management and return to the richer images of leadership. The paintings included in the journal were created using water-based media (watercolors and ink). Being water-based, they symbolically bring water—and thus life—back into those aspects of one's life and leadership that have become dry, mechanical, and thus lifeless. As you reflect, ask yourself what brings life (water) back into the dehydrated aspects of your own leadership?

Still Life: An Invitation to Reflect

Some doors open only from the inside.

—*Ancient Sufi saying*[8]

There is a tradition in the visual arts of painting a "still life," usually thought of as a centuries-old canvas filled with nicely arranged fruit or flowers. To really see the paintings, we need to still our life. We can't skim to read a painting; we have to stop to actually look at it. It is new. What do we see? How does it make us feel? What images does it conjure up in us? The journal invites us to enter into this artistic tradition and to "still" our life.

As we slow down, the paintings encourage us to notice what surrounds us— the context within which we live and lead. They encourage us to stop multitasking long enough to simply concentrate on the one thing that matters most to us right now. Without periodically stopping, it is impossible to gain the perspective needed for leadership.

An experiment conducted at Yale University demonstrated the power of viewing paintings to support professional excellence. When medical students were shown paintings in an art history course that Yale had experimentally added to their curriculum, the young doctors' diagnostic skills improved markedly (Dolev et al., 2001). Viewing the paintings taught the physicians to see their patients (and the world) more accurately. It taught them to appreciate multiple perspectives while not missing the small details. It taught them to become more comfortable with "not knowing" (what managers often refer to as tolerating ambiguity) long enough to accurately diagnose their patients' maladies rather than prematurely settling on a diagnosis based only on the initial, superficial pattern of symptoms. Much to the surprise of the medical school's leadership, viewing paintings significantly helps physicians save lives.

Experiment for a few minutes with slowing down your own fast-paced life. Choose one of the journal paintings or a painting from your own collection and view it, uninterrupted, for three to five minutes. As you stop multi-tasking and concentrate on the single painting, notice the change in the quality of your observation, insight, and experience. Then ask yourself how often you give yourself this quality of uninterrupted time and concentration? What in your life deserves this quality of attention? What in your leadership deserves this quality of attention? What in the world deserves this quality of your attention? What would your leadership be like if, as a regular practice, you gave this quality of attention to the challenges, goals, people, and dreams that matter most to you and to the people you work with (see Adler, 2004)?

The senior executive team of a major nutrition company gathered recently in Montreal to identify global strategies that could help them achieve even better performance than their current industry-leading standard. After exploring a range of strategic options, this group of extremely competent and effective executives chose to take time to reflect on what was most important to them. Individually, they asked themselves what inspired them most about working for the company. What led them, at least on some mornings, to jump out of bed, eager for another day at work?

As they shared their personal reflections with their international colleagues, a striking pattern emerged. The majority revealed that they no longer eagerly looked forward to another day at work. They confided that increasing profits, while challenging, was not inspiring. Faced with their current dwindling enthusiasm, they began to recall why they had originally chosen to work for this particular company, rather than for a firm in another industry. They remembered their desire to work for a company that helped people live a healthier life.

As the executives brought their personal observations back into their more focused discussion of corporate strategy, they almost immediately conceived a new initiative that galvanized the group: a profit-making venture to provide basic nutrition for the world's poorest people, starting with rural Africans—a population they had never considered before. As soon as the idea emerged, the executives quickly crafted innovative marketing, production, and distribution processes for Africa to make the company's products both accessible and profitable to this currently underserved market. What was most striking about the plan (beyond it being an excellent corporate initiative) was that it never would have occurred to the executives if they had not been willing to stop and to reflect back—on their core values and aspirations—and then to reflect forward about their collective dreams for the company.

Spanish artist Pablo Picasso—the founder of cubism, a multiple-perspective approach to painting that predates by a century the needs of today's leaders to see the world from multiple points of view—saw painting as just another way of keeping a journal. I first took a group of global executives to an exhibition of cubist paintings as the final session of a three-day meeting in Oslo designed to integrate the firm's latest series of intercontinental mergers and acquisitions into the company's overall strategy. Standing in the museum's cubist gallery, the CEO was astonished to discover that the cubists had captured exactly the perspective that he felt the company most needed to move from operating as a European company to succeeding as a global firm. Artists prior to the cubists had used single-point perspective—the artists painted images as if there was just one viewer standing at a specific location looking at the painted scene. The cubist revolution overthrew single-point perspective and presented the same image from multiple points of view within a single painting. Once he had seen the cubist paintings the European CEO realized that his company would be able to benefit from its recent Asian and North and South American acquisitions only if it was able to simultaneously view global markets, as well as global competitors, from multiple national and cultural perspectives. Similar to the most basic cubist paintings, competitive positioning requires creating synergy out of disparate views of reality. As the global company continued to grow, it not only became skillful at drawing on the often divergent views of its world wide network of executives and operating entities, it repeatedly positioned itself for success within its industry (see Adler, 2002).

The paintings in the journal were selected to support global managers in reflecting on their own best selves and best leadership, and to encourage them to welcome the ambiguity and uncertainty that such reflection provokes. As world-renowned Australian art critic Robert Hughes underscored, the greater the leader and "the greater the artist, the greater the doubt. Perfect confidence is [only] granted to the less talented as a consolation prize." As the Norwegian-based multinational learned, there is never just one perspective or one point of view. Global leadership demands the ability to recognize and build on differences—to create cultural synergy, not worldwide global integration (see Adler, 2002).

Reality in Translation: Asking the Right Questions

> Now that we can do anything, what do we want to do?
> —*Bruce Mau, designer (Mau and The Institute without Boundaries, 2004, 15)*

A good question always transforms how we see the world. It guides us in what we notice and what we overlook—in which patterns we emphasize and which we ignore. Throughout the *Leadership Insight* journal, questions such as the following challenge our perspective as leaders:

- What do you most want to do this year to make the world a better place?
- Why do people want to be led by you?
- With whom do you have conversations that matter?
- What do you find most difficult to face in your relationship with your work? Your career? Your life?

Because each question in the journal is printed on semi-transparent paper, they symbolically lead us to view the world through the question and thus transform our view of reality.

The semi-transparent paper for the pages with questions and the opaque paper for the blank pages bring together an Asian and a Western tradition. The semi-transparent, rice-paper-like Asian pages and ecologically certified opaque Western pages complement each other, while remaining distinct. They create a synergy—a bringing together of multiple distinct perspectives, ideas, cultures, or elements to create a whole that is greater than the sum of its parts. The journal does not combine the various types of paper into one homogeneous composite paper. Unity in diversity, not homogenization, is the physical essence of the journal. Likewise, and more important, it is the essence of well-functioning twenty-first-century companies and the core of flourishing global societies.

The Fierce Urgency of Now

Ultimately, the *Leadership Insight* journal is a call to wise action, not simply a tool for contemplation. "The fierce urgency of now,"[9] as U.S. President Barack Obama labeled it, calls on all twenty-first-century leaders to act. Leadership always happens in the moment. It does not wait until we are older, or better prepared, or have a larger savings account, or a bigger title. The call is now. The invitation to respond is now. The plea is to do so wisely, and with generosity and compassion.

Nancy J. Adler is the S. Bronfman Chair in Management at McGill University, Canada. She conducts research and consults worldwide on global leadership. She has authored 125 articles, produced two films, and published ten books and edited volumes. She is a Fellow of the Academies of Management and International Business, and the Royal Society of Canada. She is also a visual artist. Nancy J. Adler can be contacted at: nancy.adler@ mcgill.ca.

References

Adler, N. J. 2002. "Global Companies, Global Society: There Is a Better Way," *Journal of Management Inquiry* 11, no. 3: 255–60.

Adler, Nancy J. 2004. "Reflective Silence: Developing the Capacity for Meaningful Global Leadership" in Nakiye Avdan Boyacigiller Richard Alan Goodman, & Margaret E. Phillips (eds.), *Crossing Cultures: Insights from Master Teacher*. London, England: Routledge: pp. 201–218.

Adler, N. J. 2006. "The Arts and Leadership: Now That We Can Do Anything, What Will We Do?." *Academy of Management Learning and Education* 5, no. 4: 466–99.

Adler, Nancy J. 2008. "The Art of Global Leadership: Designing Options Worthy of Choosing" in Daved Berry and Hans Hansen (eds.), *Handbook of the New & Emerging in Organization Studies*. Thousand Oaks, California: Sage Publications, pp. 95–96.

Adler, Nancy J. 2010a. "Going Beyond the Dehydrated Language of Management: Leadership Insight," *Journal of Business Strategy*, vol. 31 (no. 4): pp. 90–99.

Adler, Nancy J. 2010b. *Leadership Insight*. Milton Park, U.K.: Routledge.

Adler, Nancy J. 2011a. "Leading Beautifully: The Creative Economy and Beyond", *Journal of Management Inquiry*, vol. 20 (no. 3) September, pp. 208–221.

Adler, Nancy J. 2011b. "New Times Need New Leadership" in Danica Purg (ed.), *Creating the Future: Book of the Times 2011*. Bled, Slovenia: IEDC-Bled School of Management: pp. 25–34.

Albright, M. K. 1997. Harvard commencement address. *New York Times*, June 6, p. A8.

Botkin, J. W., Elmandjra, M., and Malitza, M. 1979. *No Limits to Learning: Bridging the Human Gap—A Report to the Club of Rome*. Oxford: Pergamon Press.

Bryan, M., Cameron, J., and Allen, C. 1998. *The Artist's Way at Work: Riding the Dragon*. New York: Harper.

Dolev, J. C., Friedlaender, F., Krohner, L., and Braverman, I. M. 2001. "Use of Fine Art to Enhance Visual Diagnostic Skills." *Journal of the American Medical Association* 286, no. 9: 1020.

Drucker, P. 1999. "Managing Oneself." *Harvard Business Review*, March-April: 65–74.

Franck, F., Rose, J., and Connolly, R. (Eds.). 2000. *What Does It Mean to Be Human?* New York: St Martin's Press.

Gardner, H. 1995. *Leading Minds: An Anatomy of Leadership*. New York: Basic Books.

Hamel, G. 2000. *Leading the Revolution*. Boston: Harvard Business School Press.

Hock, D. 1998. "An Epidemic of Institutional Failure: Organizational Development and the New Millennium," Keynote Address at the 1998 Organizational Development Network Annual Conference, New Orleans, LA, available from www.hackvan.com/pub/stig/etext/deehock–epidemic-of-institutionalfailure.html.

Loehr, J., and Schwartz, T. 2001. "The Making of a Corporate Athlete." *Harvard Business Review*, January: 120–128.

Lovins, A. 2007. Keynote address at the Global Forum on "Business as an Agent of World Benefit: Management Knowledge Leading Positive Change" Cleveland, Ohio, October 27.

Mau, B. and The Institute Without Boundaries. 2004. *Massive Change*. London: Phaidon Press.

Obama, B. 1995. *Dreams from My Father: A Story of Race and Inheritance*. New York: Three Rivers Press.

Palmer, P. 2000. "Leading from Within," in *Let Your Life Speak: Listening for the Voice of Vocation*. San Francisco: Jossey-Bass, 73–94 .

Prahalad, C. K. 2006. *The Fortune at the Bottom of the Pyramid: Eradicating Poverty through Profits— Enabling Dignity and Choice Through Markets*. Upper Saddle River, NJ: Wharton School Publishing.

Roberts, L. M., Spreitzer, G., Dutton, J., Quinn, R., Heaphy, E., and Barker, B. 2005. "How to Play to Your Strengths." *Harvard Business Review*, January: 75–80.

Rumi, J. A. 1995. *The Essential Rumi*. Banks, C. with Mayne, J. (trans.), Ch. 4.

Sbarcea, K. 2007. "Corporate Sustainability and the Role of Knowledge Management: Preliminary Exploration." February, available at: http://thinkingshift.files.wordpress.com/2007/02/km-sustainability.doc.

Sharma, G. 2008. "Choosing Wisdom Through Reflection: How Businesses Can Achieve a Healthy Bottom-Line by Ensuring a Healthy Planet." *BAWB Newsletter* (on-line), May 16, available at: http://worldbenefit.case.edu/newsletter/?idNewsletter=153&idHeading=54 &idNews=630.

Warren, R. 2002. *The Purpose-Driven Life*. Grand Rapids, MI: Zondervan.

Whyte, D. 1994. *The Heart Aroused*. New York: Currency Doubleday.

Further Reading

To view Adler's *Leadership Insight* journal go to http://www.mcgill.ca/desautels/ beyond-business/art-leadership/journal. Copies of the Leadership Insight journal are available from the publisher at http://www.routledge.com/books/ details/9780415877626/ or from online bookstores. To see more of Adler's art and her work on art and leadership, go to McGill University's website at: http://www .mcgill.ca/desautels/beyond-business/art-leadership/

PART IV

RECOGNIZING AND DEVELOPING HIGH-POTENTIALS

In **Part IV, Recognizing and Developing High-Potentials**, we explore how coaches and leaders alike can spot and cultivate young leaders. Beverly Kaye and Beverly Crowell open this section with their article, "Coaching for Engagement and Retention," in which they assert that the employer and coach must determine the values, issues, and concerns of the employee through conversation and then develop a plan in order to engage and retain their high performers. In Chapter Eighteen, "Coaching Future Lawyer-Leaders," John Alexander outlines the potential for what positive effects business coaching can have on those destined to become "legal eagles." Marshall Goldsmith and Howard Morgan expand the idea of recognizing and developing high-potentials to doing this with and/or as a team in Chapter Nineteen, "Team Building Without Time Wasting." In their case study, "Leaders Building Leaders: High-Potential Development and Executive Coaching at Microsoft," Shannon Wallis, Brian O. Underhill, and Carol Hedly describe high-potential development at this corporate giant and its focus on *accelerating* the development of these individuals to advance to the next career stage. Paul Hersey describes the unprecedented investment by organizations in their high-potential pipelines in his article, "The Care and Feeding of Hi-Po Leaders." Finally, this section ends with Frances Hesselbein's article, "Mentoring Is Circular," in which she coins *mentoring* so insightfully as "coaching's companion."

CHAPTER SEVENTEEN

COACHING FOR ENGAGEMENT AND RETENTION

By Beverly Kaye and Beverly Crowell

Companies around the world are spending millions to ask employees how they feel about work. *Are you satisfied? Does your boss communicate with you daily? Do you support the company's mission and values?* These questions and others are a way to gauge employee engagement and are often a starting point for helping leaders understand their unique employee engagement and retention challenges.

Unfortunately, many of these same companies get the data, develop action plans, check off the "to do" list, and move on without ever really changing how employees feel about their work, their boss, or the company for which they work. As we move from tough economic times into calmer waters, employee engagement and retention need to be more than just a survey. It needs to be a sustained one-on-one effort to get at the heart of what really matters to employees.

After the money is spent to complete the survey, these same companies ask leaders to generate action plans that will sustain an engaged and productive workforce. These action plans generally create new programs, resources, changes in policy, and some measurable, short-term victories. What they often don't create is a change in the leader's behaviors.

In truth, it often looks like what happened at one manufacturing company. Employees cited lack of career development opportunities in the company as a key disengagement factor. The senior leaders assembled a cross-functional team to address the problem. As a result, a state-of-the art career resource center was created for employees. It was decorated with posters promoting "learn, grow, and develop." It boasted the latest in technology and access to an online university. It was highlighted in the company newsletter and heralded in all-employee meetings. Employees heard the great news and acted. As told by one employee,

"I asked my boss if I could go to the center to research career opportunities and was told, 'You don't have time for that right now. I need you to get the work done at your desk.' Imagine how engaged I felt after that comment. It was another failed promise."

For this leader and many like him, engagement and retention were defined as the annual employee satisfaction survey and the "tedious" action plan that had to be created as a result. Nowhere along the way did the leader get the message that he needed to change his ways. What he failed to realize is that all the best plans can and will fall short if they aren't supported and that he has far more influence over engagement than he ever realized. Here's where coaching for engagement and retention can create a sustained and measurable difference.

According to the U.S. Department of Labor, disengaged workers cost the U.S. economy more than $300 billion annually. The task of reengaging those who "quit and stay" falls on the shoulders of the leadership and management team. Although many leaders know the importance of engaging their talent, the "how" is often a short-term solution for what must be a long-term effort. Coaching for engagement and retention reduces the risk and empowers leaders in any organization to tap into their employees' discretionary effort and bring that energy into the workplace. When the coaching relationship is directed at these issues, it helps leaders find simple yet meaningful ways to engage their talent beyond the everyday distractions.

Engagement coaching is not unlike other coaching disciplines. Its difference is in understanding the key drivers of engagement, trends, research, and strategies to create a sustained change in workplace satisfaction. Engagement coaches are passionate about people and relationships. They have a strong understanding of the company's culture, policies, and procedures. Over time, they have built the trust and rapport of leaders and employees resulting in strong relationships. They have keen evaluative and analytical skills, the ability to listen for what lies beneath the surface, to develop and ask probing questions to understand engagement challenges, strong follow-up and feedback skills, and an understanding of available tools, resources, research, and their applicability with each person they coach. Above all else, they are passionate about developing other great engagement coaches in the leaders they grow.

Engagement coaches begin by understanding the unique employee engagement and retention challenges of each leader. The work initially is done through the leader, not directly with individual employees. If employee engagement, satisfaction, or culture surveys are readily available, the coach can work with the leader to study the results and identify key issues and opportunities. These surveys provide a great place to begin analysis as individual leaders learn about the engagement needs of their team. It is only a start, however. The true value comes from frequent conversations with every member of their team. Surveys set the tone, but it's the conversations that set the direction.

Employee surveys may not always be available to help the engagement coach. In those cases, there are some warning signs to look for as well. According to the Saratoga Institute, 80 percent of turnover is directly related to unsatisfactory relationships with the boss. In addition, research by the authors of *Love 'Em or Lose 'Em: Getting Good People to Stay* found that most retention factors are within the control of a manager. If a leader's turnover is increasing, employee complaints are up, productivity or quality are down, or people are talking, it may just be the right time for an engagement coach to step in.

Why? Employee engagement data and research continue to promote a very simple message: employees want a relationship with their leader. They feel engaged by their work and cared for by their organizations when they are able to have open, honest, two-way conversations about their ideas, careers, motivations, and challenges. They need leaders who listen to their perspectives, offer their own points of view, and provide encouragement, guidance, and opportunities. If individuals feel heard, understood. and valued by their leader, they commit more of their energy and enthusiasm.

Despite this knowledge that most leaders already have about the importance of their role, many find reasons why it won't work or why they simply "can't find the time" to invest in a relationship with their employees. Coaches must help their leaders realize that lack of time isn't what's getting in their way—they are. Engagement builds or diminishes in every interaction between leader and employee. So, it's often not just about doing more, but doing it with purpose. Purposeful engagement, simply put, is the ability to focus on every interaction with an employee as an opportunity to build a positive relationship. It's the realization that you don't necessarily have to do more to engage your employees, but you need to commit to the right actions that meet the engagement needs of each employee right where they are. You can do so by treating every interaction as an opportunity to build that employee relationship. Let us not forget, unsatisfactory relationships with the boss are a key driver of turnover. Imagine the change if leaders paid attention to their employees and learned that "it's all about me" means it's all about the employee. With that said, here's the challenge: employee engagement is an individual activity. There can be no "one-size-fits-all" approach. Every employee has values, needs, and motivations that are unique to him or her. The only way to learn these motivations is to travel down the road of discovery with each and every employee.

How do leaders discover their employees' motivations? The answer is deceptively simple. They ask and then they ask some more. It's called an engagement conversation. Engagement conversations are very different from the performance conversation leaders are already having at least twice a year with their employees. Good engagement conversations can feel like you're "peeling an onion" to get to the true motivations of each employee. The following points reveal the difference between engagement and performance engagements.

Engagement Conversations

- Emphasis on employee's career, motivators, satisfaction
- Initiated by the leader or often the employee
- Focus on the now and the future
- Leader's role is supportive and understanding coach
- Employee's role is to identify motivators and factors for job satisfaction
- Employee motivation often improves

Performance Conversations

- Emphasis on performance goals
- Initiated by the leader on scheduled timetable
- Focus on the past
- Leader's role is evaluative superior
- Employee's role is to understand and meet organizational goals
- Employee motivation varies with evaluation

Success of the engagement conversation often hinges on the authenticity of the leader. Leaders who are already disengaged themselves may find it hard to focus on the motivations of their employees, instead asking, "What about me?" What about me, indeed? If the leader's engagement is not being tended to as well, employees may find themselves the victim of an unhappy boss. Coaches can conduct an engagement conversation with the leader first to model the process and learn about their current job satisfaction. Coaches may need to work with the leader first to reenergize the job and encourage them to ask for what they need from their boss. Disengaged leaders will find it more difficult to be advocates for their employees.

After the conversations begin, an engagement coach can serve as a resource to generate ideas based on what leaders are learning in their conversations and interactions with employees.

An employee wants more opportunities to learn and grow? Consider the following:

- Conduct a career conversation to learn more about their unique skills, interests, and values. Offer your perspective, discuss trends and options, and codesign a career action plan.

- Link people to others inside or outside the organization who can help them achieve their professional goals.
- Take time to mentor your employees. Share your success stories and failures. Teach organizational realities and let your employees mentor you too.

Another employee doesn't feel valued by you or the organization? Build loyalty by trying the following:

- Recognize employees for a job well done. Offer praise that is specific, purposeful, and tailored to each employee.
- Notice your employees. Pay attention as you walk down the halls and say hello to them by name.
- Get honest feedback. Get a clear picture of how you look to others. Do you have any high-risk behaviors that may be getting in the way of your efforts?

All your employees want to work in an environment that they love. Try implementing some of the following:

- Have fun at work. Do something new or different, or create an environment where it's okay to laugh and smile.
- Show enthusiasm for what you do; it will encourage others to do the same. Disengaged leaders will have a tough time engaging their employees.
- Values define what we consider to be important. The more employee values align with their work, the more they will find it meaningful, purposeful, and important. Ask your employees, "What makes for a really great day?" or "What do you need most from your work?"

So much of coaching for engagement revolves around common-sense approaches to good leadership. Alas, common sense is often uncommonly practiced. The coaching partnership can do more than provide insight to leaders; it can also be the motivation leaders need to do what they know should be done. Leaders with engagement coaches often remark that it's the coaching that reminds them to put these common-sense strategies into practice. Here are some examples of the actions leaders in one organization implemented:

- Established the eight-foot rule with all employees. Any time the leader came within eight feet of an employee, he was committed to engaging him or her in a conversation, even if was a brief hello and "How are you today?"
- Helped a "disengaged" direct report open up about real concerns, which led to productive career discussions about future options, and receptivity to performance improvement ideas in the short run.

- Conducted a series of relationship-building phone conversations with remote employees, combined with intentional in-person get-acquainted meetings when on-site to build trust and rapport with new direct report staff.
- Conducted monthly debrief conversations after each closing period, to identify what went well and what could be improved about the closing process for the next month.
- Created motivational Monday morning e-messages to his group as a way to get the week started positively. Leader received many compliments from the team for doing this.

Success happens when leaders assume the role of engagement coaches in their organizations. Though leaders can be the catalyst for good engagement and retention, it's the employee who must step up to identify what actions they can take to find more satisfaction in the workplace. Leaders with a good handle on engagement can empower employees to take control of their workplace satisfaction.

Engagement and retention are critical in today's workplace. The coaching relationship goes beyond what a coach can do to help grow the leader, but to what they can do to help grow the organization. It's an ongoing process with no final destination. The good news—if done and done well, coaching for engagement and retention can create leaders who think of their talent first and employees who truly commit to bringing the best of their capabilities to the organization.

EXHIBIT 17.1 A PROCESS FOR ENGAGEMENT COACHING

Step 1: Meeting Preparation

- Identify the possible problems or warning signs, get your notes together, and, if possible, ask the leader what they hope to get out of the session before you meet.

Step 2: The First Meeting

- Select a neutral, private location and plan at least one hour for the session. First session should be in person.
- Turn off all electronic devices.
- Explain the overall purpose and process the coaching relationship.
- If using data or other information, share it with the leader and ask what they want to get out of the sessions.
- Ask questions to understand leader's engagement or employee engagement challenges. Tip: Read *Love 'Em or Lose 'Em: Getting Good People to Stay* by Dr. Beverly Kaye and Sharon Jordan-Evans for tips and strategies.

- Listen for and celebrate the things that are going well. Identify engagement challenges and goals.
- Identify possible tools, resources, or actions to assist leader.
- Clarify actions, deadlines, and set follow-on meeting.

Step 3: Follow-On Meetings

- Check in with the leader's commitments from the previous session.
- Discuss lessons learned, success stories, other opportunities, and possible next steps.
- If a commitment has not been completed, lead the leader to awareness that a commitment has been broken and encourage them to follow through.
- Identify additional engagement challenges and goals.
- Identify possible tools, resources, or actions to assist leader.
- Clarify actions, deadlines, and set follow-on meeting as needed.

Beverly Kaye is the founder and CEO of Career Systems International, and a best-selling author on workplace performance. She has worked with a host of organizations to establish cutting-edge, award-winning talent development solutions. Her books include *Up Is Not the Only Way; Love 'Em or Lose 'Em: Getting Good People to Stay;* and *Love It, Don't Leave It: 26 Ways to Get What You Want at Work.*

Beverly Crowell is principal consultant and founder of Crowell Consulting, and is a recognized expert and speaker in the fields of talent management, strategic business planning, and professional development. Beverly is also a senior consultant for Career Systems International (CSi), providing expertise in the areas of career development, employee engagement and retention, and coaching. Beverly authors a weekly blog and is a contributing author to *The Talent Management Handbook.*

CHAPTER EIGHTEEN

COACHING FUTURE LAWYER-LEADERS: A CASE STUDY

By John Alexander

I work well with others. Though I am naturally introverted and prefer taking on projects by myself, if I am required to work in a group, I am easy to get along with. I try to let everyone give their input and believe in facilitating communication. Nobody has all the answers and many times multiple heads are better than one.

I have high standards for others. Sometimes they are too high, and I get frustrated when I feel others are not living up to their potential. In order to work better with other people, I need to realize their self-worth and value as a group member or partner.

Currently, I will decide on a particular course of action, and (because it was my decision) I will dig a hole and fight to save it. I need to listen to others' ideas and get fresh perspectives rather than wasting time and energy preserving a system that does not work.

I often feel socially retarded. This really means I have trouble knowing how to act in certain social situations, such as meeting people for the first time. Because I am an introvert and private (and quite frankly feel that some of social engagements are silly wastes of time), I have trouble striking up meaningful conversations with unfamiliar people or making small talk. Further, and probably more importantly, because I do not have this skill, I cannot take advantage of social networking. I simply do not know how to ask certain questions tactfully or enlist assistance in an enterprise without knowing the person well.

I would like to own my own business. Set my own hours. I want to be in a position to help people. I'm also interested in politics, and being well-respected in the community might be a first step towards elected office.

Are these comments the musings of middle managers? Of mid-career government workers? Of budding entrepreneurs? Or some combination of all these? Well, not really. They are the written reflections of first-year law students at the newly minted Elon University School of Law. These students are embarking on a process of self-assessment culminating in a private one-on-one conversation with a faculty coach. Yes, really, law students—the young professionals one would think least inclined to experience this kind of coaching. Yet it is happening at Elon Law, and it is required of all first-year students, who typically number between 110 and 125 per class. The law school, which opened its doors in downtown Greensboro, North Carolina, in 2006, aspires to graduate "lawyer-leaders" who will demonstrate leadership and commitment to public service during their careers. The coaching initiative, which was introduced in the school's second year, is part of Elon Law's wider leadership development program.

Elon's Leadership Development Program

What is the actual process students undergo? The experience begins in the summer before they enroll, when each student completes the Myers Briggs Type Indicator® (MBTI®) online. The MBTI introduces the importance of self-awareness as a key component of personal and leadership development. The MBTI is debriefed during the first semester and becomes the basis of an initial one-on-one conversation with a professor regarding the student's study habits and learning style. The MBTI is then revisited during an intensive two-week leadership course in the school's January winter term. In this course, among other assignments, students divide into "firms" and participate in a number of simulations and experiential exercises that provide additional insights about their interpersonal skills, their values, ethical dilemmas that lawyers face, and the practical dos and don'ts of the legal profession.

It is in this context that coaching is introduced. Students are first asked to complete an Individual Development Plan (IDP) in which they identify strengths and developmental needs and examine and reaffirm their values. Based on this self-assessment, they identify two stretch goals they want to work on—one while in law school, and another looking at least five years out into their careers. The students then identify the action steps, time lines, and resources they will need to reach their goals. A sample short-term goal for one student reads, "I would like to work on prioritization and not getting too overwhelmed when I don't get everything done when I would like to. This will alleviate stress and allow me to complete the tasks that are most important in the manner that I would like, while also completing tasks that are less important in an efficient manner." A longer-term goal—after law school—for another student reads, "Five years from now, my goal is to be working (or have worked) for a large firm. Within the firm, I'd be practicing environmental law and have the ability to travel internationally studying green codes throughout the world."

Upon completion of this assignment, the student then meets with his or her coach face-to-face for up to one hour. These confidential meetings are the heart of the experience. The sessions are spread out over a period of two to three weeks after the classroom portion of the course is completed to allow for more efficient scheduling and greater focus. Coaches read the IDPs in advance and discuss the student's insights in the coaching session. Action steps that lead to accomplishment of the goals are also reviewed.

In the two examples cited above, the first student might be given practical tips on setting priorities and thereby lowering stress. The second student might be encouraged to seek an internship or summer job at a large law firm, and might be linked up with an attorney or law professor familiar with environmental law. In cases where action steps are too vague or unreachable, students are asked to refine their goals and action steps and submit a revised IDP to the coach for further review. Coaches encourage use of the familiar SMART approach to goal setting—Specific, Measurable, Aggressive, Relevant and Time-bound.

Elon Law School currently has a stable of ten coaches, including the school's dean, several faculty and senior staff members, one external coach, and two practicing attorneys—an interesting mix of lawyers and nonlawyers. A core group of six coaches, including this author, has been involved in the program since its inception in 2008. The coaches work as a team and typically meet before and after each winter term to compare notes. Each coach conducts, on average, between ten to fifteen individual sessions.[1]

Students are encouraged to discuss their IDPs with one another, to the extent they are comfortable doing so, and are asked to share their plans with their preceptors—attorneys in the surrounding community who volunteer as guides and mentors for the students in their first year. Students are also encouraged to pair up with another student who may exhibit the behavior or skill that the student is looking to improve, or who may be a reliable source of peer feedback.

The IDPs are officially reviewed and updated a year later, during the required winter term leadership course for second-year students. This review occurs in a small team setting, not in individual coaching sessions.

In addition, second-year students encounter a different form of coaching in this course. During the two weeks, student teams are given legal problems to solve on behalf of nonprofit clients in the Greensboro community. Each team is assigned a process coach who observes team members and gives them feedback on how they're working as a team. These coaches are drawn from the same coaching cohort. Student team members also identify behavioral goals they would like to work on during the two-week course and ask for observation and feedback from their team members.[2]

Common themes derived from the coaching sessions are understandably dictated by the early-career stages of these law students. Their focus tends to be on developing practical strategies to do well in school, gain valuable experience in summer employment, network with attorneys in practice areas that interest them, and polish job interviewing skills. Their inherent lack of emphasis on behavioral changes around intra- and interpersonal skills such as planning, communication, prioritization, time management, managing stress, working well with others, and giving and receiving feedback is a likely function of their lack of organizational work experience. The intent is that by emphasizing these behavioral areas early in their law school tenure, these law students will be better prepared to interact successfully with others and eventually demonstrate leadership—even as they assume the traditional role of interpreting and applying the law on behalf of their clients, the legal system, and a more just society.

In terms of possible differences in the perspectives of these first-year students, when compared to students from earlier decades, coaches report that they seem to be more inclined to look for *meaning* in their future work, and not just having a job that pays well. A number of them expresses interest in international service, such as helping to stop human trafficking or serving the legal needs of recent immigrant populations. In discussing their values, these students most often emphasize the importance of family—either the families from which they have come or the families they hope to start (most are not yet married or in committed relationships)—and of achieving some semblance of work-life balance. Spirituality also figures into some of their comments. These concerns contrast with today's older managers and professionals, who have typically waited to contemplate "what life's all about" until they establish themselves and reach mid-career. While it's speculative and even risky to derive generalizations from this relatively small student sample, tracking these themes over time may yield clues about the comparative values and attitudes of this generation of law students.

Practical lessons learned from the first-year individual coaching sessions include the following:

- The scheduling of more than a hundred individual coaching sessions in so short a timeframe is time-consuming and requires extensive planning. Fortunately, the great majority of students takes the process seriously; they come to the sessions prepared and on time. With a few exceptions, students are assigned to coaches randomly.

- Still, most students accustomed to competing in a graded academic environment understandably don't know what to expect once the door is closed. Other than working with a faculty advisor or favorite professor, they have probably not encountered anything resembling these coaching sessions before. A few students, especially those with prior full-time work experience, take to the process effortlessly. Others have difficulty identifying specific action steps and resources. Part of the coach's challenge is simply educating coachees about how to access the resources available all around them, starting with faculty and staff. As prospective lawyers, many of these students are independent-minded and accustomed to finding their own way without seeking help. The coaching sessions ideally encourage them to seek the ongoing support they will need to navigate successfully their course of study and their careers. At a minimum, the process gives students a tool to help them problem solve, which is something they will need as lawyers to formulate clear plans, or to strategize, rather than act spontaneously.

- For students who find the experience especially difficult or not helpful, the coaches tell them that at least they will have been exposed to a developmental process they may well encounter in organizational settings later in their careers. Then they will have a better understanding of what's required. It's ultimately up to each student to decide whether the process is useful and worth carrying forward on his or her own. By providing some up-front testimonials from students and lawyers who have benefited from the experience, we can do a better job of educating students in advance about the purpose and value of the coaching.

- Students need to be encouraged to include behavioral goals, such as improving listening or communication skills, in their plans. Otherwise, their action plans tend to revolve exclusively around improving performance in academic courses or acquisition of practical lawyering skills. While goals in these areas are appropriate and relevant, coaches work with students to explore underlying behavioral adjustments that may be needed to achieve those goals. For example, a student who wants to learn how to try a case may need to overcome "stage fright," or to hone networking skills in order to enlist attorneys who can instruct them, or to find a relevant summer job. What many students find they need is improvement of interpersonal skills—under the rubric of emotional intelligence—that will enhance their employability and their career progression, whether they intend to be solo practitioners, corporate counsels, partners at a large firm, or leaders in business and government.

• Winter term of the first year seems best in terms of timing. The first semester is too confused and busy for students to step back and reflect (plus they haven't had the experience of attending law school). Yet putting the coaching later in the first year or even in the second either crowds exams and summer plans or comes too late to be helpful in terms of action planning for school-related issues. Ideally, a final review of the IDP goals could occur early in the third year, when students are interviewing for jobs after graduation and narrowing career choices.

In terms of the *conduct* of the coaching sessions themselves, coaches report the importance of: (1) establishing trust immediately by connecting to something personal in the student's background, such as hometown, university attended, a favorite hobby, or a sports or arts interest; (2) emphasizing the confidentiality of the session; (3) maintaining eye contact throughout the session; (4) asking questions in a way that elicits more than a yes or no response; and (5) listening more than talking, despite the temptation to jump in. Of course, summarizing insights gained and action steps identified at the end of each session is a critical component.

These observations help explain the coaching process and some of the lessons learned, but they still beg a fundamental question: *why* is Elon Law School investing in leadership development for its students on such a broad scale? First, because the school's founders view leadership as an indispensable duty of lawyers in a democratic society. Second, because a whole constellation of stakeholders—including law firms, bar associations, corporations, public interest groups, and clients—are calling for a different kind of lawyer, one who combines leadership qualities with technical competence. And finally, because recent studies of legal education, most notably a major report by the Carnegie Foundation for the Advancement of Teaching and Learning, have challenged law schools to complement their traditional reliance on case analysis with what the Carnegie report calls "developing the ethical and social dimensions of the profession."[3] A program of leadership development is in part Elon Law's response to this call for pedagogical reform. And Elon Law is not the only pioneer. Several other law schools have embarked on a similar path, though features such as required leadership courses and one-on-one coaching are rare, if not unique, at this writing.

It's not coincidental that Elon Law has adopted coaching as part of its leadership curriculum. As we know, the practice of leadership coaching has grown dramatically over the past decade. Not only has coaching reached virtually every corner of the globe, it has also touched nearly every stripe of leader and type of organization. Why? Leaders and their teams, confronted by enormous and often unprecedented challenges, need help, and coaching is an increasingly essential component of any systemic leadership development initiative. Now one of the last groups to embrace leadership development—lawyers and their firms—has begun to explore coaching. Like professional consulting firms before them, traditional law firms were predicated on the ability of individual partners and senior associates to provide expert legal advice and services to their clients. But increasingly, clients of large law firms need those services across a broad array of practice areas. Clients also want lawyers to help them craft solutions to their business problems, not just tell them from the sidelines what they legally can and can't do. This shift requires lawyers to work in teams and increasingly see themselves as leaders within the firm and in managing complex client relationships.

It's no longer enough to know the law; today's lawyers must also know how to use their legal knowledge to influence others—whether colleagues in the firm, clients, opposing lawyers, or judges—to create successful outcomes in their cases. Moreover, high attrition rates among high-potential young associates have compelled some firms to offer professional development opportunities, including leadership development, as a retention strategy. (In many large companies, corporate counsels and their legal departments have long participated in company-wide performance development initiatives, including 360-degree assessment, coaching, and leadership development.)

These trends in the field have not gone unnoticed at other law schools. To the extent that they can graduate lawyers who both know the law well and have developed the interpersonal skills needed to navigate in this new environment, they will differentiate themselves and their graduates. But how will we know these innovations have had their intended impact? In the case of Elon University School of Law, it will be some years before any lasting impact can be measured. It will be verified in the testimonials and through the accomplishments of its alumni, as they evince leadership and commitment to public service in their firms, the profession, and their communities and society at large. It is a risk worth taking, for the potential rewards will be rich.

John Alexander is an executive coach, consultant, author, lecturer, and former CEO with more than thirty years' experience in the United States and abroad. He is cofounder and principal of Leadership Horizons, Inc. (LHI), an executive coaching and consulting firm. John also serves as Distinguished Leadership Coach in Residence at the Elon University School of Law in Greensboro, North Carolina, and is a special advisor to the Globally Responsible Leadership Initiative (GRLI) in Brussels, Belgium. From 1997 to 2007, John served as president and CEO of the Center for Creative Leadership (CCL). John has appeared before audiences worldwide, has been interviewed in numerous media outlets, and has published widely. For more information and to contact John, please see www.leadhorizons .com, www.ccl.org, and www.grli.org.

CHAPTER NINETEEN

TEAM BUILDING WITHOUT TIME WASTING[1]

By Marshall Goldsmith and Howard Morgan

As major organizations have to learn to deal with increasingly rapid change, teams are becoming more and more important. As the traditional, hierarchical school of leadership diminishes in significance, a new focus on networked team leadership is emerging to take its place. Leaders are finding themselves members of all kinds of teams, including virtual teams, autonomous teams, cross-functional teams, and action-learning teams.

Many of today's leaders face a dilemma: as the *need* to build effective teams is increasing, the *time* available to build these teams is often decreasing. A common challenge faced by today's leaders is the necessity of building teams in an environment of rapid change with limited resources. The process of reengineering and streamlining, when coupled with increased demand for services, has led to a situation in which most leaders have more work to do and fewer staff members to help them do it.

Our research involving thousands of participants has shown how focused feedback and follow-up can increase leadership effectiveness—as judged by direct reports and coworkers.[2] A parallel approach to team building has been shown to help leaders build teamwork without wasting time. Though the approach described sounds simple, it will not be easy. It will require that team members have the courage to regularly ask for—and learn from—regular input from team members.

To successfully implement the following team-building process, the leader (or external consultant) will need to assume the role of coach or facilitator and fight the urge to be the "boss" or "instructor." Greater improvement in teamwork tends to occur when team members develop their own behavioral change strategies rather just executing a change strategy that has been imposed upon them by the "boss."

Steps in the Process

Step One. Begin by asking all members of the team to confidentially record their individual answers to two questions: (1) "On a 1 to 10 scale (with 10 being ideal), how well *are* we doing in terms of working together as a team?" and (2) "On a 1 to 10 scale, how well *do we need to be* doing in terms of working together as a team?"

Before beginning a team-building process, it is important to determine whether the team feels that team building is both important and needed. Some people may report to the same manager, but legitimately have little reason to work interactively as a team. Other groups may believe that teamwork is important, but feel that the team is already functioning smoothly and that a team-building activity would be a waste of time.

Step Two. Have a team member calculate the results. Discuss the results with the team. If the team members believe that the gap between current effectiveness and needed effectiveness indicates the need for team building, proceed to the next step in the process.

In most cases team members believe that improved teamwork is both important and needed. Interviews involving members from several hundred teams (in multinational corporations) showed that the "average" team member believed that his or her team was currently functioning at a 5.8 level of effectiveness but needed to be at an 8.7 level.

Step Three. Ask the team members, "If *every* team member could change two key behaviors that would help us close the gap between *where we are* and *where we want to be*, which two behaviors we all should try to change?" Have each team member record his or her selected behaviors on flip charts.

Step Four. Help team members prioritize all the behaviors on the charts (many will be the same or similar) and (using consensus) determine the most important behavior to change (for all team members).

Step Five. Have each team member hold a one-on-one dialogue with all other team members. During the dialogues each member will request that his or her colleague suggest two areas for personal behavioral change (other than the one already agreed on earlier) that will help the team close the gap between *where we are* and *where we want to be*.

These dialogues occur simultaneously and take about five minutes each. For example, if there are seven team members, each team member will participate in six brief one-on-one dialogues.

Step Six. Let each team member review his or her list of suggested behavioral changes and choose the one that seems to be the most important. Have all team members then announce their one key behavior for personal change to the team.

Step Seven. Encourage all team members to ask for brief (five-minute), monthly three-question "suggestions for the future" from all other team members to help increase their effectiveness in demonstrating (1) the one key behavior common to all team members, (2) the one key personal behavior generated from team member input, and (3) overall effective behavior as a team member.

Step Eight. Conduct a mini-survey, follow-up process in approximately six months. From the mini-survey each team member will receive confidential feedback from all other team members on his or her perceived change in effectiveness. This survey will include the one common behavioral item, the one personal behavioral item, and the overall team member item. A final question can gage the level of follow-up—so that team members can see the connection between their level of follow-up and their increased effectiveness.

This four-question survey can either be electronically distributed electronically or "put on a postcard" and might look like the sample illustrated by Exhibit 19.1.

EXHIBIT 19.1 SAMPLE MINI-SURVEY

Do you believe this person has become more (or less) effective in the past six months in regards to the following items? (Please circle the number that best matches your estimate of any change in effectiveness.)

	Less Effective	No Perceptible Change	More Effective	No Change Needed	Not Enough Information
Team Item 1. Clarifies roles and expectations with fellow team members	–3 –2 –1	0	1 2 3	NCN	NI
Individual Item 2. Genuinely listens to others	–3 –2 –1	0	1 2 3	NCN	NI
General Item 3. Demonstrates effective team membership	–3 –2 –1	0	1 2 3	NCN	NI

4. How frequently has this person followed up with you on the areas that he or she has been trying to improve? (Check one.)

☑ No perceptible follow-up
☑ Little follow-up
☑ Some follow-up
☑ Frequent follow-up
☑ Consistent (periodic) follow-up

5. What can this individual do to become a more effective team leader?

_____

_____

_____

_____

_____

Step Nine. Have an outside supplier calculate the results for each individual (on all items) and calculate the summary results for all team members (on the common team items). Each team member can then receive a confidential summary report indicating the degree to which colleagues see his or her increased effectiveness in demonstrating the desired behaviors. Each member can also receive a summary report on the team's progress on the items selected for all team members.

"Before and after" studies have clearly shown that if team members have regularly followed up with their colleagues they will almost invariably be seen as increasing their effectiveness in their selected individual "areas for improvement." The group summary will also tend to show that (overall) team members will have increased in effectiveness on the common team items and overall team member behavior. The mini-survey summary report will give team members a chance to receive positive reinforcement for improvement (and to learn what has not improved) after a reasonably short period of time. The mini-survey will also help to validate the importance of "sticking with it" and "following up."

Step Ten. In a team meeting have each team member discuss key learnings from their mini-survey results, and ask for further suggestions in a brief one-on-one dialogue with each other team member.

Step Eleven. Review the summary results with the team. Facilitate a discussion on how the team (as a whole) is doing in terms of increasing its effectiveness in the two key behaviors that were selected for all team members. Provide the team with positive recognition for increased effectiveness in teamwork. Encourage team members to keep focused on demonstrating the behaviors that they are try-ing to improve.

Step Twelve. Have every team member continue to conduct brief, monthly, "progress report" sessions with all other team members. Readminister the mini-survey eight months after the beginning of the process and again after one year.

Step Thirteen. Conduct a summary session with the team one year after the process has started. Review the results of the final mini-survey, and ask the team members to rate the team's effectiveness on *where we are* versus *where we need to be* in terms of working together as a team. Compare these ratings with the original ratings that were calculated one year earlier. (If team members followed the process in a reasonably disciplined fashion, the team will almost always see a dramatic improvement in teamwork.) Give the team positive recognition for improvement in teamwork, and have each team member (in a brief one-on-one dialogue) recognize each of his or her colleagues for improvements in behavior that have occurred over the past twelve months.

Step Fourteen. Ask the team members if they believe that more work on team building will be needed in the upcoming year. If the team believes that more work would be beneficial, continue the process. If the team believes that more work is not needed, declare victory and work on something else!

Why This Process Works

The process described above works because it is highly focused, includes disci-plined feedback and follow-up, does not waste time, and causes participants to focus on self-improvement.

Most survey feedback processes ask respondents to complete too many items. In such surveys most of the items do not result in any behavioral change and par-ticipants feel they are wasting time. Participants almost never object to completing four-item mini-surveys that are specifically designed to fit each team member's unique needs. The process also works because it provides ongoing feedback and reinforcement. Most survey processes provide participants with feedback every twelve to twenty-four months. Any research on behavioral change will show that feedback and reinforcement for new behavior needs to occur much more frequently than annually or biannually. A final reason that the process works is because it encourages participants to focus on self-improvement. Many team-building processes degenerate because team members are primarily focused on solving *someone else's* problems. This process works because it encourages team members to focus primarily on solving *their own* problems!

Let us close with a challenge to you (the reader) as a team leader. Try it! The "downside" is very low. The process takes little time and the first mini-survey will quickly show whether progress is being made. The "upside" can be very high. As effective teamwork becomes more and more important, the brief amount of time that you invest in this process may produce a great return for your team and an even greater return for you organization.

Dr. Marshall Goldsmith has recently been recognized as one of the fifteen most influential business thinkers in the world, in a global biannual study sponsored by *The (London) Times*. He has also been described in *American Management Association* as one of the top fifty thinkers and leaders who have influenced the field of management over the past eighty years; in the *Wall Street Journal* as one of the top ten executive educators; in *Forbes* as one of the five most-respected executive coaches; in the *Economic Time (India)* among the top CEO coaches of America; in *Fast Company*, called America's preeminent executive coach; and he has received a lifetime achievement award (one of two ever awarded) from the *Institute for Management Studies*. Marshall is one of a select few executive advisors who have been asked to work with over 120 major CEOs and their management teams. He is the million-selling author of numerous books, including *New York Times* bestsellers *MOJO* and *What Got You Here Won't Get You There* (also a *Wall Street Journal* #1 business book and winner of the Harold Longman Award for business book of the year). Contact Marshall at marshall@marshallgoldsmith.com and www .marshallgoldsmith.com.

As an executive coach, **Howard Morgan** has led major organizational change initiatives in partnership with top leaders and executives at numerous international organizations. He was named as one of the fifty top coaches by Linkage, recognized as one of five coaches with "a proven track record of success." Howard is a pioneer in the practical understanding of how motivation, productivity, and behavior are linked to organizational values, leadership approach, and employee satisfaction. He has done significant work on measuring the impact of leaders on long-term profitability and growth. Howard is a managing director of Leadership Research Institute. Howard has published several books, including *The Art and Practice of Leadership Coaching* and *Leading Organizational Learning*. A member of the Marshall Goldsmith Group, Howard can be contacted at http://www.howardjmorgan.com and howard@marshallgoldsmithgroup.com.

CHAPTER TWENTY

LEADERS BUILDING LEADERS

High-Potential Development and Executive Coaching at Microsoft[1]*

By Shannon Wallis, Brian O. Underhill, and Carol Hedly

The opportunity for ongoing learning and development is a commitment Microsoft makes to all employees. Microsoft invests more than $300 million annually in formal education programs directed at the employee, manager, and leader offered by the Corporate Learning and Development groups and other profession-specific learning groups throughout the company.

In addition, Microsoft invests in a smaller group of employees who have the potential for, and strong interest in, taking on more senior, critical roles as individual contributors or managers. These individuals are identified and considered for more focused career development, which may include participation in one of several professional development experiences known as high-potential development programs.

In identifying employees as high-potential, it is important to appreciate that natural "gifts" are not sufficient. For an employee, reaching his or her full potential depends on a combination of natural gifts, what he or she does with that talent (hard work, perseverance, courage, and so on), the experiences he or she is given, the support of others along the way, and the context or culture within which he or she operates.[2]

At Microsoft, high-potential development goes beyond traditional management or leadership development. Instead, it focuses on *accelerating* the development

---

of these individuals to advance to the next career stage. The remainder of this chapter will present Microsoft's case for making a significant shift in high-potential development.

What Led Microsoft to Make the Change

In 2004, Microsoft had more than thirty separate high-potential programs operating around the world. The individual programs were not aligned to Microsoft's Leadership Career Model and were not easily scalable. Furthermore, consistent criteria for identifying high-potentials did not exist, and areas and segments independently determined the number of "high-potentials" that they wanted to develop. This impacted the larger talent management system and made movement among programs difficult when employees changed geographies, businesses, or functions. Given the various objectives of the programs, the experience of high-potentials was inconsistent across the company.

To build the pipeline of future leaders, Microsoft decided to align high-potential development to create a consistent experience.

Microsoft Bench Leaders Building Leaders—The New High-Potential Development Experience

Microsoft began with questions. What is a high-potential? How is high-potential talent identified? How many Hi-Pos are needed to meet future demand? Finally, how is the development of high-potentials accelerated? The answers to these questions led to a new program: Microsoft Bench Leaders Building Leaders. MS Bench is a long-term leadership development experience for high-potentials. Leaders Building Leaders is a leadership development philosophy that sets up a cascading approach to the investment of time and resources by current leaders into emerging leaders at the next career stage level. Microsoft would apply this leadership development philosophy across less than 4 percent of the population or more than 3,600 high-potentials in 107 countries. To begin, they needed to identify the high-potentials.

High-Potential Identification

Microsoft heavily leveraged the Corporate Leadership Council's 2005 empirical study, "Realizing the Full Potential of Rising Talent." A high-potential at

FIGURE 20.1. HIGH-POTENTIAL CRITERIA

Ability
A combination of knowledge, skills, and competencies an employee uses to carry out his or her day-to-day work

Aspiration
Seeks and takes on roles that offer advancement, increasing influence, greater impact and/ or recognition

Commitment
Willingness and ability to align with MSFT needs, priorities, and goals

Source: Adapted from Corporate Leadership Council High-Potential Management Survey, 2005.

Microsoft is defined as someone with the ability, commitment, and aspiration to advance to and succeed in more senior, critical roles (see Figure 20.1).

These roles include individual contributor, manager, technical and executive leadership. A high-potential differs from a high performer in that a high performer may demonstrate exceptional ability, but may not demonstrate commitment or aspiration to advance to more senior roles or to do so in an accelerated timeframe. High-potentials are a subset of high performers and are promotable into the next potential band. In other words, not all strong performers are high-potentials. A Hi-Po must have the ability (skills and competencies), commitment, and aspiration to grow and succeed and be a top performer as a people leader in an accelerated timeframe relative to high performers. The combination of the three is required, and only those employees determined to be highest on all three are selected. As they take on risky jobs, this might slow momentarily as they master new skills, which needs to be accounted for. It is expected that they will catch up and continue on a fast trajectory.

MS Bench Tiers

Once the high-potential talent is identified, Microsoft sorts them by peer level groups and career stages. Whereas in the former programs, high-potentials were

FIGURE 20.2. MICROSOFT BENCH TIERS

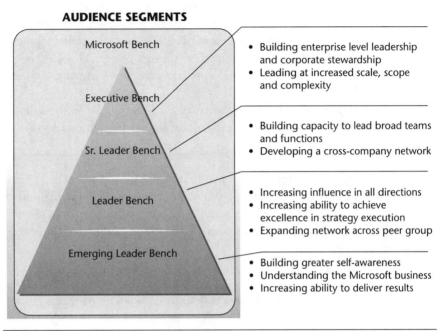

AUDIENCE SEGMENTS

Microsoft Bench

Executive Bench

- Building enterprise level leadership and corporate stewardship
- Leading at increased scale, scope and complexity

Sr. Leader Bench

- Building capacity to lead broad teams and functions
- Developing a cross-company network

Leader Bench

- Increasing influence in all directions
- Increasing ability to achieve excellence in strategy execution
- Expanding network across peer group

Emerging Leader Bench

- Building greater self-awareness
- Understanding the Microsoft business
- Increasing ability to deliver results

Source: Microsoft Leadership Development Group.

grouped regardless of career stage and received similar development opportunities, MS Bench provides differentiated development. The tiers are the organizing function for offering the development experiences based on the needs of specific peer level groups and career stages. High-potentials are segmented into a four-tier system, as seen in Figure 20.2: junior individual contributors in Emerging Leader Bench; senior individual contributors and managers in Leader Bench; managers of managers, functional leaders, and business leaders in Senior Leader Bench; and general managers and vice-presidents in Executive Bench. Each tier has a different focus area based on the unique needs of the particular career stage.

Executive Bench's development focus is building enterprise level leadership and corporate stewardship, leading at increased scale, scope and complexity. Senior Leader Bench's focuses on building capacity to lead broad teams and functions and developing a cross-company network. Leader Bench focuses on increasing influence in all directions, increasing ability to achieve excellence in strategy execution, and expanding network across peer group Emerging Leader Bench focuses on building greater self-awareness, understanding the Microsoft business, and increasing ability to deliver results.

Five Drivers of Accelerated Development for High-Potentials

Once sorted into the appropriate tiers, the high-potentials' development experience begins. Underlying all development are five drivers of accelerated development for high-potentials at Microsoft. The Five Drivers are development activities that *significantly* impact the development of high-potential leaders and are derived from two primary sources, the Corporate Leadership Council (2005) and Morgan McCall.[3]

Research indicates that five key areas, if executed effectively, have the most significant impact on high-potential development (Corporate Leadership Council, 2005):

1. Senior leadership commitment to developing leaders;
2. Manager capability and engagement in the development high-potentials;
3. A professional network that allows for contacts throughout the business;
4. A high-quality, customized stretch development plan with clear objectives; and
5. On-the-job experiences.

These five areas were used as design principles in the design of MS Bench.

Five Development Components

MS Bench allows emerging and experienced leaders to learn from each other through five developmental components that are tied to the five drivers. Each component is executed differently at each tier to provide a unique development experience that builds leader capability over the duration of the MS Bench experience. This creates consistency and integrated development for emerging leaders as they move vertically through the MS Bench tiers.

EXHIBIT 20.1 MICROSOFT LEADERSHIP COMPETENCIES (SUBSET)

Microsoft Leadership Competencies
Executive Maturity
OneMicrosoft
Impact and Influence
Deep Insight
Creative Business Value
Customer Commitment and Foresight

FIGURE 20.3. FIVE DEVELOPMENTAL COMPONENTS

What Is Microsoft Bench?

Cycle of Leaders Building Leaders

Executive Bench

Senior Leader Bench

Leader Bench

Emerging Leader Bench

One consistent and integrated development experience

Leadership Orientation

Networking + Learning Circles

In Business/ Profession Event

Career Development

Coaching + Mentoring

Five developmental components tied to the five drivers of accelerated development

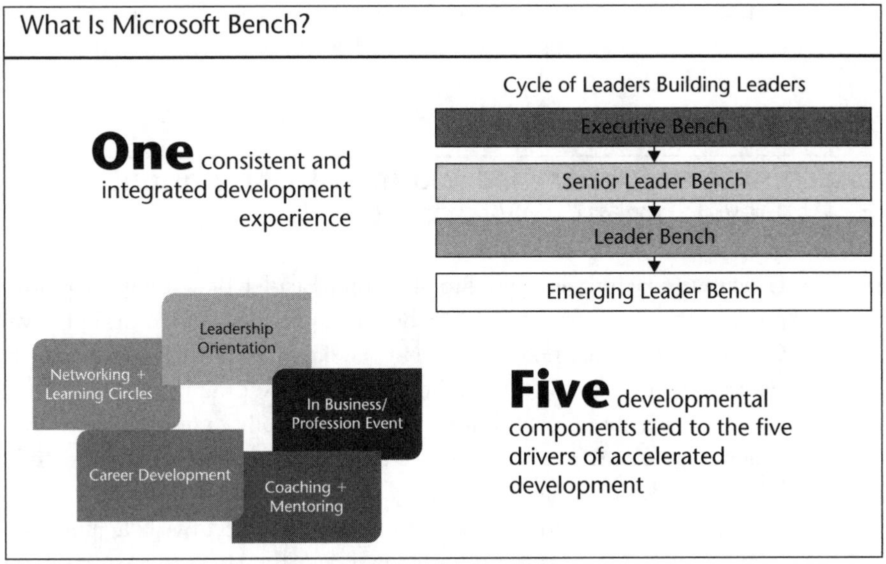

Source: Microsoft Leadership Development Group.

The five developmental components, highlighted in Figure 20.3, provide a leading-edge development experience that builds leadership capability over time.

Coaching

As a part of the overall development experience, Microsoft offers one-to-one partnerships through coaching and mentoring that involve a thought-provoking process that inspires the individual to maximize his or her personal and professional potential. Through individualized follow-up, coaching, and mentoring, they integrate learning from a variety of sources such as assessment feedback, current role experiences, and development priorities to provide a more impactful learning experience.

Coaching and mentoring enable high-potentials to:

- Build skills and close development gaps;
- Develop "big picture" understanding of Microsoft and our industry through cross-boundary and cross-role exposure; and
- Become more accountable for their own development since the coaching and mentoring process is a self-directed one.

In order to deliver MS Bench on the global scale required, partnership with external organizations was critical. As the design and implementation plans were finalized, Microsoft began a search for partners who could lend additional subject-matter expertise to a couple of key components, executive coaching and learning circles.

Coaching as a Primary Development Component for Hi-Po Development at Microsoft

Executive coaching is offered to all Senior Leader Bench high-potential participants in the first year of their MS Bench experience. Microsoft initially met with CoachSource as the potential executive coaching partner because of numerous references to the firm noted in their study of best practices.

They selected CoachSource for the availability and quality of their global coaching pool, use of technology to support the coaching process, and the flexibility they demonstrated in meeting Microsoft's needs. In the first year, approximately 214 of 250 leaders took advantage of the executive coaching program via CoachSource. The program has grown over the years to eventually serve over 700 leaders.

Why executive coaching? Microsoft believes that executive coaching provides the most effective ongoing behavioral development for leaders. Participants receive regular, individualized follow-up to help drive behavioral change over time. A coach offers a third-party, objective support for the leader's improvement efforts.

The definition of executive coaching adopted is the "one-to-one development of an organizational leader."[4] Although there are different approaches to coaching, MS Bench's focus was around the development of leaders in the organizational context. Coaching is focused on changing leadership behavior in the workplace.

Coaching Process

The coaching design allows for approximately two sessions per month, mostly via telephone (or all via telephone if participant and coach are not co-located). The coaching time line is provided in Figure 20.4. Coaching sessions are focused on feedback from the Microsoft 360-degree assessment, associated Microsoft leadership competencies, other relevant data points, and the Coaching Action Plan (CAP) crafted from the results of this assessment. (A sample is provided in Exhibit 20.2.)

FIGURE 20.4. SAMPLE COACHING TIME LINE

Sample Coaching Time line
You can manage flexibility in the framework, as required

Coaching Month	Suggested Coaching Hours, Format and Topics	Coaching/ Meeting Hours
1	Session 1 (telephone): Review Feedback Summary, goal setting and action planning Session 2 (telephone): Finalize action plan, meet with manager to gain support for action plan	1.5 0.5
2	Session 3 (telephone): Coaching on goals and action plans	1.0
3	Session 4 (telephone): Coaching on goals and action plans Session 5 (telephone): Review post-coaching development plan, meet with manager to gain support for post-coaching development	1.0 0.5
4	Session 6 (telephone): Coaching on goals and action plans	1.0
5	Session 7 (telephone): Coaching on goals and action plans	1.0
	Total Coaching Hours	7

EXHIBIT 20.2 SENIOR LEADER BENCH PROGRAM: COACHING ACTION PLAN

MICROSOFT BENCH |
Leaders Building Leaders

The purpose of this document is to provide high-potential employees a coaching action plan, agreed upon with their manager; which can complement the Bench development experience. Please work on it with your coach.

It must be completed before the fourth coaching session in order for coaching to continue.

1. Complete the Action Plan

Identify 1–3 **Leadership Competencies** you will work on (from your 360-degree results or other feedback items).

(continued)

Goals: Identify 1–3 goals that you are most passionate about working on.	**Measures:** How will each goal be measured (can be quantitative or qualitative)?	**What Specific Action Steps can you take in support of this goal?**	**Potential Business Impact:** What is the value to you and the business if you do not achieve your goal? What is the value to you and the business if you do?	**Target Date:** Set a target date for each goal.

2. Schedule the Coaching Action Plan contracting conversation with your manager

☑ **Contracting Conversation:** Set up some time to review this document with your manager and coach, ensuring a meaningful conversation and agreement regarding your development plan. Contracting is another form of commitment—commitment to working in a partnership as manager and ExPo member. Think of it as a commitment to maximize your potential; which was identified during nomination; and ensure continued strengthening of the criteria on which a high-potential employee is identified: aspiration, ability, and commitment.

3. Prepare questions which will be used to verify coaching effectiveness

At the end of coaching, a "Mini-Survey" will be conducted with your stakeholders. Here are the general questions asked:

- Has this person shared with you in the past six months about what she is working on?
- Do you feel this person has become more effective or less effective as a leader in the past six months?
- What has this person done in the past six months that you have found particularly effective?
- What can this person do to become more effective as a leader in the areas of development noted above

In addition, there are customized questions based on your particular coaching goals.

List 2–3 questions that reflect the leadership behaviors you are working on with your coach.

* The following improvement area(s) have been specifically selected by this leader. Please rate the extent to which this individual has increased/decreased in effectiveness in the following areas of development in the past six months.
    * First
    * Second
    * Third
* Examples:
    * Being less specifically directive during project work, versus being inclusive with others ideas and contributions
    * Ability to give feedback in a manner that is genuinely heard and seriously considered by others
    * Able to effectively work with conflict, remaining engaged, without attempting to avoid it or dissolve it at all costs
* List the email addresses for the leaders you will invite to give you this end of process mini-survey feedback:

_____   _____

_____   _____

_____   _____

_____   _____

_____   _____

_____   _____

4. Senior Leader Bench Learning Commitment:

Signoff:

☑ Member:

_____

☑ Manager:

_____

Please take appropriate steps to update and then periodically review your commitments in the Performance @ Microsoft tool and track resulting development activities in your Development Plan in Career Compass.

_____

This coaching process requires clearly defined goals to be created, which are outlined in the Coaching Action Plan. After the plan is created, it is shared with the program managers, allowing an additional audit that *tangible goals* are the central thrust to the coaching work. Goals have to be clearly identifiable and behavioral in nature to allow for the use of metrics to measure improvement at the conclusion of the assignment (see "Measuring Results").

Following the feed*forward* process (coined by Marshall Goldsmith; see Chapter 29), participants are encouraged to share their development objectives with their key stakeholders. Thus these stakeholders become involved in the participant's growth by being made aware of the development objectives and are able to offer future-focused suggestions related to these areas for development. Stakeholders are then surveyed at the conclusion to measure progress over time.

Coaching is seven to ten hours spread over a maximum eight-month period. After this time, unused coaching hours are lost. This is done purposefully to encourage participants to stay active with their coaches and keep momentum alive. Leaders at Microsoft are often pulled toward multiple priorities simultaneously. Enforcing a coaching deadline, as well as cancellation and no-show policies, actually helps drive greater (and more efficient) use of the service.

All coaching activity is tracked via an online web-based database. Coaches log dates of sessions, time elapsed, and any general notes to the database. Program administrators can then easily monitor progress of the pool and provide monthly reporting.

Participant-Coach Matching

Although matching is accomplished through a "full choice" process, it is also designed to operate quite efficiently. Leaders need the element of choice, which research shows increases participant satisfaction and reduces the possibility of mismatches. Prior to program start, all MS Bench coaches indicate which of the MS leadership expectations are their "sweet spots" (coaches are allowed to select up to four of the eleven leadership competencies). Simultaneously, the development needs of the MS Bench participants are gathered. Each leader is then matched with two potential coaches based on regional location, development needs, and language requirements (in that order). An automated e-mail is sent to the participant with coach biographies attached.

Participants are encouraged to review biographies and telephone interview the first coach of interest. If this seems like a match, the participant commences with that coach. If not, he or she interviews the second coach. (And if that doesn't work, additional choices are provided, along with a website of all coach bios authorized for MS Bench.)

The selection deadline date is enforced, and participants are reminded that coach availability fills up (which it often does). This seems to encourage leaders to make their selections quickly. For example, in year one, all the matching for 214 leaders was complete within only six weeks.

Measuring Results

Two key metrics are employed during the MS Bench coaching engagement. First, a coach satisfaction survey measures participant satisfaction with their coach. Secondly—and much more importantly—a "mini-survey" measures impact. This coach satisfaction survey is automatically run after four and a half hours of coaching is logged (see Figure 20.4).

The five questions asked are: How satisfied are you with your coach in the following areas:

Q1: Identifies clear priorities for my growth and development

Q2: Genuinely listens to me

Q3: Provides specific, actionable suggestions/advice

Q4: Communicates in a direct and concise manner

Q5: Overall satisfaction with your coaching experience

This graph shows high satisfaction ratings among the five questions surveyed. These data are shared with the individual coaches and adjustments or reassignments are made for any poor feedback.

The mini-survey measures improvement over time in the eyes of key stakeholders working with the executive. This is the best "impact back on the job" metric currently available. Results can be aggregated over a set of participants to show leadership impact over time. The mini uses a 7-point "less effective" (−3) to "more effective" (+3) scale (see Figure 20.5).

In the first year of MS Bench, 22 percent of raters felt the participants had improved at a +3 level; 59 percent noted improvement at a +2 or +3 level; and an impressive 89 percent of raters observed improvement to some degree with the participants (+1, +2, +3 levels). (see Figure 20.6).

Roles and Responsibilities

The participant's boss is an important part of the process. In fact, one of the coaching hours is a three-way session with the participant, his or her manager,

FIGURE 20.5. COACHING SATISFACTION SURVEY RESULTS

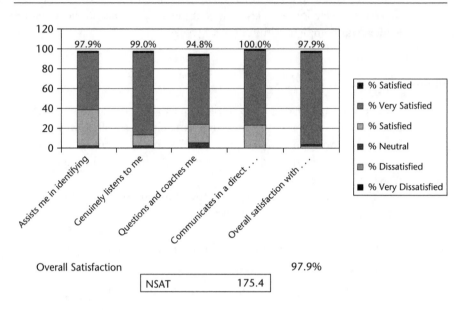

and the coach. Managers participate in follow-up metrics to measure improvement over time. Exhibit 20.1 defines the role of the boss (as well as the other key stakeholders).

Roles are clearly delineated for each of the key stakeholders in the coaching process (Exhibit 20.1). Clear responsibilities are defined for not just the participant, coach, and program manager but also for the participant's boss, skip-level boss, and human resources.

FIGURE 20.6. LEADERSHIP EFFECTIVENESS IMPROVEMENT

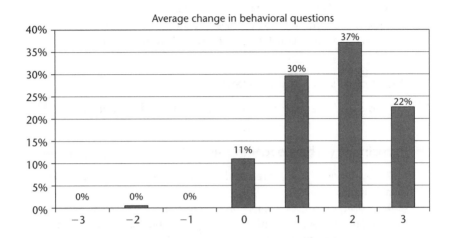

Average change in behavioral questions

EXHIBIT 20.3 KEY STAKEHOLDER ROLES FOR HI-PO COACHING PROGRAM AT MICROSOFT

Human Resources

- Program approval and general oversight
- Approval of all communication drafts before they are sent to other stakeholders

Coaching Program Manager (Program Office)

- Decide on coach selection criteria
- Source interested and qualified coaches
- Interview and select coaches
- Manage external coach-client match process
- Obtain contractual agreements with coaches
- Train coaches in MS leadership development process and external coaching process
- Manage and communicate with coaches throughout coaching process
- Assure surveys (for measurements) are designed, completed, and results reported
- Assure invoicing and payment to coaches
- Track themes that surface from clients to coaches and provide updates to HR

Participant's Manager

- Meet with coach and client ideally twice during external coaching process: once at the beginning of the engagement once at the end of the engagement

(continued)

- Approve and support client's action plan and post-coaching development plan
- Provide ongoing support throughout external coaching process (meet monthly with client and include action plan as an agenda item)
- Look for opportunities to acknowledge and support client
- Understand confidential nature of coach-client relationship

Participant's Manager's Manager

- Hold client's manager responsible to the client's development

Participant ("The Coaching Client")

- Review biographies of three coaches and call best-fit coach to make a selection by date indicated
- Take primary responsibility for the coaching experience, goals, and progress, including all meeting agendas, action plans, and post-coaching development plans
- Schedule or reschedule meetings with coach and manager as appropriate
- Attend and prepare for all coaching sessions
- Request manager's ongoing support throughout coaching process
- Complete codesigned fieldwork between coaching sessions
- Contact program manager if there is any dissatisfaction with the coaching relationship

External Coach

- Coach notifies program office when selected by a client and requests they complete an agreement
- Coach client in feedback of 360-degree assessment
- Coach client in qualifying and documenting goals and action plan steps, and in post-coaching development plan
- Support and hold client accountable in movement toward and achievement of goals in progressive sessions
- Co-design appropriate goal-oriented fieldwork for completion between sessions; hold client accountable for completing fieldwork
- Be responsive to client between meetings as needed via telephone or e-mail
- Attend two meetings with client and client's manager
- Hold client information and meetings in the strictest of confidence
- Contact HR or client's manager if client is not attending meetings or is unresponsive to contact to set up meetings (aside from a suspected law being broken, this is the only reason that the coach would contact others regarding the client)
- Collect themes and patterns of issues that Microsoft may need to be aware of (examples: special needs or additional training that may be helpful for group)

Coach Selection and Orientation

After a fair amount of research into coach qualifications, the general criteria for MS Bench coaches include the following:

- **Business or corporate experience:** Does the coach have specific business or corporate experience and/or background? Has he or she coached executives in organizations of similar size, complexity, industry, etc.?
- **Coach-specific training:** Has the coach had training in a coach-specific process and skill set? How much?
- **Experience in giving feedback on 360-degree or other assessments:** Has the coach had training and/or experience in providing feedback and developing action plans around assessments that will be used?
- **Educational background:** Does the coach have a degree, and in what area?
- **Coach credentials or base number of accrued coaching hours:** How long has the coach been coaching? How many accrued coaching hours does the coach have?
- **Willingness to subscribe to International Coach Federation Code of Ethics** (an ethical code in which the coach aspires to conduct him- or herself in a manner that reflects positively on the coaching profession, is respectful of different approaches to coaching, and recognizes that he or she is also bound by applicable laws and regulations): Does the coach subscribe to a code of ethics? If not, would he or she be willing to sign a contract subscribing to the ICF Code of Ethics?
- **Willingness to sign a contract for services:** Is the coach willing to sign a contract or agreement (with all of its organizational specifics) for the coaching?
- **Availability/capacity to take on new clients:** How much space does the coach have in his or her schedule to take on the number of new clients you need to have coached?
- **Specific language requirements:** Is the coach fluent in a specific language needed to coach participants?
- **Location of coach and participant:** Is the coach located in a specific time zone? Although most coaching can be done over the telephone, time-zone proximity will make scheduling easier.

Using the number of MS Bench participants and their regions, a forecast is made on how many coaches are needed in each region (based on a 4:1 or 5:1 ratio). In the Americas, a group of Microsoft coaches already met these criteria, and a majority of those were invited to return to MS Bench. Outside of the Americas, the worldwide resources of CoachSource were brought to bear to screen and bring this talent on board. CoachSource screened the coaches according to Microsoft's criteria and brought the international coaches into the pool. Local Microsoft human resources professionals reviewed these biographies and selected coaches for the pool.

Approved coaches then indicated their maximum capacity for MS Bench leaders, so Microsoft wouldn't overload them. Currently, the MS Bench pool includes fifty eight coaches located in fifteen countries, speaking ten languages.

Coaches then attended two virtual teleconference orientations of two hours length, the first focusing on the Microsoft business, the second specifically highlighting the details of the MS Bench program (coach expectations, the process and time line, coach-participant matching, manager engagement, coaching success measures, and invoicing process). Coaches already working with Microsoft were exempt from the first orientation, but all coaches were required to join the second session. Microsoft's own LiveMeeting technology was used for these sessions.

International Coaching Forum

One of the most rewarding endeavors was the Coaching Forum, held in Microsoft's headquarters in Redmond, Washington. All coaches were invited for the two-day forum. It began the night before the two days with a welcome reception. Day one included presentations by Microsoft executives and coach round-table discussions. The day wrapped up with a special dinner at the Seattle Space Needle. Day two began with joint time between coaches and Microsoft HR, presentations from several executive coaching thought leaders, a tour of the exclusive Home/Office of the Future demo, followed by a visit (and discounts) to the company store.

Coaches were paid a small stipend, and their expenses were covered once they arrived in Seattle. They were not compensated for airfare or professional fees for the two days. Despite this limitation, 70 percent of the pool attended, including coaches from as far away as China, Ireland, England, Peru, and Australia. Feedback from the two days was overwhelmingly positive: the wealth of best-practice sharing, networking, and overall goodwill generated by the event made it worthwhile for all.

Conclusion

Microsoft has a strong commitment to building leaders at all levels. The MS Bench Leaders Building Leaders program is an integrated and comprehensive high-potential development program encompassing multiple learning methodologies, tailored to each leader's level in the organization. The research-based design includes elements of assessment, coaching, mentoring, learning circles, action learning, and business conferences.

Designed into the program was an expectation that participants will give back to the program over time. As the program progresses into its fourth year, initial MS Bench participants are now participating as conference instructors and mentors for new participants. In this way, participants are learning that they are part of a community that continues to grow and develop itself beyond the initial experience.

Shannon Wallis is the former global director of global high-potential leadership programs and was responsible for the development of top-tier talent at Microsoft. She is an executive coach, consultant, and teacher with more than twenty years of international work experience in leadership development and organizational change. Prior to her current role, she consulted to and held management positions in Fortune 100 businesses as diverse as Coca-Cola and Universal Studios. Her degrees include an MBA from Duke University and a BS in human development and social policy from Northwestern University in the United States. As a speaker, she has addressed Linkage, the Society of Industrial and Organizational Psychology, OD Network, and regional ASTD and industry events, as well as multiple women's conferences throughout the United States. She resides in Fairfax, Virginia, with her family.

Brian O. Underhill, PhD, is an industry-recognized expert in the design and management of worldwide executive coaching implementations. Dr. Underhill is the author of *Executive Coaching for Results: The Definitive Guide to Developing Organizational Leaders* (Berrett-Koehler, 2007). He is the founder of CoachSource and the Alexcel Group and previously spent ten years managing executive coaching operations for Marshall Goldsmith. Dr. Underhill is an internationally sought-after speaker, addressing The Conference Board, Linkage, and regional ASTD, SHRM HRPS, and PCMA events. He has a PhD and an MS degree in organizational psychology from the California School of Professional Psychology (CSPP) and a BA in psychology from the University of Southern California. He holds advanced certification in the Goldsmith Coaching Process. Dr. Underhill resides in Silicon Valley.

Carol Hedly is a Leadership Development Consultant for Microsoft Corporation. She is globally responsible for managing a Senior Leader Bench segment of Microsoft Bench. Carol manages Executive Coaching for Microsoft Bench, and is additionally responsible for Microsoft's global High Potential Identification Process. Carol was a key leader in the development and implementation of Microsoft's talent management platform, Career Models. Prior to Microsoft, Carol held a myriad of management positions for a world leader in workforce management services and human resources solutions. She resides in Kirkland, Washington, with her family.

CHAPTER TWENTY-ONE

THE CARE AND FEEDING
OF HI-PO LEADERS

By Paul Hersey

Mark Zuckerberg, the young upstart CEO of Facebook, recently declared that "someone who is exceptional in their role is not just a little better than someone who is pretty good," he said. "They are 100 times better."[1] Whether his multiplier is accurate, Zuckerberg's comment certainly spotlights the attention companies are paying to the value of key talent. Strategies for recruiting, developing and retaining high-potential leaders now range from conventional, internal succession planning to aggressive, external "acquiring"—buying a company primarily to capture its exceptional talent. Organizations are investing in their Hi-Po pipelines as never before. These rising stars are often publicly identified in order to reinforce their value, signal the company's commitment to developing them, and, they hope, to improve the likelihood of retention—and success—once they transition into leadership roles. They are trained and mentored, offered stretch assignments and executive coaching to prepare and sustain them for the rugged corporate rodeo. So why all the focus on the care and feeding of the elite and the exceptional?

Given the convergent trends of economic distress (do more with less), flattening organizations (manage more people), and the hyper-complexity and pressured pace of today's business environments (navigate perpetual whitewater), even seasoned leaders find themselves gasping for air as they try to keep up, much less see ahead of the competitive curve. Top executives have calendars that rival those of a campaigning politician. A recent report indicates that 47 percent of managers now sleep within reach of their iPhone or Blackberry. The volume of e-mail has exploded, with leaders often cc'd for information's sake; even so, more than 90 percent of them still respond. Virtual teams that operate across time zones call for distance leadership that can build collaboration and bridge cultural differences with little or no face-to-face contact. Managers must assemble and deploy project teams, which may well include members who are not their direct reports, to deliver results quickly. Is it any wonder that the "exceptional" few are at the center of talent wars? Or that those seen as tomorrow's leaders need to begin preparing today?

The Hi-Po Paradox

Flattering as it may to be regarded as an emerging leader, it is also the portal to what we call the "Hi-Po Paradox": it is estimated that 70 percent of high-potentials are courted, groomed, and subsequently promoted because of their technical prowess and individual outcomes—both of which become immediately, and almost completely, irrelevant in their new roles. Instead, they need to rely on influence, networking, strategic thinking, emotional intelligence, and resilience as the arsenal of effectiveness. It is as if you were promoted based on your reputation as a solo contemporary dancer, and now in the new job you are expected to choreograph an international dance troupe. So what happens? Consider this statistic: 43.6 percent of new-to-role leaders underperform in their role.[2] And this problem is quickly compounded by the ripple effect that their initial struggles have on others in the organization, dragging productivity in the decidedly wrong direction.

The Triple Threat

For the new-to-role leader, there are three significant issues of capability at stake:

1. Transition Capability: Actively managing the transition itself
2. Position Capability: Exercising the skills necessary for effectiveness in the role
3. Development Capability: Simultaneously developing one's self, the team, and the organization

In cases where the new leader is transitioning from individual contributor to managing others for the first time, the learning curve is precipitously steep. The basic deficit of all these capabilities—which are unrelated to the individual's existing technical or functional expertise—comprise a serious triple threat. If the new-to-role leader has managed others before, position capability may be less of an issue, but the need for transition and development strategies still looms.

Transition Capability

The transition itself is the first hurdle that threatens to dim the potency of the Hi-Po upon moving into a leadership role. While the job description clearly details what *the* job is, it does not address how to get started in *this* job with this team, this boss, at this moment in time. What should my priorities be? How can I get to know my team and their current issues? What are my boss's expectations? How quickly am I expected to deliver changes? Who are my peers and how can I begin building partnerships with them? These are the kinds of key questions that must be clarified before a new manager can begin to focus on developing position capability. And they point to the fact that effective transition plans are fundamentally about relationship building, which include the previous manager, new boss, colleagues, and the new team.

Position Capability

Speed to proficiency in a new position certainly serves the organization well, minimizing the inevitable disruption that accompanies a promotion from Hi-Po to new manager. But "speed" does not mean it happens instantaneously. And without a supported transition plan, a new-to-role manager can easily sink into quicksand: business pressure to produce quick results, or self-imposed pressure to be fully effective right away. This sense of urgency can lead to "me-driven" mistakes (see Table 21.1.)

The desire to establish "my" credibility, based on one's own thinking, effort, and decisions, is not surprising. Why? Because that is the way these leaders have gotten results in the past! Michael Watkins, who has written extensively on the critical nature of the first ninety days in a new role, concurs that "perhaps the biggest pitfall you face is assuming that what made you successful in your career to this point will continue to do so."[3]

For executive coaches, helping a new-to-role manager make the shift from a "me" to "we" mindset and skill set is central to accelerating position capability.

TABLE 21.1: ME VERSUS THEM

It's About Me	It's About Them
Taking credit	Giving credit
Having all the answers	Asking the right questions
Discounting the perspectives of direct reports	Actively seeking and listening to their views
Withholds information	Shares information
Micromanaging	Empowering strengths

Let's go back to our example of the contemporary dancer who was selected for a coveted role as a choreographer. She will now have to design the movements of the troupe, not execute them flawlessly as an individual performer. She will have to give directions, not take them. She will have to choose who gets the spotlighted solo, not position herself for the opportunity. What she needs most now are people skills, not technical dance skills, to effectively motivate, facilitate, coordinate, communicate with, and influence the members of the troupe.

Once a Hi-Po enters a transition, the value of effective people skills will forever outweigh and add more value than the technical skills that were once the basis of proficiency. Research has shown that the greatest impact on leader performance (57.9 percent) comes from people management skills, particularly team building and developing direct reports.[4]

Many organizations define position capability from "successful manager" profiles or leadership competency models they have developed. Manager skill-building programs are usually built around these models, which are often level-specific. While the training experience may be a dynamic launch to developing people skills, application, and follow-up are the mitochondria that can truly drive skills into leaders at a more cellular than surface level. Becoming competent at using people skills requires people interaction: using that four-quadrant model to coach and adapt your style to one of your direct reports, asking your boss or coach for feedback, soliciting ideas for improvement from coworkers.

As leaders gain vital people skills, the cycle may repeat again. Being promoted to a more senior level is likely to require more conceptual skills, strategic thinking, and business acumen. Consider that our choreographer has now become director of the dance company. Her concerns shift again: How can we sustain our fundraising efforts in the current economic climate? How many new members of the company should we hire this season? How can we capitalize on the current resurgence of interest brought on by competitive dance shows on television? But the ability to think and act with the entire company in mind is an additive skill set to the people skills, which now become exercised more politically and systemically than in the previous role.

Development Capability

Although the disruptive nature of the transition may take many forms—an upward or diagonal move from individual contributor to manager, a shift across functions or businesses, a stretch rotation (which could mean a new product, service or geography), or a highly visible strategic project—the need to develop oneself continually as a leader and to develop others in their roles is imperative. Development capability is about learning how to learn, being continually ready to recognize what you don't know, to be vulnerable and uncomfortable. It is also about building the next level of proficiency within the same skill set or competency. For example, cultivating emotional intelligence (EQ) has exponentially increasing relevance and impact, transcending any one leader's self-awareness or ability to "read" others. Strong EQ fuels the ability to coach individual direct reports effectively at different levels of ability and willingness. It also shapes a team as it creates emotionally intelligent behavioral norms that support and build trust, group identity, and group efficacy. This is more complex and challenging than it is for individuals. Why? Because the team must pay attention to the emotions of its members, its own emotional currents, and the emotions of other relevant groups and individuals outside its boundaries.[5] At more senior levels, EQ will influence buy-in to large-scale changes and encourage organizational learning, even create partnerships with other organizations.

Hamlet for Hi-Pos: Its Relevance and Relationship to Situational Leadership®

In Shakespeare's great tragedy *Hamlet*, the protagonist repeatedly ruminates about when to take action, memorably concluding, "The readiness is all."[6] The concept of readiness remains evergreen and highly relevant for those coaching Hi-Po leaders—and the leaders themselves. The Situational Leadership® Model provides coaches with a framework for assessing the Performance Readiness® of the Hi-Po leader committed to building transition, position, or development capability. After all, executive coaches must first help their transitioning clients identify clear goals through initial assessment, and what and how to focus their efforts.

Once those goals are established, the executive coach must consider the client's readiness for each action step needed to develop the desired capabilities and then coach appropriately.

Performance Readiness® in Situational Leadership® is defined as the extent to which a leader demonstrates the ability and willingness to accomplish a specific task in a given situation. In this model, "ability" is the demonstrated knowledge, experience, skill, and "willingness" is the extent to which the individual has demonstrated confidence, commitment and motivation. Even though the concepts of ability and willingness are different, it is important to remember that they are an interacting influence system. This means that a significant change in one will affect the whole. The extent to which leaders bring willingness into a specific situation affects the use of their present ability, and vice versa. It is critical that the assessment of readiness is task specific, not a global description of the person or a high-level competency. Why? Because task specificity increases the likelihood of success, or at least completion of a task. Additionally, readiness varies from task to task. For example, a Hi-Po might excel at budget projections and not need any coaching. The same Hi-Po, for the task of providing feedback to their team members, may need a lot of hand-holding to accomplish the task.

Meeting Them Where They Are

As described in earlier editions of this book, Situational Leadership® has been adapted for executive coaching. The executive coach who can accurately diagnose Performance Readiness® has an excellent platform for designing coaching interventions. The level of Performance Readiness® can help the coach define and delimit not only what the appropriate intervention might be, but how the coach can best adapt his/her style to meet clients where they are. Coaches often have ideas for interventions at the ready, and it is easy to succumb to the trap of prescribing what the client needs to do. Like the client he is coaching, style flexibility is a strength for executive coaches, allowing a far greater range of interventions over time as the client faces different tasks and situations and continues to develop.

Whether the Hi-Po client needs to create a transition plan, develop key skills for a new role, or identify development strategies for the team, an executive coach has an opportunity to model the kind of style flexibility the leader ultimately needs to demonstrate. Of course, executive coaching may be only one possibility integrated within a broader talent management strategy, given that many companies are investing in their Hi-Po pipeline with an entire portfolio of targeted learning and development offerings for their future leaders. Other companies and clients fumble forward without them, some to astounding success. A recent *New Yorker* profile revealed that during the early years of Facebook, there was a fast-revolving door of senior executives, some coming and going within ten days of being hired.[7] Apparently, the company has stabilized since then! But the war for talent rages on. And executive coaches may well find themselves on its front line.

Paul Hersey is chairman of the Center for Leadership Studies, Inc., providers of leadership, coaching, sales, and customer service training. He is one of the creators of Situational Leadership®, the performance tool of over ten million managers worldwide and has personally presented Situational Leadership in 117 countries, influencing the leadership skills of four million managers in over a thousand organizations worldwide. He is the coauthor of the most successful organizational behavior textbook of all time, *Management of Organizational Behavior*, now in its seventh edition, with over one million copies in print. Contact: www.situational.com; ron.campbell@situational.com.

CHAPTER TWENTY-TWO

MENTORING IS CIRCULAR

By Frances Hesselbein

The early 1980s brought two great thought leaders and two great friends into my life. In 1981, when I was CEO of the Girl Scouts of the USA I met the "father of modern management," Peter Drucker. His philosophy and his work had played a critical part in my development as a leader from those beginning years in the mountains of western Pennsylvania.

In May, 1970, the first day I walked into the offices of the Talus Rock Girl Scout Council, in Johnstown, Pennsylvania, as its new CEO, under my arm were copies of *The Effective Executive* by Peter Drucker for each staff member. I had never met Peter Drucker, but had every book and film he had ever done. I just knew his philosophy was exactly right for our Girl Scout Council, its board and staff, thousands of girls, and their leaders.

In four years to support a powerful, contemporary program for girls, we had developed a girl- and program-focused circular management system. It worked so well that the central Pennsylvania Penn Laurel Girl Scout Council, York and Lancaster area, called and I went. That remarkable board and staff adopted the same mission-focused, values-based circular management system with the same success.

Then eighteen months later, Girl Scouts of the USA, the national organization, the largest organizations for girls and women in the world called looking for a new CEO. I agreed to come to New York to meet with the search committee and a few days later they offered me the position and I accepted. I was the first CEO of the Girl Scouts of the USA to come from the field in sixty seven years. So, July 4, 1976, my husband, John, and I arrived in New York.

Everything I had learned, experienced on the ground in two local Girl Scout Councils I carried with me. Circular management, managing for the mission, managing for innovation, managing for diversity worked in a powerful way.

In just five years, 1976–1981 those 700,000+ inspired and inspiring Girl Scout volunteers and staff had transformed this largest organization for girls and women in the world, over three million members sharing a Promise. Harvard Business School Faculty wrote a case study of the transformation of the Girl Scouts of the USA used in business schools all over the world.

In 1981, we met Peter Drucker and he studied us, on the ground, gave us two or three days of his time for the next eight years and pronounced the Girl Scouts as "the best managed organization in the country"—in all three sectors.

In 1982, my second greatest leader and my second greatest friend came into my life, and this time not anyone I had ever even heard of, or read about. A handsome young man walked into my office at Girl Scout National Headquarters, and said, "I am Marshall Goldsmith. I have developed a new program, a 360-degree Feedback tool and I want to give it to you and the Girl Scouts, and work with you in its use." He showed me the 360-degree tool, I was intrigued, and the day ended with a plan.

Marshall would work directly with my management team, and me, and then we would move it across the National staff, and local Girl Scout council staff. We did and Marshall's contribution to Girl Scouting made a positive difference.

In 1981–1982, Peter Drucker and Marshall Goldsmith became two of our strongest, most generous supporters. Eight years later, at the end of my thirteen-year tenure, Girl Scouts of the USA had achieved the highest membership, the greatest diversity, and the greatest cohesion in our history.

And in late 1989, as I was leaving Girl Scouts of the USA, at the wonderful staff celebration of my thirteen exuberant years with "the greatest organization in the world," both Peter and Marshall were there, speaking, celebrating with almost five hundred Girl Scout executives from all over the country.

Six weeks after I left the Girl Scouts of the USA, on January 31, 1990, the Peter F. Drucker Foundation for Nonprofit Management was born, and I found myself the president and CEO of the smallest organization in the country—with no money, no staff, and in offices that were a gift of Mutual of America Life Insurance Company. And who was the first board member to be invited to serve with Peter? Marshall Goldsmith, of course. And he serves to this day on the Drucker (now Leader to Leader) Institute board.

All of this is simply the backdrop for the article on coaching Marshall invited me to write. I am going to take a different track, and write about coaching's companion—mentoring.

While companies are investing in the growth, effectiveness, in the performance of their people through coaches and coaching, and no one is a greater coach than Marshall Goldsmith in our country or globally, there is another powerful force, running on parallel tracks—mentoring.

For a long time, I have personally engaged in mentoring several young women and continue to do so. These are my formal commitments. However, frequently, I am introduced before a speech as the introducer's "mentor." Although, we do not have a formal relationship, it is obvious the Drucker Foundation/Leader to Leader Institute's twenty-seven books in thirty languages, *Leader to Leader Journal*, and our global webinars all connect in a way that engages leaders in a personal way, and "mentor" becomes part of the language.

Almost fifteen years ago, a young Coast Guard Lt. Commander came to see me, explained that she had a grant that would enable her to go with me, wherever I would speak, to "shadow me for six months." She had the funds to do it and live in New York. Tempted as I was, for traveling alone several times a week, and several times a year, abroad, I could use a bright, young, eager leader of the future as a fellow traveler. However, I thought of what would be the right decision, in her best interest. So I said, "As much as I am tempted to say yes, it wouldn't be fair to you. You would spend most of your time in airports. Instead, do use your grant where it will result in the greatest learning experience. And, if you like, I would be honored to be your mentor."

Fifteen years later, Commander Carla Grantham, U.S. Coast Guard (Ret.) and I have had hundreds of shared travels, conferences, celebrations, and mentoring sessions. And in fifteen years, not one disappointing moment. And her husband and two teenagers are part of my family. With Carla, I learned that mentoring is circular. The mentor learns as much as the one to be mentored, the richest possible experience. And it does not end.

The second adventure in mentoring is totally different. Eleven years ago, speaking on mission, values, and leadership in Shenzhen, China, when my speech was over, among the warm responders coming up to greet me, came a young Chinese couple with their eighteen-year-old daughter. The mother was a journalist, the father, a lawyer. The father said, "This is our daughter, Youchen Lin, and we want you to be her mentor." They explained why, and I replied, "I would be honored. With e-mail we can easily work together." I gave them all the ways to reach me, and we parted in a touching, inspiring way. These young Chinese parents wanted a wider world for their only child.

I flew back to New York. End of story. No Youchen Lin e-mail, nothing. Then six months later, a phone call. "Mrs. Hesselbein, this is Youchen Lin. I am in Staten Island, in college, a freshman. I am ready to be mentored." That was ten years ago. Today, she has a masters degree in auditing, has a very good job, and our mentoring sessions involve dinners, luncheons, her attendance at our conferences, celebrations, gatherings. She calls her parents in China when the event is over and our relationship has new titles—her wish. I am now Youchen Lin's "Godmother," she is my "Godchild." Her family part of mine.

From these two remarkable young women I continue to "mentor" I have learned, indeed, that "mentoring is circular." When we are mentors, we learn even more than the leaders we are mentoring. And lives are changed, theirs and ours.

I began this, "Mentoring Is Circular," chapter with warm appreciation of coaching and one of the greatest coaches of our times—Marshall Goldsmith. I believe he is the greatest, and my evaluation, my appreciation of Marshall began in 1982, twenty-nine years ago, with never one disappointing moment. We've traveled the world together. I can call him on the telephone and ask, "Marshall, can you go to Poland with me?" His reply, "When do we leave?"

Marshall has redefined "coaching" for our times, and in my life he, Lyda, Kelly, and Bryan have defined love, friendship, and family for me. Wherever I go, whatever I do, Marshall is there. And it is circular.

Frances Hesselbein is the president and CEO of the Leader to Leader Institute (formerly the Peter F. Drucker Foundation for Nonprofit Management) and its founding president. She was awarded the Presidential Medal of Freedom, the United States of America's highest civilian honor, in 1998, and serves on many nonprofit and private sector corporate boards. She was the Chairman of the National Board of Directors for Volunteers of America from 2002 to 2006 and is the recipient of twenty honorary doctoral degrees. In 2009 the University of Pittsburgh introduced The Hesselbein Global Academy for Student Leadership and Civic Engagement. Among many other awards, Mrs. Hesselbein was inducted into the Enterprising Women Hall of Fame at the Seventh Annual Enterprising Women of the year Awards Celebration and was named a Senior Leader at the United States Military Academy, 2008 National Conference on Ethics in America. Mrs. Hesselbein is editor-in-chief of the award-winning quarterly journal *Leader to Leader* and coeditor of the Drucker Foundation's three-volume *Future Series*. Mrs. Hesselbein is the coeditor of twenty-seven books in thirty languages. And she is the author of *Hesselbein on Leadership* and the recently published *My Life in Leadership* (2011).

PART V

INTO ACTION

The articles in **Part V, Into Action,** are included to help guide high-potentials themselves to success. We open this section with "Effectively Influencing Decision Makers" by Marshall Goldsmith. In his article, Marshall puts forth eleven guidelines, which are intended to help high-potentials do a better job of influencing decision makers. High-potentials who read "From the FastForward Playbook: Successfully Transition into Bigger Roles" by Patricia Wheeler before they begin their upward journey, will greatly benefit from her Playbook, which offers clear action steps and words of wisdom from those who've already made successful transitions. In Chapter Twenty-Five, "Strength in Numbers: The Advantage of Being a Top Team," Lawrence S. Levin discusses "Top Teams" that are such because they vigilantly examine and reexamine their stated focus in order to adapt successfully to the ever-changing environment and economy in which they do business. In "Double Your Value," Mark C. Thompson and Bonita S. Buell-Thompson reveal nine steps that will help high-potentials dramatically increase their value. Finally, Stephen A. Miles and Nathan Bennett propel the analogy of coaches, teams, and individual players on the sports field to their relevance in the corporate arena in "Creating Winners in the Career Game: What Every Player and Coach Needs to Know."

CHAPTER TWENTY-THREE

EFFECTIVELY INFLUENCING DECISION MAKERS

Ensuring That Your Knowledge Makes a Difference

By Marshall Goldsmith

The great majority of people tend to focus downward. They are occupied with efforts rather than results. They worry over what the organization and their superiors "owe" them and should do for them. And they are conscious above all of the authority they "should have." As a result they render themselves ineffectual.

—PETER DRUCKER

Peter Drucker has written extensively about the impact of the knowledge worker in modern organizations. Knowledge workers can be defined as people who know more about what they are doing than their managers do. Many knowledge workers have years of education and experience in training for their positions, yet they have almost no training in how to effectively influence decision makers.

As Peter Drucker has noted, "The greatest wisdom not applied to action and behavior is meaningless data."[1]

The eleven guidelines listed next are intended to help you do a better job of influencing decision makers. In some cases, these decision makers may be immediate or upper managers—in other cases they may be peers or cross-organizational colleagues. I hope that you find these suggestions to be useful in helping you convert your good ideas into meaningful action!

1. Every decision that affects our lives will be made by the person who has the power to make that decision—not the "right" person, or the "smartest" person, or the "best" person—make peace with this fact.

   As simple and obvious as this statement may seem, I am amazed at how few (otherwise intelligent) people ever deeply "get" this point. When your child comes home from school and complains, "It's not fair! The teacher gave me a C and I really deserved an A!" We, as parents, should say, "Welcome to the real world, kid! In life you have to accept the fact that decision makers make decisions—and that you are not always the decision maker." Once we make peace with the fact that the people who have the power to make the decisions always make the decisions—and we get over whining because "life isn't fair"— we become more effective in influencing others and making a positive difference. We also become happier!

2. When presenting ideas to decision makers, realize that it is your responsibility to sell—not their responsibility to buy.

   In many ways, influencing ultimate decision makers is similar to selling products or services to external customers. They don't have to buy—you have to sell! Any good salesperson takes responsibility for achieving results. No one is impressed with salespeople who blame their customers for not buying their products.

   While the importance of taking responsibility may seem obvious in external sales, an amazing number of people in large corporations spend countless hours "blaming" management for not buying their ideas. Former Harvard professor Chris Argyris pointed out how "upward feedback" often turns into "upward buck-passing."[2] We can become "disempowered" when we focus on what others have done to make things wrong and not what we can do to make things right.

   If more time were spent on developing our ability to present ideas, and less time were spent on blaming others for not buying our ideas, a lot more might get accomplished.

   A key part of the influence process involves the education of decision makers.

   To again quote Drucker, "The person of knowledge has always been expected to take responsibility for being understood. It is barbarian arrogance to assume that the layman can or should make the effort to understand the specialist."[3]

   The effective influencer needs to be a good teacher. Good teachers realize the communicating knowledge is often a greater challenge than possessing knowledge.

3. Focus on contribution to the larger good—not just the achievement of your objectives.

An effective salesperson would never say to a customer, "You need to buy this product, because if you don't, I won't achieve my objectives!"

Effective salespeople relate to the needs of the buyers, not to their own needs. In the same way effective influencers relate to the larger needs of the organization, not just to the needs of their unit or team.

When influencing decision makers, focus on the impact of your suggestion on the overall corporation. In most cases the needs of the unit and the needs of the corporation are directly connected. In some cases they are not. Don't assume that executives can automatically "make the connection" between the benefit to your unit and the benefit to the larger corporation.

4. Strive to win the "big battles"—don't waste your energy and "psychological capital" on trivial points.

Executive's time is very limited. Do a thorough analysis of ideas before "challenging the system." Don't waste time on issues that will only have a negligible impact on results. Focus on issues that will make a real difference. Be willing to "lose" on small points.

Be especially sensitive to the need to win trivial nonbusiness arguments on things like restaurants, sports teams, or cars. People become more annoyed with us for having to be "right" on trivia than our need to be right on important business points. You are paid to do what makes a difference and to win on important issues. You are not paid to win arguments on the relative quality of athletic teams.

5. Present a realistic "cost-benefit" analysis of your ideas—don't just sell benefits.

Every organization has limited resources, time, and energy. The acceptance of your idea may well mean the rejection of another idea that someone else believes is wonderful. Be prepared to have a realistic discussion of the costs of your idea. Acknowledge the fact that something else may have to be sacrificed in order to have your idea implemented.

By getting ready for a realistic discussion of costs, you can "prepare for objections" to your idea before they occur. You can acknowledge the sacrifice that someone else may have to make and point out how the benefits of your plan may outweigh the costs.

6. "Challenge up" on issues involving ethics or integrity—never remain silent on ethics violations.

Enron, WorldCom, and other organizations have dramatically pointed out how ethics violations can destroy even the most valuable companies. The best of corporations can be severely damaged by only one violation of corporate integrity. Ideally, you will never be asked to do anything by the management of your corporation that represents a violation of corporate ethics. If you are, refuse to do it and immediately let upper management know of your concerns. This action needs to be taken for the ultimate benefit of your company, your customers, your coworkers, and yourself.

When challenging up try not to assume that management has intentionally requested you to do something wrong. In some cases, a seemingly inappropriate request may merely be the result of a misunderstandings or poor communication. Try to present your case in a manner that is intended to be helpful, not judgmental.

7. Realize that powerful people are just as "human" as you are—don't say, "I am amazed that someone at this level . . ."

It is realistic to expect decision makers to be competent; it is unrealistic to expect them to be anything other than normal humans. Is there anything in the history of the human species that indicates when people achieve high levels of status, power, and money they become completely "wise" and "logical"? How many times have we thought, "I would assume someone at this level . . ." followed by "should know what is happening," "should be more logical," "wouldn't make that kind of mistake," or "would never engage in such inappropriate behavior"?

Even the best of leaders are human. We all make mistakes. When your managers make mistakes, focus more on helping them than judging them.

8. Treat decision makers with the same courtesy that you would treat customers— don't be disrespectful.

While it is important to avoid "kissing up" to decision makers, it is just as important to avoid the opposite reaction. A surprising number of middle managers spend hours "trashing" the company and its executives or making destructive comments about other coworkers. When reviewing summary 360-degree feedback on leaders, the item "avoids destructive comments about the company or coworkers" regularly scores in the "bottom ten" on coworkers satisfaction with peers.

Before speaking it is generally good to ask four questions:
- Will this comment help our company?
- Will this comment help our customers?
- Will this comment help the person that I am talking to?
- Will this comment help the person that I am talking about?

If the answers are no, no, no, and no—don't say it! There is a big difference between total honesty and dysfunctional disclosure. As we discussed earlier, it is always important to "challenge up" on integrity issues. It is inappropriate to stab decision makers in the back.

9. Support the final decision of the organization—don't say, "They made me tell you" to direct reports.

Assuming that the final decision of the organization is not immoral, illegal, or unethical—go out and try to make it work! Managers who consistently say, "They told me to tell you" to coworkers are seen as "messengers," not leaders. Even worse, don't say, "those fools told me to tell you." By demonstrating our lack of commitment to the final decision we may sabotage the chances for effective execution.

A simple guideline for communicating difficult decisions is to ask, "How would I want someone to communicate to their people if they were passing down my final decision and they disagreed with me?" Treat decisions makers in the same way that you would want to be treated if the roles were reversed. For example, if you stab your boss in the back in front of your direct reports, what are you teaching your direct reports to do when they disagree with you?

10. Make a positive difference—don't just try to "win" or "be right."

We can easily become more focused on what *others* are doing wrong, than how *we* can make things better. An important guideline in influencing up is to always remember your goal—make a positive difference for the organizations.

Corporations are different than academic institutions. In an academic institution, the goal may be just sharing diverse ideas, without a need to impact the bottom line. Hours of acrimonious debate can be perfectly acceptable. In a corporation, sharing ideas without having an impact is worse than useless. It is a waste of the stockholders' money and a distraction from serving customers.

When I was interviewed in the *Harvard Business Review*, I was asked, "What is the most common 'area for improvement' for the executives that you meet?" My answer was "winning too much." Focus on making a difference. The more *other* people can "be right" or "win" with your idea, the more likely your idea is to be successfully executed.

11. Focus on the future—"let go" of the past.

One of the most important behaviors to avoid is "whining" about the past. Have you ever managed someone who incessantly whined about how bad things were? When people consistently whine, they inhibit any change they may have for impacting the future. Their managers tend to view them as annoying. Their direct reports view them as inept. Nobody wins.

Successful people love getting ideas aimed at helping them achieve their goals for the future. They dislike being "proven wrong" because of their mistakes in the past. By focusing on the future you can concentrate on what can be achieved tomorrow, as opposed to what was not achieved yesterday. This future orientation may dramatically increase your odds of effectively influencing decision makers. It will also help you build better long-term relationships with people at all levels of your organization.

In summary, think of the years that you have spent "perfecting your craft." Think of all of the knowledge that you have accumulated. Think about how your knowledge can potentially benefit your organization. How much energy have you invested in *acquiring* all of this knowledge? How much energy have you invested in learning to *present* this knowledge to decision makers—so that you can make a real difference? My hope is that by making a small investment in learning to influence decision makers, you can make a large, positive difference for the future of your organization!

Dr. Marshall Goldsmith has recently been recognized as one of the fifteen most influential business thinkers in the world, in a global biannual study sponsored by *The (London) Times*. He has also been described in *American Management Association* as one of the top fifty thinkers and leaders who have influenced the field of management over the past eighty years; in the *Wall Street Journal* as one of the top ten executive educators; in *Forbes* as one of the five most-respected executive coaches; in the *Economic Time (India)* among the top CEO coaches of America; in *Fast Company*, called America's preeminent executive coach; and he has received a lifetime achievement award (one of two ever awarded) from the *Institute for Management Studies*. Marshall is one of a select few executive advisors who have been asked to work with over 120 major CEOs and their management teams. He is the million-selling author of numerous books, including *New York Times* bestsellers *MOJO* and *What Got You Here Won't Get You There* (also a *Wall Street Journal* #1 business book and winner of the Harold Longman Award for business book of the year). Contact Marshall at marshall@marshallgoldsmith.com and www .marshallgoldsmith.com.

CHAPTER TWENTY-FOUR

FROM THE FASTFORWARD PLAYBOOK

Successfully Transition into Bigger Roles

By Patricia Wheeler

As the musician and poet Bob Dylan so aptly put it, "The times, they are a-changing." The rate of change has never been so intense as we have experienced over the past few years. High-potential leaders within the global landscape couldn't ask for a richer climate than they now have. Economic upturns and downturns, increasing globalization, technological innovations, and an environment poised for change create many opportunities for executives on an upward path.

And business is no longer "business as usual." A recent Booz and Company report shows that companies across many industries and geographies are hitting the "reset button"; making changes to their portfolios, their business and operating models, their processes and infrastructure, all through a lens focused more closely on what truly creates value for their companies and their customers.[1] Many companies have acknowledged that their executive pipelines need to be more robust,[2] so it is indeed an opportune time for motivated high-potential leaders to become part of the solution to this organizational issue.

Moving Up: What Matters Most

We're seeing an upswing in the rate at which executives are moving into new roles; transitions take place as organizations merge or are acquired, reposition their business models, grow into different segments and geographies, and as the previous generation of senior leaders continues to retire at a rapid rate. Since 2007, our global coaching alliance Alexcel has partnered with the Institute of Executive Development to study executive transitions: what makes them succeed, and what predictable obstacles high-potential leaders face as they move into more senior roles.[3]

In our research, we examined how *senior leaders* (defined here as executives within the top 5 percent of their organizations) best navigate their promotions, whether they entered a new organization or were promoted internally, as well as how many of these senior leaders did not fulfill the promise of their positions. We gathered responses to an online survey from more than 350 leaders and talent professionals across many organizations and geographies consisting of eighteen multiple-choice questions plus more than fifty in-depth interviews to gain additional insight.

We believe that these findings are important to high-potential leaders for the following reasons. First, this is the level to which many high-potentials aspire. In addition, knowing the culture, success factors, and "watch-outs" for the top layer has great implications for determining who will successfully move up . . . and who won't.

So what did our research uncover? We found that the rate of failure at the top 5 percent of the organizations we surveyed continues to be unacceptably high. One in three leaders brought into these roles from other organizations were not successful in meeting organizational expectations by the two-year mark.

The more surprising finding is that one in five leaders promoted to the top from within failed to meet their organization's criteria for successful performance within two years. This bears repeating: 20 percent of leaders who were *successful enough* in their roles to earn a promotion or lateral move to a bigger and broader role did not succeed in the new role. They weren't necessarily fired—companies are loath to dismiss many of these internally grown leaders—but their lack of success likely meant the end of the road for their upward mobility.

What is the clear learning from our survey? We're confirming that, to paraphrase Marshall Goldsmith, what gets you to one level won't necessarily be sufficient at higher levels.[4] Let's take a closer look at our findings.

What derails leaders at the high-potential and senior levels? Failure here is seldom about technical knowledge; it's more about relational intelligence and cultural alignment. Seventy-three percent of our survey participants listed interpersonal and leadership skills as a significant factor in executive underperformance. For one in three respondents, it was listed as the most important factor. So as individuals move up the leadership pipeline,[5] keep in mind that relationships are an increasingly important factor in more senior roles. Why? Simply put, each turn of the pipeline increasingly forces leaders to get more done through others. So we recommend that executives who want to climb the corporate ladder find ways of addressing this challenge. This includes understanding how others see you, developing conscious awareness of the culture, and learning to flex your own leadership and communication style. In this way, good intentions have a greater probability of being perceived clearly by others.

The Leader's Journey

One senior leader whom we interviewed commented, "Last year I hired four MBAs from the most competitive business schools. Within a year, we fired them all." He went on to say that although all four were blazingly smart, driven, and had great technical skills, they were arrogant know-it-alls convinced that they had all the right answers to the business challenges facing them. They didn't take time to understand and respect the culture of the business units and teams they inherited, pushing so hard that they engendered great resistance from their stakeholders. Morale plummeted, turnover increased, and results suffered.

In our work we see this scenario all too often, which is the reason we created the FastForward program for leaders moving into new roles. It's not easy balancing new role demands, new matrix and reporting relationships, as well as the pressure for results and often the mandate for implementing change. Too often the relational aspects of a new role are left to languish.

Contrast the failure cited above to the case of one leader, whom we'll call Mitchell. As part of his company's program to develop high-potentials, he was moved from a corporate marketing role to a regional operations role in an underperforming region; in this role, he was expected to drive higher performance in sales and production. Mitchell felt good about this move; as he was close to the global strategy team, he felt that he knew the business inside and out. He saw his move as an opportunity to shine as he imagined teaching the region more about the "view from the strategic balcony."

What Mitchell did not anticipate was the difference in the culture of the regional business, and the degree to which his regional colleagues felt at odds with corporate initiatives, which were often seen as unrealistic and short-lived. He quickly saw that he needed to consciously navigate his new territory and that he needed more than a good strategy and business case to assure his success. Triumph in this role demanded that he rapidly build trust within his new matrix.

As Mitchell and I worked together to craft a six-month plan for his transition, I asked him to reflect on the culture within his new team and the regional business. What were its hallmarks? What was the balance between the emphasis on stabilizing process and the emphasis on innovation? Was the culture more collaborative or bottom-line driven? What was Mitchell used to and how did his current situation echo or differ from the type of culture that was most comfortable for him? He described his former culture as strategic and innovative. "I was encouraged to think up new ideas for how we could establish beachheads in the marketplace," he recalled, "whereas in the region, our focus is on efficiency and process." Clearly he needed to shift his perspective and his style to fully appreciate and adapt to his new culture.

Next, I had him map his matrix of new stakeholders and create a template of conversations he needed to have to understand the different points of view he must navigate. His task was to go on a "listening tour,"[6] which is different from the "speaking tours" on which many leaders embark. In these conversations, he discovered important events in the region's history, key sources of information and influence, and the political minefields that existed. He identified two potential mentors who could help him with ongoing connections and sponsorship for the change initiative he was tasked with executing.

Mitchell also took time to reflect on what he knew about himself. His strength for driving business results became a liability when he drove himself and others so hard that he neglected to acknowledge others' contributions. To ensure this did not delay building trust within his role, he decided to deliberately practice seeking others' input and asking questions before expressing his opinions, so that others (especially his direct reports) would feel comfortable telling him the difficult truths. He quickly learned that if he slowed the pace of his communication, he was more effective at getting his point across. These are simple practices, but ones that high-potential leaders often forget to exercise in the urgency of seeking results.

When I suggested that Mitchell ask his manager and other key stakeholders to define "success" in his role, he initially pushed back. He had that discussion in his job interview, and he'd attended the town hall meetings. He eventually relented and was surprised to find that some of his manager's measures of success had not been on his radar screen at all. He had not anticipated, for example, that he would be measured on his development of others as well as on quarterly results. Knowing this, he was able to decide on which "early wins" would signal that he was developing his people, and he had to ensure that he carved out time on his schedule to address this, which was new for him.

I encouraged Mitchell to continue seeking regular input to ensure that his progress was perceived as forward movement by key stakeholders. His discipline allowed him to catch early mistakes and misalignments and "course correct" before trust was eroded. This was important for Mitchell given his tendency to rely on hard numbers as measures of progress; yet many early "wins" do not yet translate into hard numbers.

One year later, Mitchell has seen visible progress in turning his region around. He's in the succession pipeline for an even bigger role. He's already doing some preliminary investigation about the microculture he will enter in that geography and business unit. Through his developmental roles, he's gathering both the breadth and depth, about the organization and about himself as a leader, which will enable him to move into broader enterprise-wide roles.

Accelerating Success in New Roles: Actions You Can Take

If, in addition to your technical and business knowledge, you can, as a high-potential, successfully navigate the interpersonal, political, and cultural challenges as you take on new roles, you will be positioning yourself for success as you advance in your organization. Following are a few areas to consider as you move into bigger and broader roles.

Prepare for Challenge

- Assess the culture and know that there are many microcultures within each organization. You must understand and acknowledge culture before you have any chance of producing lasting change.
- Assess yourself and be conscious of your default settings. Our greatest strengths, taken to excess, become weaknesses; and we're often the last to notice when we cross that boundary.
- Ask yourself and others: what's the new "balcony position" you must adopt? Each successive move up the pipeline presents new strategic demands . . . and to effectively act on strategy, you will need to let go of some tactical activities.

Develop Your Network

- Peer relationships are of increasing importance for high-potentials. They encompass centers of influence, knowledge, and connection. Don't underestimate their importance.
- Leverage multiple mentors to get the view from different perspectives. You can never have too much assistance on the way up.
- Actively develop others and serve as a mentor yourself. You'll create a great learning experience for yourself as well as for those you take under your wing.

Measure Success

- Ask your manager and other key stakeholders: what will success in my role look like six months down the road? Don't assume you know the correct answers.
- Follow up regularly and seek future-oriented feedback. By doing so, you will create a climate of open dialogue where misalignments can surface and be managed before they become immovable obstacles.

- Celebrate success regularly. Remember, in the fierce urgency of now, to pause and acknowledge benchmarks, milestones, and even small wins, to yourself as well as to others.

Patricia Wheeler, PhD, is managing partner of The Levin Group, a global leadership advisory firm, and an expert in leadership development and executive coaching. Her specialty is helping technically talented executives become more effective leaders, raising the bar for their own performance and the performance of their teams. She holds a PhD in psychology; she served as assistant professor for the Emory University School of Medicine and is guest lecturer in the Robinson College of Business at Georgia State University. She publishes the executive resource *Leading News* (www.LeadingNews.org) in collaboration with leadership expert Marshall Goldsmith, and is a contributor to the *Best Practices in Leadership Development Workbook* and the *AMA Handbook of Leadership*.

CHAPTER TWENTY-FIVE

STRENGTH IN NUMBERS

The Advantage of Being a Top Team

By Lawrence S. Levin

For the past twenty years, we at the Levin Group have worked closely with executive teams within global Fortune 1000 and midcap companies across the span of health care, financial services, manufacturing, life sciences, and technology.

We've helped senior teams learn to navigate growth, manage significant and complex change, and address the new and ever-changing global marketplace and economies. These experienced teams have had to react to sudden shifts in political and economic conditions and commodity prices, as well as to global mergers and rapid, unexpected market changes. They have had to think simultaneously of how to grow a business courageously while "bottom-proofing" it against a downturn. These are smart people doing what is "business as usual" for a Top Team—or at least should be. And these teams are both committed and ultimately responsible for setting and executing strategy, for ensuring financial results, and for securing a future for their employees.

As the speed of change continues to accelerate, and as volatility, complexity, and ambiguity increase, the interconnectedness of the global marketplace becomes even more apparent. These are tough times for top executive teams, who are faced with a new series of challenges and paradoxes that require new mindsets and thinking about driving success. The questions they must ask themselves are many and difficult. For instance:

- How do we set a strategy when external forces and technologies shift so quickly?
- How do we bottom-proof our company and grow at the same time?

- How do we focus on innovation while ensuring we really pay attention to the "basics" of our businesses?
- How can we think together as a team and align the organization behind our most critical priorities, which can and will shift and change in response to the changing world?
- How do we get the most out of our teams and our people?
- How do we develop our best and brightest talent—our High-Potentials?

Top Teams Versus High Performance Teams

It is no exaggeration to say that leadership, more than ever, is a team sport. As high-potentials develop, an essential area of their expertise must be in building and developing the quality of the teams on which they serve and those teams that report to them. For many years, the gold standard of teams was the "High Performing Team." But in today's environment, the elements found in a good High Performing Team are now the ticket of admission to being a Top Team—an exceptional, high-caliber, super-performing team that can drive growth in a world of increased volatility, complexity, ambiguity, and speed of change. This is about how good teams get even better to become great teams in a more complex world.

Developing the High-Potential Leader

Evolving and high-potential leaders today require a different skill set than leaders of the past. They are asked to do more, handle more complexity, and deal with more paradox than leaders who preceded them.

Leading in the Now and the New

Irial Finan, head of Coca-Cola's Bottling Investment Group, tells his emerging leaders that they have to be able to manage multiple and seemingly conflicting demands simultaneously. They have to be strong general managers who know the details, issues, operational and performance metrics of their business, and drive "the fierce urgency of execution." And they have to know how the business makes money.

Yet at the same time, they have to have the strong strategic competencies that allow them to understand evolving social, geopolitical, and economic issues, and broadly think "over the horizon" about competitive differentiation. As one of our pharmaceutical clients said, "In the fierce urgency of the now, you earn the right to implement tomorrow's future by executing today."

We call this leading in the "Now and the New." A paradox to be sure, but one essential to navigate. Leaders must have the ability to zoom into the details and zoom out to the bigger context in which they play.

Being Truly *for* Something: The Power of a Collective Future

What represents the first critical waypoint in a Top Team's journey, is the articulation of a uniting common purpose and a clear and agreed vision of a desired future—in other words, what the team is truly *for.* This is the key aligning principle of a Top Team and the start of its journey as it begins to define the intersection of leadership direction, organizational concern, and current reality. To be sure, this is a very different process from writing a typical vision or mission statement, which often becomes more of a slogan than a deep source of gravity, focus, and commitment. To go through a process of defining what a Top Team is *for* requires honest, deep, and ongoing dialogue among the members of a senior team and throughout the organization about current realities, real possibilities, and what must and must not change in order to secure the future of the organization.

As Mickey Connolly writes, "The source of teamwork is a common future."[1] Everything must be on the table as teams redefine success and survival. As a senior leader in a large pharmaceutical company told us, "We have to get past how we have historically looked at things; overcome our classic objections, such as, 'We've never done it that way' or 'That won't work here'; and move the conversation forward." This sounds easier than it is. In debriefing our *Top Teaming Assessment* with senior leadership teams, the first question "We clearly understand our senior purpose—what we are *for* as a team" has often been the driver of several hours of intensive dialogue. Because the corporate environment today is not business as usual, Top Teams must continually reexamine how they work together in the service of the mission. In other words, they must constantly redefine themselves as a team.

One Size Does Not Fit All

Once a team has begun the process of articulating its senior purpose, it needs to define what kind of team it must be to accomplish it. There is no textbook answer. Simply put, the type of team that is needed and how members must operate together depends completely on what this team needs to do in the service of the organization's strategic and critical priorities. Teams that are tasked with growth are different from teams that are tasked with maintaining stability. A team that requires high interdependence on one another is different from a team that represents a portfolio of businesses (a "bowling team"). Though there is no one right

way to design a team, most intact teams express a clear need for higher interdependency as they set and begin to move toward more ambitious and higher-level
goals. They know, as Marshall Goldsmith (2007) would say, "what got them here
won't get them there."[2] And there are organizations that are specific about exactly
where they must be more collaborative as a team and where they can continue to
operate as they are. Simply put, there is no one "right" type of team or structure.
It completely depends on what a team is tasked to do—again, what it is *for*.

Once a team has defined how it needs to be structured in order to accomplish
the senior purpose, there are some difficult conversations that must occur. Often these
take place between the leader and his or her trusted advisors, and sometimes they
occur in the room within the team. The question of whether the team has the "right
people on the bus," as Jim Collins states in *Good to Great*,[3] is a difficult yet essential
question. In our work as executive coaches, we are often called upon to help assess
and develop executives who have to grow in their roles and capabilities to contribute
to a Top Team. It is a demand and a stretch to play at this level. And it must be a
conscious process for those evolving leaders who have been asked to operate in a new
and critical role.

One of the common observations we hear from senior leaders about teams
that are described as exceptional is that the individual intelligence and experience
of the team members is a given. What is different is how people "show up" with
one another to utilize their experience and intelligence. Top Teams bring tremendous expertise, experience, and collective intelligence to address the most complex
issues. Simply put, if they didn't have this capability, they wouldn't be considered
a Top Team for long. Yet it is in harnessing the dialogue and intellectual rigor
needed to balance the complex paradoxes that they face on a regular basis where
Top Teams shine. We have a bias for dialogue within Top Teams about the most
essential and difficult issues. We absolutely believe that Top Teams must be able
to put the most complex issues they face on the table and talk about them.

Trust over Peace: Addressing and Resolving the Issues That Matter

One of the most essential yet difficult variables that distinguishes Top Teams
from most other executive teams is their ability to engage in this honest, candid,
and authentic dialogue. Dialogue (from the Greek *dia-logos*) literally means an
exchange of ideas. In our work with teams, and in our observation of Top Teams,
there is a high premium put on addressing the most important and often the
most difficult issues within the team setting, with an eye toward resolving them.
Jake Jackson, retired executive of a large financial institution, talks about how
teams can choose to prioritize peace over trust or vice versa. Most of us have
experienced this when we have participated in polite, careful, and indirect teams.

In this dynamic, issues may be noted, but they are not explored in depth. At worst, civility in public gives rise to passive-aggressive or indirect behavior in private as members of teams talk over the watercooler or an adult beverage about those very issues that should be on the table.

In Top Teams, the opposite must occur—trust must be even more important than keeping the peace. This requires leaders to encourage, demand, and ensure that it is safe to talk openly about anything. As Sidney Taurel of Eli Lilly was widely attributed as saying when opening the dialogue up for honest interactions, "Put the moose on the table." This is far easier said than done, as the culture of many firms is deeply "nice," yet indirect. Periodically, we hear the horror story of the executive who was shunned, banned, or fired for being too honest. In truth, this is rare. For many new team members, however, political correctness, carefulness, and less-than-direct conversations often occur as they become familiar with the culture and earn their stripes. Yet one of the greatest differentiators between adequate teams and Top Teams is in the harnessing and integrating of their members' experience and wisdom accomplished by deliberate and focused dialogue. Another way of stating this is if people didn't want to hear what you had to say, you wouldn't be sitting in the chair.

Defining and Managing the Critical Intersections

As teams come together and begin to have the forward-thinking dialogue about how they need to operate, several critical conversations begin to occur. The first is deciding how best to structure given the expressed level of interdependency. Matrix organizations are designed to maximize flow of products or services by minimizing the numbers of redundant functions within each division or unit and by increasing collaboration between operational and functional areas. Yet matrix organizations are often seen as unwieldy and hard to navigate. This is where the process of identifying and managing critical intersections occurs.

Simply put, the easiest and most elegant way to navigate a matrix is to map the organization, identify those people with whom you have to have successful outcomes, then go out and, as one of our favorite leaders says, "Make and cut your deals." What he means is that people who are involved in any critical intersection—whether it involves working across a matrix, in an intersection between a functional and an operational area, or who operate as teams of people that pursue similar customers—must connect with one another, define what is important to them, listen for what is important to others, affirm what is important to the organization, and then make (and keep) agreements. This is relational intelligence (RI) at its finest, which accomplishes several things concurrently: it builds those critical relationships within the informal organization; it accelerates decision making and accountability as the right people are talking directly to one another about what matters; and it makes a complex structure significantly easier to navigate in the service of the customer. It also serves to free up senior leaders, who are not asked nearly as often to make day-to-day decisions and can thus spend more time on the larger issues critical for the senior team.

A CFO of a major financial institution commented that the "ticket of admission" for her to think strategically was how well the people who reported to her were handling operational issues across the global organization. She was surprised at how few ties she had to break and how few impasses made it to her desk.

Shaving the Tiger: Understanding and Recalibrating the Default Setting of a Team

Part of understanding the collective self-knowledge that comprises the emotional intelligence (EI) of a team is to understand its default setting—what it is likely to do when under stress or operating on automatic pilot. Teams that have a history of operational focus go directly to the numbers and root-cause discussions when pressured. Health care teams almost immediately argue about outcomes and support these arguments with data (then often argue about whose data is better). This default setting is not unlike our individual default settings when under stress. Do I move toward or away from others when pressured? What happens to my ability to trust? How do I cover my derriere when under threat? We know from the studies on EI that self-awareness is the first key step in recognizing our own default settings. It is equally true, though sometimes more difficult to recognize, what a team's default setting is when under the gun.

I was amazed (but somehow not surprised) to see, while watching a recent *Animal Planet* program, that when tigers are shaved, their stripes are also present in their skin. This says something about our fundamental personality or wiring, as the "who we are" goes deep—down to our very skins. Thus it is important to know (from an EI standpoint) who we are and what our default settings are likely to be individually and collectively. This is where people receive great value from leadership style instruments such as the Meyers-Briggs, Hogan Suite, CDR 3-D Suite, DISC®, and our Top Teaming Assessment.

Being "That" Person: Great Teams Need Great Leaders

While it would seem logical that great teams would be comprised of great leaders, this is not always the case. In fact, it would be more accurate to say that great teams are made up of people who are committed to being even better leaders—people who are conscious and deliberate about their own learning and effectiveness as leaders and equally committed to growing their understanding of how teams continue to grow and develop. Just as there is no one right type of team—the structure, makeup, and focus depend on what the strategy requires—it is equally true that there is no one right type of leader within a team. Leaders come in all sizes, shapes, and styles—from extroverted to introverted, from warm and caring to businesslike, from participative to command-and-control. What is true about good leaders who build and comprise great teams is that they are very aware of their leadership style and about what the team must continue to do. If they were to have an autopilot setting, it would be in the "off" position much of the time.

Seldom do good teams become great teams by accident. There is purposefulness about their evolution and a definite series of practices they follow. Think about any teams that have a moderate to high degree of interdependence—from sports teams to elite military teams. In most cases, they begin with people who are highly qualified and have earned their stripes by being serially successful at the fundamentals of their jobs. In their track records of success, they have learned to play well with others—to blend support of others with a tough-minded, edgy, playing-flat-out approach to the outside world. They push each one another and demand only the best. They almost always have a coach—either someone who has been there before or sees a future state and the road map to get there. Again, this is true in sports, the military, medicine, and business. There is someone or something that pushes the group to look more deeply and achieve more than they could have done by themselves.

Building Emotional, Relational, and Collective Intelligence

It is a given that leaders must know themselves and have the requisite emotional intelligence that allows them to understand their style, default settings, hot buttons, and hard wiring. What is less well understood is the importance of what we call relational intelligence, which is how we interact with others, understand the social/relational milieu, and communicate our histories, values, and intentions. This is where trust is built and absolutely critical when it comes to playing well and hard on teams. And this is mostly accomplished in informal settings, over lunch or an adult beverage. Leaders of highly diverse organizations and those in which people rotate on and off teams are extremely aware of the criticality of building these relationships. To the extent that we can develop the requisite EI and RI and then apply them within a global world, we become wiser human beings. And through fully integrating our own knowledge, specialization, and wisdom with that of the people we work with most closely, we can create and fully mine our collective intelligence (CI), which is the great differentiator between good teams and Top Teams. How we do this is largely dependent on creating a deliberate atmosphere, clear expectations, and agreed-upon processes that can drive requisite dialogue forward.

Demonstrating Courage in the Face of Uncertainty: Top Teams in Tough Times

There are no straight lines in the art and practice of leadership. It is in the constant journey of leaders and the learning that occurs through dialogue and correction that great teams get it (mostly) right. Leadership sets the tone for either candor or carefulness. Unresolved issues limit an executive team and restrict what is possible for the company. *If you cannot talk about it, how can you address it and continually improve?* On the Mississippi River, tugboat captains have the pattern intelligence that comes with navigating an organic and ever-changing system and the necessary willingness constantly to adjust to their environment. Thus it is with Top Teams in setting and following strategy within a flexible and movable environment. Flexibility wins, and dialogue is the currency of the land.

Creating and sustaining Top Teams is largely a dialogue process in which team members fully and completely talk about the stuff that matters. There is a Rule of One—that it only takes one person who knows something important and doesn't get the full attention of his or her peers or partners to destroy a business, a space shuttle, or the credibility of leadership. So whom do the people at your level talk to? The obvious answer should be that you talk openly and honestly to one other. This dialogue builds trust, as leaders must be able to address anything and everything with one another. Yet, as stated earlier, this doesn't always come easily or naturally, even for the best leaders.

Over the past twenty years, we have coached a lot of people across a wide range of industries. One of the things we quickly learned is that *unless* we understood the unique business the executives are in, with the specific demands, intellectual requirements, structure, strategic direction, organizational and cultural history, key players, and more, our effectiveness as an influencer of behavior and as an advisor was limited. Our clients were always the first ones to know that. So our strong belief, shaped by many years of doing this, is that good coaching always occurs in the context of a specific business, and in that unique milieu; those are the teams where the leaders sit. You have to know the territory.

Without question, one of the most important responsibilities of leadership teams is to develop the next generation of leaders. But how good is their thinking about developing the next generation of teams? Do they (or do you) spend the time and resources and possible investment to build team capabilities one to three levels down the organization? Are future leaders exposed to the organization's strategic worldview and to emerging trends and technologies? Do they have a point of view about leadership that compels them to look both inside and relationally, at EI and RI? No doubt future leaders and high performers have to perform well and execute flawlessly, but how well are they trained to be more deliberate, conscious, and disciplined members of Top Teams? These competencies are of increasing importance as Hi-Pos move up the organization and hold roles of greater importance. Those high-potential leaders who master the skills needed to build and operate within Top Teams are poised to make a real difference in their business, their career, and for the enterprise.

With executives stressed beyond comprehension, due to the increased complexity, volatility, ambiguity, and rate of change within the world of business, leaders within Top Teams have a responsibility to be straightforward and demanding with clear expectations of one another. This is yet they must be aware of the humanity and personal sacrifice entailed in such leadership and look for the opportunities to support one another in this adventure.

Lawrence S. Levin is founder and senior partner of The Levin Group LLC, a consulting and advisory firm with over twenty years of experience in improving senior team effectiveness, organizational performance, and leadership solutions for CEOs, top executives, and senior teams. Larry specializes in working with leadership teams in Fortune 500 companies and mid-sized organizations on understanding and improving the dynamics and capabilities of executive teams, utilizing team-based interventions and coaching to drive business success and improve C-level effectiveness. He also specializes in accelerating significant change within complicated systems, usually as a result of rapid growth, major technology insertions, mergers and acquisitions, and other complex culture changing initiatives. Larry is a frequent speaker at conferences and association meetings. He has been featured on CNN as well as other national and local media, and has written for many publications. His book *Top Teaming: A Roadmap for Teams Navigating the Now, the New, and the Next* was published in June 2011.

CHAPTER TWENTY-SIX

DOUBLE YOUR VALUE

By Mark C. Thompson and Bonita S. Buell-Thompson

Value is a perception—not a fact—and everybody has different ideas about what is most valuable. We develop these ideas early on, based on both our experiences and inherent inclinations. In doing research for our book, *Success Built to Last*, we discovered a number of techniques that can be used to determine what's valuable to your boss and coworkers. Following are nine steps that will help to dramatically increase your value.

1. Two Interests Are Better Than One

First and foremost, most people treat themselves as a commodity—something that can be replicated and therefore isn't unique or has value that's more or less equivalent to that of other commodities like it.

Instead, think about how you can combine several of your special interests, skills, and passions into a role in your company. The late Steve Jobs was a great example of this. He was an adoptee who started Apple in his adopted parents'garage. But he dropped out of a liberal arts college when it failed to inspire him, not wanting to waste his folks' money on something he didn't feel was special or unique. Instead, he started taking art classes, particularly calligraphy, where he discovered what technology was missing most: a sense of beauty and an ease of use.

Jobs' ability to combine his dual passions for engineering and art into exquisite industrial design is legendary. Rather than following a linear path toward a career or job, you're better off combining your multiple passions to make what you do more unique.

When coauthor Bonita Thompson started out in HR thirty years ago, she combined her love for organizational behavior with her interest in statistics. She became a compensation specialist, which at the time was valued at a real premium over being an HR generalist. It was very rare to find an HR person who loved both people and math, so Bonita was able to capitalize on that. She then went on to earn an MBA, with a concentration in management information systems. Her interest eventually led her to develop the world's first corporate intranet for human resources. She created that innovation at Levi Strauss—and the idea sprang from both her interest in HR and her passion for using technology to improve service. Nobody else in the world has the same combination of experiences, talents, and interests as you, so use them to your advantage!

Two or three passions are better than one if you want to offer your company something unique.

2. Sign Your Name

It's really important to give your product a personal imprint, and more so, to show that you're willing to take the responsibility to put your name on the door—at least, metaphorically. Show that what you've created is so special that you are willing to brand it.

When Bonita was working in a cubicle amidst dozens of others as an HR job analyst for Bank of America, she found a way to brand her special way of analyzing over 100,000 positions at that bank and it separated her from the pack. Bonita created the brand name of "Market Analyzer," which turned an average project into a special *product* that distinguished her work as strategic to the organization.

Sign off on all the unique work you do—make it clear *who you are* and how important your projects are to your organization.

3. Know What Your Client Values

Understanding what your boss wants and values is not always as obvious as you might think. To figure it out, you've got to actually go and observe them—spend *real* time figuring out your boss! Most supervisors appear to be clear about what they think you should be doing on your job, but have you found out how they are evaluated by *their* bosses? In other words, do you know what makes your boss successful? What is she or he stressing out about, and how might you think of ways to help?

When Bonita was an HR officer, she noticed that her manager was scrambling to keep up with current events in the international markets where the company had many offices and branches. She took it upon herself to scan the relevant publications and pull out articles for him that related both to his job and to the company's priorities. This ended up becoming a highly valued skill and Bonita's boss became seen as an important source of strategic and up-to-date information by other senior executives

If you want to be highly valued, don't wait to be told how. Go find out what's challenging your boss and clients—seek to help them long before you're asked.

4. Know *Who* They Value

It's vital not only to know what your clients value, but *who* they value. Who matters to their success? A study recently emerged showing certain nonprofits that had actually *grown* during the economic crisis—nonprofits were obviously among the hardest hit, but there was a group that mysteriously managed to grow anyway. They succeeded by making it their business to find out who was most important to their various donors or organizations and which individuals or outlets those donors would want recognition from. Save the Children, for example, put out press releases and sent notes to the communities and people *who mattered to their donors*, emphasizing how much of a difference that donor's contribution had made. These nonprofits effectively used both flattery and public promotion.

It's definitely good to keep in mind that flattery can be overused and end up appearing fake or off-putting. But if it's given for specific behaviors that people take seriously, flattery has tremendous value.

In fact, Cliff Nass, a professor at Stanford, recently conducted a research study on flattery and criticism and surprisingly discovered that people appreciate and respond to flattery far more than they'd like to believe. People actually love to be patronized!

Nass also discovered that people criticize others much more than they flatter, meaning when we do praise someone or something, it's more cherished.

If you want to be more valuable, give more status and recognition to the good work done by those around—even your boss—and it will call your attention to the ways in which you should be valued, too.

5. The Three P's: A Three-Part Secret to Success

We all too often separate our passion from the work we do for others, and this is *such* a big mistake! We conducted a World Success Survey of 110 nations for our best-selling book *Success Built to Last*, which determined that people who had continued success and impact in their field or profession—for twenty years or more—had *all* three traits in common. Those who had success year after year, through both thick and thin, all defined success in three distinctive ways that were necessary for them to have success that was sustainable. We call them "the 3 Ps" as part of their value equation: Passion, Purpose, and Performance.

In our jobs, we're all held accountable for goals, and that's what we mean by *Performance*—we have to deliver on our promises and deliver them well.

But successful people don't just work for a company or a job, per se. We have to also be serving a *Purpose* that's larger than ourselves. Most people need to have a cause that motivates them—something that we feel makes a difference.

At the same time, we need to be doing something *we care about* and have *Passion* and heart for—that's what recharges our batteries and gets us through setbacks. Otherwise, during tough times, how would you scrape yourself off the floor, get back up and out, if you have no fundamental connection to what you're struggling with? We have to pursue something that serves the market, which serves customers *and* serves something we care about and want to deliver year after year.

6. Get Known

In this day and age, there are so many techniques available to help get the word out about what you're doing. Start by creating a connection to social media—blog about what you've been doing and whom you've been helping. Mention case histories, what problems have come up for you or your organization, and how you solved them.

Guy Kawasaki is a great example—he separated himself from the pack of early Apple folk by blogging his thoughts and experiences for many decades now. He'd left the company early on, so he never became as wealthy as those who stayed. But he has had so many valuable things to say about his profession in general, and Apple in particular,, that he's became a sought-after speaker and consultant.

Joining professional associations is another effective way to both get known and have impact: they're always looking for more hands, hearts, and brains. Offer to help out and you'll probably be asked to join the board. Reach out to reporters who write for your professional magazines and newsletters. Eventually you will be quoted, and before you know it, you'll be better known in your industry. Make sure that you can serve others, and in so doing, gain visibility for your valuable services.

7. Build Trust: Offer a Sense of Security

One of the best ways to be seen as valuable is to make people feel secure that you can get the job done right. In our research, we found three steps that are most valued in building trust. We call them the 3Rs.

Responsibility: People need to feel they can count on you, but there's more to it than that: if you make a mistake, avoid playing the blame game. Don't waste energy deciding who's most at fault, or finding excuses for why something went wrong. Instead, take responsibility for the mistake or problem, take accountability, and offer solutions that can solve the problem.

Your credibility can actually increase *more* when you make a mistake—if you show the ability to take responsibility and accountability even when things aren't rosy.

Reliability: Show up as the same person every time—people will not trust you if you're someone different every time they meet you. Be consistent and behave consistently in all of your interactions.

Responsiveness: Do it quickly! Deliver on whatever promises and commitments you've made in a timely way—get it done. The faster you follow through, the more credibility you will have.

8. Always Get Better

What can you do better next time? This step might also seem obvious, but it's one of the most difficult to implement. When we fail, we again tend to play the blame game, focusing all of our energy on fault as opposed to what can be done to succeed in the future. Worse yet, we decide not to try again.

But success isn't a good teacher either. Most people have difficulty finding ways to get better at what they do when they're already succeeding. We don't see the incentive to get better. We've won. How could we possibly improve? The people who are valued most in an organization over the long term focus on how to do *even better* next time around.

9. Create a Place for Your Goal

To make something happen and get something done, we've got to be with the right people, at the right time, in the right space with the right tools. Make sure your work environment has everything you need to succeed with your goal—all the tools and files and information that will help make progress the moment you turn your attention to it.

A successful entrepreneur that we know wanted to fulfill a lifelong dream of making a movie. But to make that happen, he realized he needed to move to Hollywood or New York—he needed to start to access a community of people in that field to build a network. Another friend wanted to learn a new programming skill for her HR work, so she made sure that she always kept a special place on her desk with all the books, software, and tools together in that place—ready for her work every day. Studies show that people who lay out their gym clothes the night before a workout are many times more likely to actually work out the next day.

Perhaps most important, if you want to be more valuable in your role or position in an organization, make it your business to meet other people who are valuable in the type of job that you're striving for. When you dive into the nine steps we have outlined in our research, start by observing and befriending people you value and respect, those you know are valued in their professional community. What are they doing and how are they interacting with others? Spend less time with toxic friends and invest more time with people who inspire you. How were they driven to do more and be more valuable? It's a good bet they're doing something they love with people who support their passions—and that is essential to success that is built to last.

Bonita S. Buell-Thompson is a thirty-year veteran of human resources and industrial psychology at Bank of America, Catellus, Pacific Telesis, Genentech, and other leading organizations. She holds an MBA in information systems from U.C. Berkeley and was research director for *Success Built to Last*, the sequel to *Built to Last*, and the *Leaders of the New Century* series.

   Mark C. Thompson is former SVP of Charles Schwab, an executive coach and venture investor in Best Buy, Facebook, and Apple's leading iPhone and iPad applications companies. He is a founding advisor of the Stanford University Venture Design Lab and best-selling author of *Success Built to Last* and *Now, Build a Great Business*!

CHAPTER TWENTY-SEVEN

CREATING WINNERS IN THE CAREER GAME

What Every Player and Coach Needs to Know

By Stephen A. Miles and Nathan Bennett[1]

In our work with executives at all career stages we have become fond of the game metaphor as a way to frame productive, strategic coaching sessions focused on resolving challenging career decisions. We like the metaphor because it is easy for executives to grasp and leverage. They quickly recognize that in their career game, there are positions they hope to obtain that reflect their own idea of winning. It is easy to see how there are other players who can have an impact on their game, such as competitors, mentors, coworkers, and family members. Each of these players has their own motives in the game that may make them at times allies or adversaries. And, finally they understand how games are won when players smartly execute the right moves. When it comes to demonstrating a readiness to join a C-suite, there are three such moves. Making these moves in an effective manner requires that executives see the value in each and that they are coached up so that they understand what they need to do to earn and then execute each move.

Executive coaches play a critical role when they properly explain the relevance of each move and help their clients recognize and develop the competencies needed to excel with each move. Each move requires the executive to add range to his or her style, and in some cases, add new ways of leading. As Marshall Goldsmith has stressed, executives have to understand that what got them where they are won't necessarily get them where they want to go. When a coach can't help a client do an honest inventory and then garner their commitment to doing the work necessary to play their career game well, the executive runs a risk of derailing.

The Moves That Matter Most

What preparation does it take for an executive to convince others they are ready to take on a role in the C-suite? There is no shortage of recommendations about how to prepare to be, for example, CEO. A quick perusal of bestselling titles reveals an emphasis on how to "think and to act like a CEO." These books note the personality traits leaders must demonstrate and tout the importance of "executive presence." The predominant focus on who you are—or, more aptly, who you appear to be—quickly becomes apparent. There is little doubt that we hold stereotypes about the way leaders should look and act. It is easy to poke fun at many of them and it is easy to find examples of people who are successful in spite of displaying characteristics that contradict these preconceptions. In the end, these stereotypes about appearances and personality are not particularly useful predictors of ability. Much better conclusions about leadership potential can be reached by focusing on the developmental experiences an executive has had. In our work we have interviewed dozens of executives who were remarkable for the career progress they had demonstrated. We have identified three moves critical to the development of an executive capable of leading at the highest levels in a company. Together, these moves can help rising stars differentiate themselves from other hopefuls by opening the door to the ultimate opportunity: a position in the C-suite.

Move #1: Find Something Broken and Important and Fix It

It can be difficult to distinguish yourself early in your career, particularly in a large company. One way to make a mark is to find something that is undeniably broken and fix it. Positions in these areas often aren't hard to get because the competition is typically low. And the risk in these turnaround opportunities is usually less than one might suspect. Should you fail, many will understand the difficulty of what you took on and be more forgiving. As an example, consider Ted Mathas, president and CEO of New York Life. Early in his career, he was offered a job that no one else wanted—running two struggling businesses: NYLIFE Securities and Eagle Strategies. These were small and self-contained divisions that were far removed from the core activities of New York Life. Because the businesses were a bit off the radar—and weren't performing that well—Mathas could try ideas, experiment, and learn. He hired his own team, developed a strategy, and turned the operations around. Because he was successful, his role in this turnaround was visible at the highest levels of company.

A similar example can be found with Alex Vanselow at BHP Billiton. Hired away from Anderson Consulting, Vanselow was given three choices for a first assignment, and he intentionally picked the worst. There were several professional challenges in this new position. First, the group had not had a finance manager for a year and a half. Second, the group leader at this division was vocally opposed to the creation of a finance manager position and was dismissive of Vanselow during the brief interview process. But the new role was going to be a challenge personally, too, because the location was undesirable. Rather than bringing his wife to see things for herself, he made a video to play for her. As he noted to us, you can't feel the heat of Port Hedland (a particularly hot town in western Australia) on a video. His logic for choosing this assignment was that he would have a difficult time quickly making a visible contribution at a location where things were working well. Once at BHP, he succeeded at winning over his new boss, and it wasn't long before his efforts earned him the first in a series of promotions.

What is it about these opportunities to fix something that make them such great learning experiences? There are several ways that leading a turnaround develops executive capability:

- It requires the executive to understand deeply the way an operation works, as well as the most critical levers to pull to recover performance.
- Speed is nearly always of the essence; learning to make good, quick decisions is a result.
- The context places a premium on the ability to develop, articulate, and build commitment to a strategy so that the team is motivated to follow.
- Hiring and firing decisions matter more; it forces executives to be honest about who is an asset and who is a liability and to manage accordingly.
- The lack of slack means incredible discipline around operational efficiencies must be honed.
- The executive has to be comfortable working without a lot of support and to be entrepreneurial in the way resources are acquired.

For an executive to succeed while executing this move, the coach should focus on helping the executive understand and amplify their frontline leadership skills. People are often already motivated by the burning platform; as the cliché goes, a crisis shouldn't be wasted. These scenarios usually have low or lower expectations, because something is widely seen as fundamentally broken. The leader has higher degrees of freedom to change people and business processes; doing so requires great speed and disciplined tactical execution. Making the most in this move happens by getting quick wins and creating positive momentum.

Move #2: Show You Can Make a Healthy Business Even Better

Turnarounds provide dramatic stories about an executive's abilities, but to be ready for the C-suite, an executive also needs to prove an ability to take a healthy business and improve it further. After all, few companies are in a constant state of turnaround. The "burning platform" that can help leaders engage followers is less available in a healthy company. As most will quickly agree, it is more difficult to effect change in a culture of success. Issues with complacency abound—it's too easy to say that if nothing is broken, then there is nothing to fix. And, unlike a turnaround where any move seems to make progress, improvements to a healthy system are harder to identify. Finally, executives must overcome action anxiety—a fear of making a move that upsets the current equilibrium.

To be effective in a thriving business, leaders have to develop different capabilities from what a turnaround requires by finding ways to innovate and improve without rocking the boat. Dan Palumbo, an executive with experience at Proctor & Gamble, Kodak, and the Coca-Cola Company, emphasized the importance of a process focus and the ability to "helicopter up and down" to manage the issues that matter immediately and the issues that are on the horizon. If executives want to be trusted with C-suite positions, they have to be able to point to proof that they can manage a steady ship. Improving a healthy business develops and demonstrates a number of important capabilities:

- It positions you as a true general manager with final P&L responsibility.
- It provides exposure to the CEO and board.
- It requires you to develop the ability to negotiate with the C-suite as you look to balance the interests of your business unit with those of other business units.
- It requires you to think broadly about the business and its industry in terms of positioning, go-to-market strategies, the competition, and future sources of revenue.
- It demands that you learn to use functional experts (legal, human resources, and so on) both in your business and from corporate.

During this move, the coach must frame the situation so their client understands how leadership needs to be demonstrated. In situations like this—where there isn't a burning platform and their marching orders from above often don't amount to much more than "don't screw it up"—there isn't much of a mandate for change. And as a result these leaders have less freedom to do things differently during this career move. They often inherit a team that has had success and is comfortable doing what it has always done. Yet, change will be needed to make the operation better. The coach needs to help the executive see how to lead without the burning platform. The ability to articulate and communicate a vision in a compelling way—a way that really sells a team that may not see that "winning more" is important—is the critical skill for an executive to develop during this career move.

Move #3: Make an Impact While Serving in a Staff Role

A career move that is often dismissed may be one of the most instrumental in efforts to prepare for the C-suite: serving a rotation in a corporate staff role. Too often, executives view a staff role as a ticket to watch from the sidelines. But staff rotation offers exposure—*of* you to board and top management team members and *for* you to everything going on at the company. A staff role provides tremendous access to everything that comes across the desk of the executive you work for. In this role, you attend the majority of senior-level meetings and have a front-row seat to understanding how the business is run, how the members of the top management team interact, and the interpersonal relationships among them. This in itself is a powerful learning experience, but the position provides even more opportunities. Ursula Burns, now CEO at Xerox, credits her time as executive assistant to previous Xerox CEO and Chair Paul Allaire as a critical experience in her development as a leader—and in her fully understanding the company.

First, many executives—particularly those who are rapidly promoted—are given a staff position because they are being noticed and rewarded for their ability to drive results. Rapidly promoted people are, more often than not, very directive in style and narrow in their exposure to the company. For such an executive, the staff role is a tremendous place from which to develop tools to address these gaps—soft management skills and an understanding of the "big picture." The staff role teaches how to lead with force of personal influence rather than with force of position, so the executive learns to manage rather than direct an outcome.

A corporate staff role also teaches executives how the headquarters office works. In doing so, the value that can be created at the HQ level becomes clear. When people miss this rotation before becoming CEO, they often discount the HQ functional staff and create an unproductive rift between HQ and the field and distract everyone from a focus on the business. If a new CEO discounts the value of corporate functions like legal and human resources, they typically do not recruit the best people into these roles; the failure to add value becomes a self-fulfilling prophecy. They also don't learn how to use the corporate staff as true advisors, which decreases their overall effectiveness as leaders. Knowing how to be effective in an HQ environment makes you even better when you return to the field.

To get a client ready for a staff role the coach will likely need to first help the client understand how this move is smart in his or her career game. This is not always an easy conversation—in our experience we have seen operating executives visibly wilt when the possibility of a headquarters role is mentioned. Coaches need to see—and then share—how these roles are tremendous developmental roles. Nothing better teaches an executive how things work at the corporate level. Tasks have to be accomplished without much positional authority, and those who succeed must build a broad set of relationships that allows them to get work done without relying on formal relationships. Further, these opportunities allow executives to see the full company view rather than a business or function view. Finally, in these roles executives get exposure to the senior management team and the board of directors. There is great value in these positions—and there are important interpersonal skills that coaches can help their clients develop.

Now the Next Move

These moves—finding something to fix, making a healthy business better, and having a positive impact in a staff role—are instrumental in providing the experiences and exposure necessary to prove readiness for the C-suite. Though the moves do not need to come in a particular order, we advocate focusing early in your career on finding something to fix. These opportunities have risk, but this risk is much easier to take early in a career when there is more time to recover.

The first two moves allow executives to develop and demonstrate their abilities as a "field general." The leader is closely embedded with the people doing the work. The mission is more clearly defined. The time horizon under which results are required is shorter. And the leader more likely has his hands on the financial and operational levers that direct the enterprise.

The third role, a staff assignment move, provides the opportunity to exercise abilities as a "Pentagon general." Much of the attention is focused further into the future, and a greater emphasis is put on engaging field generals, through participation and inspiration, to execute longer-term, more abstract goals. The ability to influence without direct authority is tested regularly in these sorts of roles.

We have seen in our work that success in these three experiences provides a strong body of work to open the door to the C-suite. Individuals who have demonstrated the ability to execute each of these roles become lower-risk choices in succession planning. Boards can measure individuals' experiences in these areas as important criteria in evaluating succession candidates.

For executives, these recommendations can help in personal career planning. By seeking and excelling in these roles, an executive can create a strong narrative as to why he or she is ready to lead. Having the experience isn't enough. You must be able to talk about how these moves prepared you for a C-level position and gave you the breadth and depth to be able to handle the role. Those who can tell this story in a compelling way to decision makers will have the advantage over those who think the work speaks for itself.

What makes a compelling narrative? First, think about the context for each career move you've had. Dan Palumbo offers the recommendation to frame moves as chances to run toward an opportunity where you could learn rather than as a chance to run from a situation that was undesirable. Hewlett-Packard's Brian Humphries emphasizes that your narrative should make it clear you have been purposeful in your career—not what he would call a "drifter." You want to show you have continually leaned in to your career to keep its momentum. Perhaps most important, as BHP Billiton's CEO Marius Kloppers suggests, is that you be able to point to what is demonstrably better in each of your previous positions due to your efforts.

Through these moves, rising executives can propel and steer their careers, rather than just ride the tide. These thoughtful actions can make a critical difference in pushing through to attain their desired leadership position. For coaches and mentors, understanding these moves and their role in developing an executive is also important because it obviously is not enough to simply ask for a turn in each role—the executive has to be able to demonstrate their preparation and suitability for each opportunity in order to earn it.

Stephen A. Miles is vice chairman of Heidrick & Struggles, overseeing worldwide leadership advisory activities. Having coauthored *Riding Shotgun: The Role of the Chief Operating Officer*, he is a recognized expert on the subject and consults on establishing the role and the transition from COO to CEO. His CEO advisory services were profiled in the *BusinessWeek* article "The Rising Star of CEO Consulting." Stephen is regularly featured in *Forbes, BusinessWeek, Directorship*, and *The Wall Street Journal*.

Nathan Bennett is the Wahlen Professor of Management at Georgia Tech. He is coauthor (with Stephen Miles) of two books, *Riding Shotgun: The Role of the Chief Operating Officer* and *Your Career Game: How Game Theory Can Help You Achieve Your Professional Goals*. His current research interests include power, leadership, top management team effectiveness, and leadership transitions.

PART VI

COACHING MODELS AND TOOLS

Part VI, Coaching Models and Tools, puts forth models and tools used by some of the world's leading coaches. We begin the section with "Coaching Tools for the Leadership Journey" by Ken Blanchard, Madeleine Homan Blanchard, and Linda Miller. In this chapter, the authors define "relationship mapping" and "leadership point of view," discuss their pivotal roles in coaching a new leader to success, then follow one man on his journey from Project Developer to CEO. Marshall Goldsmith describes his fun and successful technique in Chapter Twenty-Nine, "Try Feed*Forward* Instead of Feedback." And, though the title, "Three Types of Hi-Po and the Realise2 4M Model: Coaching at the Intersection of Strengths, Strategy, and Situation," may sound like a complicated mathematical formula, Professor P. Alex Linley and Nicky Garcea's article is actually a straightforward, highly pertinent discussion of the types of high-potential leaders and the differences in how they approach their environments in order to succeed within them. The final chapter of Part VI, "Coaching High-Potential Women: Using the Six Points of Influence Model for Transformational Change" by Barbara Mintzer-McMahon, presents a model for transformational change that is a key resource for addressing and mastering challenges that many high-potential women face today. It is an appropriate and superb finale for our printed book.

CHAPTER TWENTY-EIGHT

COACHING TOOLS FOR THE LEADERSHIP JOURNEY

By Ken Blanchard, Madeleine Homan Blanchard, and Linda Miller

The road to effective leadership can be a rocky one and the way ahead is not always clear, particularly for new managers. In his book *The First 90 Days*[1] Michael Watkins reveals that it normally takes more than six months for leaders in new positions to start contributing to the bottom line. Coaching can shorten that time period, as well as establish a firm foundation for exceptional leadership over the course of a lifetime.

In this article we'll discuss two coaching tools that are particularly effective in accelerating the new leader's journey to effectiveness: Relationship Mapping and Leadership Point of View.

Leadership Is a Journey

Just as a Sherpa guide knows the way up the mountain, so the executive coach knows the steps along the leadership journey. In fact, the stages people go through on their leadership journey are fairly predictable.

When people join companies—especially young people trained in specific skills—they usually start as individual contributors. They have key responsibility areas directly linked to their particular expertise. They may be part of a team, but as individual contributors they are judged by the quality of their individual work.

Tom's leadership journey is a good example. Tom came into the company as a product developer. His job was to find out which new products had been approved for the pipeline and to shepherd them through the development cycle.

He worked with the marketing and sales departments, but he was an individual contributor with high individual effort and no direct reports. (See Figure 28.1.)

As individual contributors increase their technical competence, they frequently are promoted into management roles. Often, they have no management experience and limited interpersonal skills, especially if their fields are highly technical.

When Tom was promoted into management, his effort as an individual contributor decreased as his number of direct reports increased. Tom no longer had the freedom to get the job done on his own. He had to get it done through others. (See Figure 28.2.)

FIGURE 28.1. LEADERSHIP EFFECTS OF COACHING

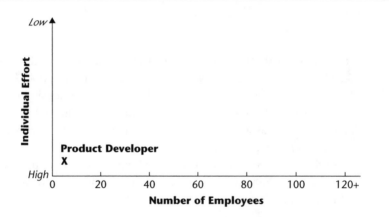

FIGURE 28.2. LEADERSHIP EFFECTS OF COACHING

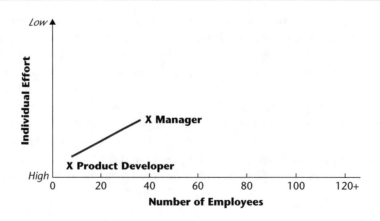

One of the hardest things for technically proficient, smart people to realize is that as they assume more and more leadership responsibility, they must continue to increase their dependence on the goodwill and help of people at all levels of the organization. Each of these "others" is an individual who needs to be seen, heard, and understood by their leaders in order to maximize the potential they offer. At this point, Tom's organization provided him with a coach who introduced him to a tool called Relationship Mapping.[2]

The Relationship Mapping Tool

It was critical for Tom to map his key relationships to understand how each could impact his performance. Relationship Mapping is an ideal tool to use when strategizing a new project, beginning a new role, or running into unexpected obstacles in a specific area. The secret to using this tool effectively is to know and be able to articulate:

- Key goals and milestones
- The plan to achieve goals
- Who will be affected by the achievement of goals
- How each of these people can either help or hinder success
- What can be done to leverage helpers
- Tactics for possible damage control

The Relationship Mapping Process

Taking the time to really think through relationships requires a great deal of discipline and adherence to a specific process. To begin, Tom's coach had him take a large piece of flip chart paper and clearly identify what, exactly, needed to be accomplished. Because there were several goals, Tom's coach had him create a relationship map for each. Next, Tom drew a box for *each* person who might be affected by the efforts involved in achieving the goal. Like many people working on Relationship Maps, Tom worried about going overboard, but his coach assured him it was best to think of as many people as possible and then scale back, if needed. Tom included all relevant senior leaders, colleagues in the industry, peers in other departments, direct reports, functional reports, and dotted-line team leads.

Once all possible stakeholders were on the map, Tom answered the following questions for each person:

- What are their main goals and objectives?
- How will it serve them for me to succeed—or fail?

- What is needed from them?
- How can they help—or hurt—the project?
- What is the person's thinking style? What will be needed to most effectively communicate and influence him or her? For example, does she like a lot of detail or would she prefer the executive summary?
- What attitudes does the person have about me? Is there respect, credibility, trust?
- How do I feel about the person? Is there any judgment or bad history to complicate things?

Once this process was completed for each person, Tom thought about what he had learned. He immediately saw that some individuals were less important to the success of the project or goal than he had previously thought, whereas others were more important and might have been overlooked.

Creating Action Plans with Relationship Maps

At this point in the Relationship Mapping process, Tom needed to create a mini action plan for deepening his relationship with each individual on the map. Action plans can include spending time together, going to the person to ask for advice, or picking up the phone simply to get an opinion about something. Tom planned several lunches and coffees with the individuals he needed to get to know better. It was a real stretch for him to overcome his introversion, but he made himself do it and found that it wasn't as hard as he'd initially expected. He began to include several new people on relevant e-mails, and made it a point to drop by certain cubicles that were not on his regular path.

With one particular person, Tom realized that mistakes had been made and that past misunderstandings were getting in the way of clear communication. The air needed to be cleared. Tom forced himself to pick up the phone and ask for a meeting to discuss what had happened in the past, forge an improved relationship, and agree on a new way to move forward. This proved to be a critical and extremely positive decision.

Action plans for each individual should include methodically paying attention to how people use language. In Tom's case, he needed to understand what was important to others, what they focused on, how they thought, and how they approached things.

How people communicate their understanding offers useful clues to how they process information. If they say "I *see*," in all likelihood they are literally swayed by visual images and graphics. "I don't *feel* comfortable" is often used by kinesthetic learners who respond better to a document in their hand than to an electronic copy. Those who remark "I *hear* what you're saying" are likely to be auditory learners who respond best to verbal communication.

As Tom learned to listen carefully—to assess whether someone wanted to be told or shown, whether they wanted the detailed plan or the cut-to-the-chase outcome—his effectiveness soared. Tom began to develop a reputation for being an excellent communicator who got the job done.

This is a critical point in coaching. Leaders on an upward path must decide if they want to continue their upward movement, or not. In Tom's case, he had to think about whether he wanted to retain some pieces of his role as an individual contributor or transition to a predominantly leadership position, depending on and developing others.

Tom found that he loved leading others and excelled at it. As a result, he was given increasingly more responsibility. Over time, top management was so impressed with his ability to build relationships while maintaining his technical expertise that he was promoted to divisional vice president with new responsibilities. (See Figure 28.3.) Tom no longer did much individual technical work because he set the strategic direction for an entire division. He thrived with the change.

Leaders at this level in the organization are responsible for getting almost all their work done through others. Tom now had eighty people reporting either to him directly or through his direct reports, and his division was responsible for $35 million in revenue. It was at this point that Tom realized he had too many employees under him for all of them to know him well. He needed to find a way to be a truly inspirational leader without having personal contact with everyone. Again, Tom's coach was there with a tool that helped him make the crucial shift from manager of processes and people to leader: The Leadership Point of View.

FIGURE 28.3. LEADERSHIP EFFECTS OF COACHING

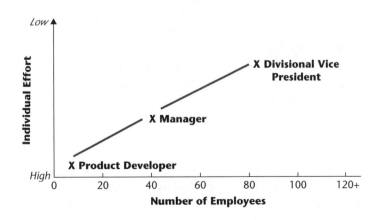

The Leadership Point of View

Leadership Point of View[3] (LPoV) is a credo that encompasses not just a leader's vision for the work, but also shares personal background that has influenced the leader's beliefs and expectations about leadership. The LPoV expresses what is most important to the leader and offers examples that help people understand and remember what has been shared. Whereas the Relationship Mapping process focuses on the leader's development, the LPoV focuses on others, telling them what they need to know about their leader to work effectively with him or her.

Tom's coach explained to him that his LPoV would express what he expected of others and what others could expect from him. By sharing his LPoV, Tom would make explicit what had up to now been implicit. He would set an example for his people and encourage them to think about their own beliefs about leading and motivating people. Finally, Tom's LPoV would serve as his road map for actions he would choose when stressed or in a crisis.

Tom was delighted by this assignment, although it was harder than he initially expected. He was not nearly as clear about his LPoV as he thought he would be, and he had to work on it in stages.

Ken and Margie Blanchard developed the Leadership Point of View process after reading Noel Tichy's book, *The Leadership Engine*.[4] Tichy's extensive research has shown that the most effective leaders have a clear, teachable LPoV, and they are willing to share it with others.

The Leadership Point of View Process

To develop his LPoV, Tom needed to answer some questions. The answers to these questions generated more questions, required a great deal of thought, and in the end yielded rich and varied answers. Tom began his LPoV exploration by asking: who are the leaders who have inspired me and had an impact on my beliefs about leading and motivating people? He thought about all kinds of people from the past and the present, real and fictional. One of Tom's favorite leaders was Abraham Lincoln, whose humility he loved. Another leader, known only to Tom, was his middle school soccer coach, Mike. What a motivator he had been! Tom created a list of these leaders.

Once his list was finished, Tom took each of the leaders from the list and asked:

- What qualities does this person have that I find so impressive?
- What have they done that I find so inspiring?
- What lessons am I learning from them about leadership?

One of Tom's personal examples was Atticus Finch, the protagonist of the novel *To Kill a Mockingbird* by Harper Lee.[5] Atticus Finch was a caring and committed parent, yet he chose to stand up for justice in his small town at great risk to himself and his children. By thinking about why he found Atticus Finch so inspiring, Tom realized that he was committed to doing the right thing even when it wasn't popular or convenient.

The list of qualities and actions revealed what Tom thought was important for a leader. These were his leadership values. These values, it turned out, were different from any official corporate values his company had. Because these values were personal and drove his behavior, he saw that it was critical to know what they were and share them with his people.

Using his list of qualities and actions, Tom was able to reflect on the next question:

- Is there something about me that would be helpful for others to know that would make them more effective in working with me?

Through his LPoV work it became clear to Tom that although he believed a leader should be kind and appropriate at all times, this would be a lifelong challenge for him personally. He knew that despite his best efforts, his dry and mischievous sense of humor would cause him to fail sometimes to live up to his own standards. Because he might occasionally slip up and crack inappropriate jokes, Tom decided that part of his LPoV would be to prepare and warn people about this.

This led Tom to the next question:

- What can people expect from me?

His coach convinced Tom that letting people know what they could expect from him would demonstrate Tom's belief that good leadership is a partnership. It would also give his people a picture of how things would look under his leadership.

In reflecting on what he expected and what people could expect from him, Tom knew that he wanted people to win. Therefore, they could expect him to roll up his proverbial sleeves and help, whether they needed a sounding board or someone to brainstorm solving a problem.

As Tom thought about this aspect of his LPoV, it felt risky to share with his people exactly what they could and shouldn't expect from him. He realized that it gave implicit permission for them to call him on his behavior when what was promised went undelivered. In talking to his coach, he realized that although sharing was risky, it was the only way to foster the trusting environment he wanted for his people.

The next question forced even more clarity for Tom:

- What do I expect from my people?

Tom realized in talking with his coach that expectations can go from the explicit—like accomplishing agreed-upon goals—to the implicit—such as, "I expect my people to do what they say they are going to do." Tom intuitively understood that people like to know what is expected of them. They want a clear picture of what the leader thinks a good job looks like, because it provides them with a sense of safety. That certainly was true for him.

In talking with him about what people could expect from Tom and what Tom could expect from people, Tom's coach emphasized how important it was that he give an example for each major expectation, so that they could see themselves within each expectation.

After many hours and much thought, Tom created a draft LPoV in writing. His first attempt was ten pages long, which he finally whittled down to a three-page document. Once that was complete, he had to answer the last key question about his LPoV:

- How will I share this information with others?

He knew that reading the document to people would not be very motivating. Instead, he committed his LPoV to memory, so that when he shared it with his people he could look them in the eye and make a sincere presentation. Tom's coach encouraged him to make a date with himself to revisit his LPoV annually to see if it needed to be updated.

Tom also came to rely on his LPoV as a working document for himself. As he recently told his coach, "I refer to it when I have a hard day and forget who I am. I've been glad to have it in this downturn. It's like an emergency kit I keep on hand."

Putting the LPoV to Work

For coaches who want to do Leadership Point of View work with their clients, it is important to remember that creating a LPoV is a process that takes time. The work can be done in a number of ways. Each client is going to have a different thinking and learning style. Visual leaders are going to want to see the questions in writing. Auditory ones will want to be talked through it. Very few will be able to answer the questions off the top of their heads. Many will want time to reflect and make notes.

One client who worked insane hours and went home to three kids designated a couple of her driving commutes to thinking through the questions, and then she left voice mails for her assistant to transcribe and e-mail back to her. A highly extroverted, "think out loud" entrepreneur hosted a dinner party with his most interesting friends during which he conducted a lively guided discussion around the questions. He gleaned amazing thinking, and as an added bonus he received some keen insights into what leadership attributes he already had. Another leader got the best results from long, solitary walks, after which she wrote up some notes. There is no right way to generate answers, but the coach can help each individual find the best way for him or her. Once the process begins, it will be a work in progress over the course of the leadership tenure. For some that will mean the rest of their lives.

Finding Your Leadership Point of View

- Who are the leaders who are inspiring to you?
- What qualities do they have? What did they do that you found inspiring?
- Can you do these things? Do you possess these qualities? If not, can you develop them? If not, what will you do about it?
- What do you expect of yourself and others?
- What can others expect of you?
- How will you share this information with others?

An Inspirational Leader

Tom's record as a divisional vice president was exemplary. So when the CEO retired, no one was surprised that Tom was promoted to the top spot. When leaders are promoted to CEO, they are fully responsible for creating, establishing, and living the organization's vision, values, and mission. They must focus on strategy and building a leadership team. They must network with other CEOs and learn quickly what is working and what is not. They must make hard decisions about how to solve problems, often with no road map.

The technical skills Tom brought to his organization have long since been set aside. They once served him well, but no longer. As CEO, Tom now produces all results through the work of others and is held responsible by all stakeholders for the company's success or failure. (See Figure 28.4.)

FIGURE 28.4. LEADERSHIP EFFECTS OF COACHING

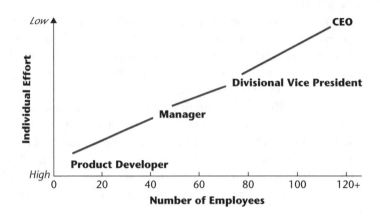

Getting things done with and through others is an executive trait. To master this skill, it helps to have a detailed map of every single person who is going to make a significant contribution, so Tom uses Relationship Mapping to this day.

At their best, executives lead others to excellence so that the entire organization succeeds. Tom regularly shares his LPoV, as does each member of his executive team, increasing the level of trust and the quality of conversations in the organization. Tom now spends every hour of every day helping others achieve their goals, connecting them with the best resources, and removing the obstacles in their paths. All the while, he inspires them with the organization's vision and values.

Ken Blanchard is one of the most influential leadership gurus in the world, respected for his groundbreaking work in leadership and management. He is the author of dozens of books, including the blockbuster international bestseller *The One Minute Manager*® and the giant business best-sellers *Raving Fans* and *Gung Ho!* His books have combined sales of nearly 20 million copies in more than 27 languages. In 2005, Ken was inducted into Amazon's Hall of Fame as one of the top 25 bestselling authors of all time. He is the cofounder and chief spiritual officer of The Ken Blanchard Companies, an international management training and consulting firm headquartered in San Diego, California. The College of Business at Grand Canyon University bears his name.

Madeleine Homan Blanchard is the team lead for Blanchard Certified, an online leadership development system, and she is a cofounder of Coaching Services for The Ken Blanchard Companies. A coach since 1989, Ms. Homan

Blanchard was instrumental in developing the core curriculum for Coach University, where she was a founding advisory board member and senior trainer. She was a founding board member of the International Coach Federation, where she served on the board for six years. Previously, Ms. Blanchard founded Straightline Coaching, a coaching service firm devoted to life and work satisfaction for creative geniuses. She spent two years as the program director for a coaching program that rolled out to 2,100 individuals globally for the IT division of an international investment bank. She is the coauthor of three books: *Coaching in Organizations*; *Leverage Your Best, Ditch the Rest: The Coaching Secrets Executives Depend On*, and *Leading at a Higher Level*. She is also coauthor of The Ken Blanchard Companies' coaching skills program *Coaching Essentials for Leaders*.

Linda Miller is the Global Liaison for Coaching at The Ken Blanchard Companies. In this role Linda has coached and trained leaders from Europe, Asia, and Central and South America. In addition, she is known for her ability to communicate what coaching is and how it can be applied in organizations. Since 1996, Linda has been an active member of the International Coach Federation and is a founding recipient of the Master Certified Coach designation. She and Madeleine Homan Blanchard are coauthors of *Coaching in Organizations: Best Practices from The Ken Blanchard Companies®*. During the 2008 and 2010 election cycles Linda moderated political debates at the legislative level throughout Arizona. In 2009, she was awarded an honorary doctorate recognizing her contributions to the field of coaching.

CHAPTER TWENTY-NINE

TRY FEED*FORWARD* INSTEAD OF FEEDBACK[1]

By Marshall Goldsmith

Providing feedback has long been considered to be an essential skill for leaders. As they strive to achieve the goals of the organization, employees need to know how they are doing. They need to know if their performance is in line with what their leaders expect. They need to learn what they have done well and what they need to change. Traditionally, this information has been communicated in the form of "downward feedback" from leaders to their employees. Just as employees need feedback from leaders, leaders can benefit from feedback from their employees. Employees can provide useful input on the effectiveness of procedures and processes and as well as input to managers on their leadership effectiveness. This "upward feedback" has become increasingly common with the advent of 360-degree multirater assessments.

But there is a fundamental problem with all types of feedback: it focuses on the past, on what has already occurred—not on the infinite variety of opportunities that can happen in the future. As such, feedback can be limited and static, as opposed to expansive and dynamic.

Over the past several years, I have observed more than thirty thousand leaders as they participated in a fascinating experiential exercise. In the exercise, participants are each asked to play two roles. In one role, they are asked to provide feed*forward*—that is, to give someone else suggestions for the future and *help as much as they can*. In the second role, they are asked to accept feed*forward*—that is, to listen to the suggestions for the future and *learn as much as they can*. The exercise typically lasts for ten to fifteen minutes, and the average participant has six to seven dialogue sessions. In the exercise participants are asked to:

- Pick one behavior that they would like to change. Change in this behavior should make a significant, positive difference in their lives.
- Describe this behavior to randomly selected fellow participants. This is done in one-on-one dialogues. It can be done quite simply, such as, "I want to be a better listener."
- Ask for feed*forward*—for two suggestions for the future that might help them achieve a positive change in their selected behavior. If participants have worked together in the past, they are not allowed to give ANY feedback about the past. They are only allowed to give ideas for the future.
- Listen attentively to the suggestions and take notes. Participants are not allowed to comment on the suggestions in any way. They are not allowed to critique the suggestions or even to make positive judgmental statements, such as, "That's a good idea."
- Thank the other participants for their suggestions.
- Ask the other persons what they would like to change.
- Provide feed*forward*—two suggestions aimed at helping the other person change.
- Say, "You are welcome" when thanked for the suggestions. The entire process of both giving and receiving feed*forward* usually takes about two minutes.
- Find another participant and keep repeating the process until the exercise is stopped.

When the exercise is finished, I ask participants to provide one word that best describes their reaction to this experience. I ask them to complete the sentence, "This exercise was . . ." The words provided are almost always extremely positive, such as "great," "energizing," "useful," or "helpful." One of the most commonly mentioned words is "fun"!

What is the *last* word that comes to mind when we consider any feedback activity? Fun!

Eleven Reasons to Try Feed*Forward*

Participants are then asked why this exercise is seen as fun and helpful as opposed to painful, embarrassing, or uncomfortable. Their answers provide a great explanation of why feed*forward* can often be more useful than feedback as a developmental tool.

1. *We can change the future.* We can't change the past. Feed*forward* helps people envision and focus on a positive future, not a failed past. Athletes are often trained

using feed*forward*. Race car drivers are taught to "Look at the road ahead, not at the wall." Basketball players are taught to envision the ball going in the hoop and to imagine the perfect shot. By giving people ideas on how they can be even more successful (as opposed to visualizing a failed past), we can increase their chances of achieving this success in the future.

2. *It can be more productive to help people learn to be "right" than to prove they were "wrong."* Negative feedback often becomes an exercise in "let me prove you were wrong." This tends to produce defensiveness on the part of the receiver and discomfort on the part of the sender. Even constructively delivered feedback is often seen as negative as it necessarily involves a discussion of mistakes, shortfalls, and problems. Feed*forward*, on the other hand, is almost always seen as positive because it focuses on solutions—not problems.

3. *Feed*forward *is especially suited to successful people.* Successful people like getting ideas that are aimed at helping them achieve their goals. They tend to resist negative judgment. We all tend to accept feedback that is consistent with the way we see ourselves. We also tend to reject or deny feedback that is inconsistent with the way we see ourselves. Successful people tend to have a very positive self-image. I have observed many successful executives respond to (and even enjoy) feed*forward*. I am not sure that these same people would have had such a positive reaction to feedback.

4. Feed*forward* can come from anyone who knows about the task. It does not require personal experience with the individual. One very common positive reaction to the previously described exercise is that participants are amazed by how much they can learn from people that they don't know! For example, if you want to be a better listener, almost any fellow leader can give you ideas on how you can improve. They don't have to know you. Feedback requires knowing about the person. Feed*forward* just requires having good ideas for achieving the task.

5. People do not take feed*forward* as personally as feedback. In theory, constructive feedback is supposed to "focus on the performance, not the person." In practice, almost all feedback is taken personally (no matter how it is delivered). Successful people's sense of identity is highly connected with their work. The more successful people are, the more this tends to be true. It is hard to give a dedicated professional feedback that is not taken personally. Feed*forward* cannot involve a personal critique, since it is discussing something that has not yet happened! Positive suggestions tend to be seen as objective advice—personal critiques are often viewed as personal attacks.

6. Feedback can reinforce personal stereotyping and negative self-fulfilling prophecies. Feed*forward* can reinforce the possibility of change. Feedback can reinforce the feeling of failure. How many of us have been "helped" by a

spouse, significant other, or friend who seems to have a near-photographic memory of our previous "sins" that they share with us in order to point out the history of our shortcomings. Negative feedback can be used to reinforce the message, "this is just the way you are." Feed*forward* is based on the assumption that the receiver of suggestions can make positive changes in the future.

7. Face it! Most of us hate getting negative feedback, and we don't like to give it. I have reviewed summary 360-degree feedback reports for over fifty companies. The items "provides developmental feedback in a timely manner" and "encourages and accepts constructive criticism" both always score near the bottom on coworker satisfaction with leaders. Traditional training does not seem to make a great deal of difference. If leaders got better at providing feedback every time the performance appraisal forms were "improved," most should be perfect by now! Leaders are not very good at giving or receiving negative feedback. It is unlikely that this will change in the near future.

8. Feed*forward* can cover almost all of the same "material" as feedback. Imagine that you have just made a terrible presentation in front of the executive committee. Your manager is in the room. Rather than make you "relive" this humiliating experience, your manager might help you prepare for future presentations by giving you suggestions for the future. These suggestions can be very specific and still delivered in a positive way. In this way your manager can "cover the same points" without feeling embarrassed and without making you feel even more humiliated.

9. Feed*forward* tends to be much faster and more efficient than feedback. An excellent technique for giving ideas to successful people is to say, "Here are four ideas for the future. Please accept these in the positive spirit that they are given. If you can only use two of the ideas, you are still two ahead. Just ignore what doesn't make sense for you." With this approach almost no time gets wasted on judging the quality of the ideas or "proving that the ideas are wrong." This "debate" time is usually negative; it can take up a lot of time, and it is often not very productive. By eliminating judgment of the ideas, the process becomes much more positive for the sender, as well as the receiver. Successful people tend to have a high need for self-determination and will tend to accept ideas that they "buy" while rejecting ideas that feel "forced" upon them.

10. Feed*forward* can be a useful tool to apply with managers, peers, and team members. Rightly or wrongly, feedback is associated with judgment. This can lead to very negative—or even career-limiting—unintended consequences when applied to managers or peers. Feed*forward* does not imply superiority of judgment. It is more focused on being a helpful "fellow traveler" than an "expert." As such it can be easier to hear from a person who is not in a

position of power or authority. An excellent team building exercise is to have each team member ask, "How can I better help our team in the future?" and listen to feed*forward* from fellow team members (in one-on-one dialogues).

11. People tend to listen more attentively to feed*forward* than feedback. One participant is the feed*forward* exercise noted, "I think that I listened more effectively in this exercise than I ever do at work!" When asked why, he responded, "Normally, when others are speaking, I am so busy composing a reply that will make sure that I sound smart—that I am not fully listening to what the other person is saying I am just composing my response. In feed*forward* the only reply that I am allowed to make is 'thank you.' Since I don't have to worry about composing a clever reply—I can focus all of my energy on listening to the other person!"

In summary, the intent of this article is not to imply that leaders should never give feedback or that performance appraisals should be abandoned. The intent is to show how feed*forward* can often be preferable to feedback in day-to-day interactions. Aside from its effectiveness and efficiency, feed*forward* can make life a lot more enjoyable. When managers are asked, "How did you feel the last time you received feedback?" their most common responses are very negative. When managers are asked how they felt after receiving feed*forward*, they reply that feed*forward* was not only useful, it was also fun!

Quality communication—between and among people at all levels and every department and division—is the glue that holds organizations together. By using feed*forward*—and by encouraging others to use it—leaders can dramatically improve the quality of communication in their organizations, ensuring that the right message is conveyed, and that those who receive it are receptive to its content. The result is a much more dynamic, much more open organization—one whose employees focus on the promise of the future rather than dwelling on the mistakes of the past.

Dr. Marshall Goldsmith has recently been recognized as one of the fifteen most influential business thinkers in the world, in a global biannual study sponsored by *The (London) Times*. He has also been described in *American Management Association* as one of the top fifty thinkers and leaders who have influenced the field of management over the past eighty years; in the *Wall Street Journal* as one of the top ten executive educators; in *Forbes* as one of the five most-respected executive coaches; in the *Economic Time (India)* among the top CEO coaches of America; in *Fast Company*, called America's preeminent executive coach; and he has received a lifetime achievement award (one of two ever awarded) from the *Institute for*

Management Studies. Marshall is one of a select few executive advisors who have been asked to work with over 120 major CEOs and their management teams. He is the million-selling author of numerous books, including *New York Times* bestsellers *MOJO* and *What Got You Here Won't Get You There* (also a *Wall Street Journal* #1 business book and winner of the Harold Longman Award for business book of the year). Contact Marshall at marshall@marshallgoldsmith.com and www.marshallgoldsmith.com.

CHAPTER THIRTY

THREE TYPES OF HI-PO AND THE REALISE2 4M MODEL

Coaching at the Intersection of Strengths, Strategy, and Situation

By Professor P. Alex Linley and Nicky Garcea

The need for learning and change in a dynamically complex global environment has never been greater. The increasing pace of globalization. The emergence of the BRIC economies—those of Brazil, Russia, India, and China—as major global players. The talent tidal wave that has been unleashed through the economic emergence of China and India. The Great Recession of 2008–2009. How the Hi-Pos (those with high potential) cope with—or even capitalize upon—these circumstances will determine if, how, and how far they succeed as they become the next generation moving into the corporate C-suite. Their Hi-Po type will also be instrumental in the pathways that might be open to them and the development they will need to succeed. Our experiences suggest there are three types of Hi-Pos: the Hard-Wired Hi-Po, the Hard-Working Hi-Po, and the Humble Hi-Po. Each has its own different development needs and performance trajectories. Determining the Hi-Po type with whom we are working helps us to better understand what they need in order to succeed, and what we can best do to help them.

The Hard-Wired Hi-Po

The Hard-Wired Hi-Po has grown up with the belief that they are the best of the best. Prep school, private school, Ivy League or Oxbridge university. top of the class, house captain, member of the varsity elite. Then graduate entry and leadership fast-track with the heavy label of "High-Potential." OK—we stereotype to draw the caricature—but our point is a simple one. With this gilded existence helping them to glide into the elite, these Hi-Pos can wear their labels as a badge of honor, but also as a heavy burden of expectation to bear—and one which is exacerbated by the curse of the *fixed mindset*.[1]

The fixed mindset can be an unwitting consequence of high intelligence, precocious success, and early achievement. It is the view that *"I'm one of the brightest people in this company, so everything should be easy for me."* Unfortunately, for people with a fixed mindset, the implication is that everything should be easy and that they don't need to put in the effort—that they should never fail, that mistakes are something confined to lesser mortals. As is apparent, the fixed mindset is anathema to the deep requirements for learning and change that pervade modern corporate life. The fixed mindset leads to the belief that "I will be found out because I can't actually do what is expected of me—and I'm too afraid to try in case I might fail."

The consequences for the Hard-Wired Hi-Po can be debilitating. On the one hand, they expect (and believe that others expect of them) that success is a given, to be assumed, rather than earned. Their superior talent, ability, intellect, or charisma is all they need to float to the pinnacle of whatever they desire. Hard work, effort, failure, learning—*"These don't come into it. They're for others, not for me."* The fixed mindset is the belief that everything I have is what I deserve and what I was born with. As a result, anything that challenges this belief, that causes the Hard-Wired Hi-Po to think that they might not just be so special after all, presents a major threat. It is easier to walk away than to fail, easier not to try than to admit defeat—and so self-sabotage can be a key indicator of when the fixed mindset is at work in the Hard-Wired Hi-Po.

The Hard-Working Hi-Po

In contrast, the Hard-Working Hi-Po is characterized by the abundance of learning, change, and growth that they have enjoyed (and endured) along the way. This may often have been as a result of challenge, disappointment, and trauma—but all will have been used as the crucible of experience to forge their growth mindset and resilience for success. Such Hard-Working Hi-Pos will undoubtedly be intelligent—but they will never have taken that intelligence for granted, and their intelligence will likely be more street smarts than just book learning.

The work ethic, commitment, and engagement of the Hard-Working Hi-Po will be predictive of the sheer effort they have expended in their desire to learn, to adapt, to change, and to progress through the vicissitudes of life. As the Hi-Po talent pool has widened immeasurably with the growth of the BRIC economies and the earlier emergence of the Asian tigers (the highly developed economies of Hong Kong, Singapore, South Korea, and Taiwan), so has the breadth and diversity of the Hi-Po population—and the experiences they have had, the mindsets they bring with them, and the assumptions that they consider normal.

With this fundamentally different attitude and mindset, the Hard-Working Hi-Pos see every challenge as an opportunity, welcome the unknown as potential to be embraced, and use adversity as stepping stones for their further change, learning, and growth. In contrast to their Hard-Wired Hi-Po colleagues, the Hard-Working Hi-Po is characterized instead by their *growth mindset*—the belief that their destiny was not fixed at birth, but instead that their trajectory can be shaped and influenced by the effort they put in and the learning they pick up along the way.

The Humble Hi-Po

The third of our class is the Humble Hi-Po—the genuine contender who can't really see that they are that special or why they should be where they are. Although in some ways this might be seen as a variant of the imposter syndrome that has been recognized for the last thirty years,[2] there are subtle differences. The Humble Hi-Po may be confident in himself to an extent, but equally cannot see how he is special compared to others—a phenomenon that we have often observed in high-achieving women and especially high-achieving Asian women (a possible gender and gender X culture interaction difference). They attribute the credit for their successes and achievements to circumstance, good fortune, the efforts of others, or the serendipity of finding themselves in the right place at the right time. All of these may indeed have had a part to play—but the Humble Hi-Po risks losing sight of his or her own contribution and significance if he or she plays this hand of humility too far. As ever, the balance to be struck is a sensitive one that calls to mind Aristotle's "golden mean"—the right thing, to the right amount, in the right way, at the right time.

Equally, the Humble Hi-Pos may be seen as strong leadership candidates, naturally possessing the attributes of the Level 5 leadership virtue of humility, espoused by Jim Collins, amongst others.[3] We have been struck by just how often we have seen humility feature as a team strength in the Realise2 Team Profile[4] of high-performing leadership teams—but interestingly, a lot less frequently in leadership teams that are not high performing.

In sum, the humility of the Humble Hi-Pos can become debilitating when it starts to undermine the contributions they genuinely make and the impact they exclusively have. In this way, humility overplayed becomes a weakness, as it trips up the Humble Hi-Pos from doing what they need to do and being recognized for it. In the alpha-male environment of some organizations, humility is tantamount to career suicide. Humble Hi-Pos have to recognize this and dial back on their humility if they are to succeed. Crucially, this doesn't mean that they have to become something they are not—just that they need to develop the situation-sensing agility of knowing when it is right to speak up for themselves, and when it is right to let others take the credit—which they will always be willing to take!

Helping the Hi-Pos: The Realise2 Strengths Model

On one level, the Hard-Wired Hi-Po, the Hard-Working Hi-Po, and the Humble Hi-Po have very different development needs to address. On another level, they share a common humanness. This can be captured by the strengths approach that helps ground them in a surer sense of who they are at their best, what they do well, and what they love to do.

Strengths are the things that we do well *and* love to do. In traditional thinking on strengths, they are simply understood in terms of *performance* (*"What I am good at"*). But this isn't enough, since a strength is also characterized by the experience of *energy* when we're using it (*"What I enjoy and what gives me energy"*). Further, for a strength to deliver outcomes, it has to be used, and *use* in itself is by definition variable, situational, and dynamic.

Taking these three elements together, we define a strength as being comprised of *performance, energy,* and *use.* These three dimensions combine in a number of different ways along a high-low axis, and together represent the four possible combinations of energy, performance, and use, which define the four quadrants of the Realise2 4M Model[5] (see Figure 30.1):

1. A realized strength is characterized by high energy, high performance, and high use.
2. An unrealized strength is characterized by high energy and high performance, but lower use.
3. A learned behavior is characterized by lower energy but high performance, while use may be variable.
4. A weakness is characterized by lower energy and lower performance, while again use may be variable.

These four characteristics—realized strengths, unrealized strengths, learned behaviors, and weaknesses—together make up the four quadrants of the Realise2

FIGURE 30.1. THE REALISE2 4M MODEL

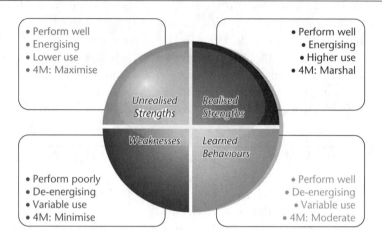

- Perform well
- Energising
- Lower use
- 4M: Maximise

- Perform well
- Energising
- Higher use
- 4M: Marshal

Unrealised Strengths

Realised Strengths

Weaknesses

Learned Behaviours

- Perform poorly
- De-energising
- Variable use
- 4M: Minimise

- Perform well
- De-energising
- Variable use
- 4M: Moderate

4M Model. The four "Ms" refer to the advice that follows from the model, following clockwise from the top right:

1. **Marshal** realized strengths—use them appropriately for your situation and context
2. **Moderate** learned behaviors—use them in moderation and only when you need to
3. **Minimize** weaknesses—use them as little as possible and only where necessary
4. **Maximize** unrealized strengths—find opportunities to use them more.

Coaching Hi-Pos with the Realise2 4M Model

The first fundamental of strengths coaching with the Hi-Po population is that it can help them to achieve a grounded understanding of their strengths, but also their learned behaviors and their weaknesses. This grounding of strengths helps to underpin the personality integration that is integral to their realizing their potential and moving on and up to deliver greater success. The impact of this is subtly different for each of the three Hi-Po types:

- For the Hard-Wired Hi-Po, understanding the situational context around strengths, and appreciating the dynamic interaction between strengths and situations, can help them to recognize that their internal world is not as fixed as they might first have thought. This reframing toward adaptability and agility can transform their mindset and outlook, enabling them to transform their performance as a result.

- For the Hard-Working Hi-Po, the distinction between strengths and learned behaviors is often experienced as the light bulb moment. This group is most likely to have understood their strengths as *"what I am good at"* and so to have confused their learned behaviors in this way, accepting that hard work and effort are the entry ticket to success. When they start to recognize that high performance can be something that you deliver by doing things you enjoy—as well as sometimes knuckling down and just doing the things that need to be done—their perspective and performance can quickly step up a level.

- For the Humble Hi-Po, the recognition, acceptance, and reinforcement of the strengths they have can help to unlock their sense of their own value, and release them from the prison of feeling like an impostor to their own success. As they develop a language for, and integration of their strengths, they grow into their own skins, increasing their authenticity, confidence and performance as a result.

With the identification and recognition of strengths firmly under way, our coaching then typically moves on to helping the Hi-Pos work around the four quadrants of the Realise2 4M Model:

1. Marshal your realized strengths and align them to your goals and objectives, because you are more likely to achieve them by using your strengths.
2. Watch out that you moderate your learned behaviors, using them as much as appropriate but not too much. Learned behaviors are there to be called on when needed—but not overused.
3. Learn how to minimize your weaknesses, so that they don't have a negative impact on your performance. You might do this by finding ways to use your strengths to compensate, working with other people, in partnership or in teams, or even learning how to develop the weakness so that it's "good enough."
4. Find opportunities to maximize your unrealized strengths and use them more in achieving what you want. Your unrealized strengths are a goldmine of untapped potential.
5. Having worked through the cycle, put it into practice. After a month, three months, or six months, come back and review. Strengths are dynamic, situations are ever changing. See what has changed for you and what you need to do about it, so that you can continually perform at your best through realizing your strengths, moderating your learned behaviors, and minimizing your weaknesses.

Crucially for Hi-Po development, the Realise2 4M Model is a dynamic model, and Realise2 is a dynamic assessment tool. As situations change, so might the strengths we use in those situations change as well. It's called adaptation, something that we humans have been doing for hundreds of thousands of years through our evolution to become the people and the species that we are today. Unfortunately, on the fast track to success, Hi-Pos don't always recognize this need for adaptation, and instead think that they need to do what they have always done, and then do more of it as they strive to succeed ever more. Situational judgment here comes into its own. The need for the practical wisdom which Aristotle defined as *phronesis*—the ability to judge, decide, and practice doing the right thing in the right way to get the right result—has the potential to become the sine qua non of future C-suite success.

As we work with Hi-Pos on coaching them for their strengths, it is therefore critical to recognize that their strengths are just one part of the three axes of the individual-organizational-environmental triangle with which they need to contend if they are to step up to the mark and deliver the leadership performance their organizations require. The other two axes relate to strategy (organizational direction) and situation (environmental context), which together form the 3S-P Model that we have developed in conjunction with colleagues Laurence Lyons and Anna Bateson.[6]

The 3S-P Model: Performance at the Intersection of Strengths, Strategy, and Situation

The central premise of the 3S-P model is very simple. *Strengths* used in the absence of context (situation) and direction (strategy) are just hobbies. *Strategy* in the absence of environmental awareness (situation) and an understanding of the capabilities to deliver it (strengths) is just a wish upon a star. *Situation* knowledge provides context, but in the absence of a direction of travel (strategy) and a means to get there (strengths), it is just wallpaper—providing a nice backdrop to what is going on around us. However, at the intersection of these three factors when they come together, we find the necessary foundation and sufficient capability for the delivery of *Performance*—thereby defining the 3S-P Model (see Figure 30.2).

Our coaching of Hi-Pos is therefore structured to take account of these three domains. Typical coaching questions include:

1. Strengths
   - What strengths can you use to help you achieve your objectives?
   - How are your strengths perceived within the organization?
   - Are there strengths that you need to dial up or dial down?

FIGURE 30.2. THE 3S-P MODEL

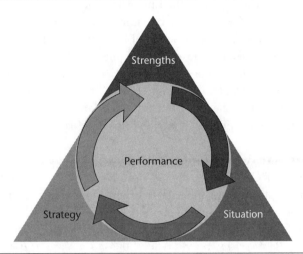

2. Strategy
   - What are you trying to achieve and why?
   - What are the major impacts that will help or hinder you getting there?
   - Why is doing this the right thing for the organization to do? How can you ensure it will help the organization achieve its mission and purpose?
3. Situation
   - What is your current context and how does this impact you?
   - What is changing in the world that will influence the decisions you're making?
   - Is there a match between your strengths and strategy and your situation? If not, what can you do about it?

As the coaching session works through the deeper understanding and dynamic integration of strengths, strategy, and situation, so a more complex but complete and integrated perspective emerges of the Hi-Po and what he or she needs to do to deliver performance. Of course, the reality in our modern world is that situation and strategy can change from one situation to the next, so although our coaching is of necessity adaptive and dynamic, there are also underpinning fundamentals that provide the framework for why we do what we do.

The first of these fundamentals is that people always perform better when they are working from their strengths. Second, as defined by Revans's axiom, the rate of learning in the individual and the organization must always be greater than, or at least equal to, the rate of change in their environment if they are to survive and thrive. Third, by maximizing the dynamic intersection of strengths, strategy, and situation, we will enable people to deliver the performance that is needed to succeed in our ever-changing world. The world that the Hi-Pos will inherit is replete with perils and pitfalls, but also possibilities and potential. Like Virgil guiding Dante through the *Divine Comedy*, our role is to help them navigate this world as best they are able, for the Hi-Pos' stewardship of their organizations for future generations will have an impact on us all.

Professor P. Alex Linley, Capp, is a chartered psychologist and founding director of Capp (www.cappeu.com). He works as an organizational consultant applying strengths psychology to organizational development and people practices, serving a range of major global clients. Alex has written, cowritten, or edited more than 150 research papers and book chapters, and seven books, including *Positive Psychology in Practice* (Wiley, 2004), *The Strengths Book* (CAPP Press, 2010), and the *Oxford Handbook of Positive Psychology and Work* (Oxford, 2010).

Nicky Garcea, Capp, is a chartered occupational psychologist and advisory director of Capp (www.cappeu.com), where she leads the advisory team delivering work in Capp's key areas of assessment, development, performance management, and change. Her own areas of specialty include organizational development, strengths-based talent management, coaching, and female leadership development. Nicky has delivered work in the Americas, Europe, and West Africa. In 2010, she coedited the *Oxford Handbook of Positive Psychology and Work*.

CHAPTER THIRTY-ONE

COACHING HIGH-POTENTIAL WOMEN

Using the Six Points of Influence Model for Transformational Change[1]

By Barbara Mintzer-McMahon

Recently I spent the weekend with my husband at our favorite seaside resort. We had stopped at a local market to pick up a few last-minute items when I eyed a postcard display of pithy sayings and began to entertain myself. There was one in particular that grabbed me. It asked the question: "Are you one of those folks who, when opportunity knocks, you respond, 'Can somebody get that?'"

I can't tell you how many women leaders I have worked with who have struggled to find the right response to this knock of opportunity. Why? Why is it so hard for women to fully embrace and engage in possibility? I have coached many women, some of whom, struggling with a crisis of self-confidence, find themselves reluctant to believe in or accept new opportunities when they are offered and others who find it difficult to believe that they can engage in an old and familiar situation in a new way. And then there are the brave few who actively seek out these precious points of entry or opportunities for engagement only to find themselves waiting endlessly for someone to let them in. This chapter presents a model for transformational change that is a key resource for addressing and mastering challenges such as these.

To ask "Why?" is especially timely; for example, in the United States the workforce is undergoing a radical change. Baby Boomers, 60 percent of whom are white males, are beginning to retire. They are being replenished by a brand-new labor force that has the potential to revitalize and rejuvenate the system. Women are projected to account for 51.2 percent of the increase in total labor force growth between 2008 and 2018.[2] This opens up more opportunity for high-potential women.

Consequently, it is a critical time for women to populate the workforce in such significant numbers, especially as they are overwhelmingly responsible for consumer buying decisions. In the United States, women make 85 percent of consumer purchases and influence decisions in more than 90 percent of all goods and services sold. As business futurist Faith Popcorn said, "The companies, from Fortune 500 to mom and pops to startup entrepreneurs, that do the best job of marketing to women will dominate every significant product and service category." [3]

This points to the inevitable realization that having women in leadership and decision-making roles in the organization is vital to reaching consumers and anticipating their needs. Those organizations that effectively serve their most important customers clearly have to know them well. And, who better to understand the choices, likes and dislikes, of women customers than women themselves?

Identifying and nurturing these new women leaders is critical, and this brings us to the next call to action: if organizations are to be successful, they must figure out how to recruit, sustain, and involve high-potential women at every level of business.[4] This insight is supported by recent McKinsey research, which reveals that companies that promote women to high levels are the most profitable. McKinsey's 2010 report on women showed that companies with higher numbers of women in their executive committees outperformed other companies, earning up to 41 percent higher returns on equity.[5]

Ascending the Corporate Ladder

With women having such potential to smooth the transition from Baby Boomers to New Workforce, we must ask: How are we doing? Are we making sure that women are ready for organizational life—and that organizations are ready for them?

It is evident from the increasingly growing numbers of women entering MBA programs around the world that women are acknowledging their commitment and desire to prepare to enter the world of business. In an April survey, thirteen of fourteen Forte member schools said that China or India accounted for the largest number of overseas women in their classes. Members in the Forte group include Harvard Business School, University of Chicago, and University of Pennsylvania.[6]

The question becomes: are we actively planning to develop these high-potential women who might be prepared and willing to assume more senior positions of leadership? That seems to differ depending on culture or country. The statistics in the United States suggest that there is more work to be done. Management and professional roles are currently split roughly equally between men and women. Yet, women are concentrated at the base of the hierarchical pyramid, whereas men occupy the upper levels. Only 14 percent of Fortune 500 officers are women, and—remarkably—less than 2 percent ever make it to the CEO level.[7] This suggests a developmental opportunity for these U.S.-based organizations. In sharp contrast, women now hold 34 percent of senior management roles in China, excluding Hong Kong.[8] That said, this seemingly enlightened progress is tarnished by the fact that many of these women remain unmarried in their mid-thirties and older and are perceived as *shengnu,* or "leftover women."

As they ascend the corporate ladder, many working women find they suffer from directional challenges. Partnerships, marriage, motherhood, and community often vie with work responsibilities, thereby making it difficult to juggle the competing demands and desires of work and a personal life. Most women will recognize the sense of being overwhelmed by multiple roles.

For high-potential women, the pressure is especially intense. While working their way up their organizations, they find that their prizes come at a price. They tackle the challenges of new responsibilities and stretch assignments. They don't want to disappoint the people who have championed them as they climb the ranks at work; furthermore, they don't want to give up their competitive standing, nor do they want to disappoint family and friends. The clash between their personal and professional visions intensifies as they strive to navigate across and between two very different worlds.

So, why are all these women getting stuck, and how can they avoid the pitfalls? How can organizations best cultivate the talents of this elite and critical workforce?

The Six Points of Influence Model for Transformational Change

The Six Points of Influence Model for Transformational Change (Six Points Model) is a systemic coaching model used for breaking big changes down into manageable parts. It is especially pertinent in cultivating and coaching talent and has been effectively applied to the challenges that high-potential women now face. The unifying goal when using the Six Points Model is to support sustainable transformation.

Within the model there are four interactive components (the Four Ps): Perception, Practice, Partnership, and Performance. Due to its systemic nature, a change around any of the Four Ps potentially affects the other three. The success of mastering any of these four components is achieved through using a balance of Reflection and Discipline. All told, these elements comprise the Six Points of Influence for Transformational Change.

Defining the Six Points of Influence

Perception   *Perception* is how we see ourselves, how we see others, how others see us, and how all involved see or understand the situation, business, or experience that has our attention.

Practice   *Practice* is what we do, our habits, our patterns of behavior. It is the set of competencies we choose to focus on. It is the way we deal with the change, our reaction to it, and our choice of how to engage.

Partnership   *Partnership* is the way we choose to engage dynamically with others and perhaps more importantly, it is the way we teach them to engage with us.

Performance   *Performance* is the actuality of how things unfold compared to the vision we want to create through the change.

Reflection and Discipline   To use the Four Ps successfully, leaders must integrate them with reflection and discipline.

Reflection is the time we spend considering the *what-happeneds* and the *what-ifs?* It holds the memories and emotions garnered from our experiences, and our understanding of the past—as well as our anticipation, both positive and negative, for how the change will affect things moving forward. All of these thoughts influence our decisions and the decisions of others, *all* of which affect what comes next.

Discipline is commitment combined with ability to stand up and take action.

A balance between discipline and reflection is necessary for success even though the natural tendency, when feeling stressed or threatened, is to ground oneself in one over the other. Reflection without action gets you nowhere, and action without reflection can result in hurtling at warp speed toward disaster.

Reflection and discipline are not exclusively solitary pursuits. They must also take place within the context of relationships with the principal people in the leader's life. A coach's responsibility is not only to work with the individual in developing an action plan, but also to ensure that the leader involves appropriate stakeholders. Developing a feedback loop with those stakeholders is bound to keep things on track.

Finally, for transformational change to stick, the envisioned outcome must be anchored in the values of the individual(s) embarking on change. The high-potential leader has to uncover her own values, both organizational and personal—a process that is often accomplished with the help of a coach—so that she can answer the so what? question. So what if I make this change? She must reflect on her personal perceptions and consider what it means for her, for her boss, organization, partner, family, and so on. Before she decides whether a change is worth making, the high-potential should consider the upsides and downsides for all the people in her circle of influence.

FIGURE 31.1. THE SIX POINTS OF INFLUENCE MODEL FOR TRANSFORMATIONAL CHANGE

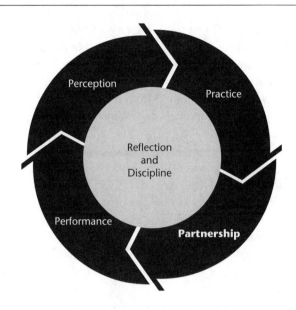

Getting Started with the Six Points of Influence

Let's recall for a minute our high-potential leader who hears opportunity knocking but is somehow stopped from opening the door. How can she apply this model? Imagine, for example, that the opportunity is the possibility of filling the vacancy her boss will leave now that he has announced he is moving on.

To start using the Six Points Model, the coach should introduce her to the Six Points: perception, practice, partnership, performance, reflection, and discipline. The high-potential should choose in which area she feels most comfortable beginning. If she struggles with the way she sees herself and the way she's seen by others, she may shy away from applying for the job because of her lack of confidence. In that case, she would want to begin coaching on the Perception "P." If, on the other hand, she were concerned that she didn't have a clear vision for her team, she might choose to begin with the Performance "P."

Using the Six Points of Influence to Accelerate the Hi-Po's Career Path

A lack in any of the six areas can prevent high-potentials from being promoted. Let's consider how the Six Points affect common obstacles that these leaders face when trying to break through the infamous glass ceiling and how the leader along with her coach can work to move them aside. Sometimes these obstacles relate solely to one of the points and sometimes they tie into two or more of the points.

Too many roles: Directional challenges from trying to be everything to everybody. This is a problem of perception, failing to have a clear vision for herself in a chosen role, and practice, constantly taking on more tasks and failing to be disciplined in drawing boundaries.

Boys' club: Being excluded from a heavily male environment. This can be avoided by reflecting on one's stakeholders, identifying key players, and cultivating partnerships.

Succession planning bias: Being overlooked. The culprit may be other people's perceptions, as women are often seen as support people rather than leaders, or because male leaders assume that a woman wouldn't want to be away from home to fulfill the added travel and responsibilities of stretch assignments. Senior management often lacks women, who might be likelier to propose other female candidates.

Always settling for support roles: Care-giving habit is deeply ingrained. This is usually due to perception, especially self-perception. The leader must be disciplined to reflect regularly on what she gives her time to. Will this create the legacy she wants to leave?

Going it alone: Too few alliances. Women have many reasons for going it alone. This may be due to the practice of trying to be perfect and avoiding asking for help or delegating to others. Women are culturally taught to do for others, so often a female boss takes it upon herself to pick up her team's slack. Insisting on doing everything solo could also be because of insufficient partnerships, or a worry about perception. What will other people think of her if she asks for help, or doesn't know the answer to every question? Some women worry that their coworkers will think they're unprepared or incompetent if they work with a coach, sponsor, or mentor.

Cloudy vision: One example of cloudy vision is when a high-potential leader wants more than what she has settled for. She knows she can contribute in a stronger and more meaningful way yet doesn't have a clear sense of what that vision or contribution might be. Or when she does have that vision but it conflicts with how her boss believes her work should be measured. These are both challenges of performance.

Case Illustrations of the Six Points Model at Work

Having described the model and provided some examples of how to identify and master obstacles and challenges, let's explore how I coached two high-potential women leaders to create sustainable transformational change in their lives using the Six Points Model.

Greta and Donna

In the first case, Greta heard the knock of opportunity yet was resistant to answer the door. She was afraid that it would be disruptive to her family. In the second case, Donna was also challenged by the faint knocking of opportunity. The uniqueness of her situation was that she was not ignoring others, but herself.

Case Study #1: Greta's Story

Greta found herself in a situation familiar to many women: torn between her family and career. Because she was a high potential (Hi-Po), the career opportunities were especially enticing. When Greta learned that she was short-listed to be the next CEO of one of the world's biggest manufacturing companies, the validation she received was like the rush of endorphins that one can get during exercise, making her feel energized and strong. For high-potentials, their expanding sense of capabilities and this validation from others can be addictive. It is easy to overindulge in a can-do campaign only to wind up disappointing oneself by making mistakes in one's personal life. As Greta was given more stretch assignments in preparation for her new role, her concerns mounted. She realized she could not continue at this accelerated rate while maintaining all her other commitments and responsibilities.

The tipping point came when she was assigned a new project that would require frequent travel out of the country. Not even Greta could stretch herself this far. She needed to rethink and renegotiate her ideals for herself and her family. She turned to her coach for help. We reflected together on the *so what* factor. We considered what new behaviors she would adopt and actions she might take. We considered the upsides and downsides to the changes and proactively prepared for both. Greta completed the following sentence: "If I take on this new assignment then I _____?" She filled in the same sentence with the names of her various stakeholders, considering the impacts on her husband, family, team, and organization.

Greta set aside some quality time to meet with her husband and kids. Together *they* reflected on the sacrifices and added responsibilities everybody would have to shoulder, and assessed *whether the promotion* was worth it. They examined the short- and long-term rewards, and the financial upsides for the family: more security, money for college, and family vacations.

The deal-clincher was when Greta told her family that if she was successful on the assignment, she would split her large bonus with them. Now everybody was working together for the bonus, rather than sacrificing while she alone reaped the rewards. This

(Continued)

created a marked difference in their *partnership*. The kids enthusiastically discussed a strategy and divvied up the extra chores and responsibilities they would take on during Greta's absence.

Greta also engaged in *reflecting* with her boss about her visioning process. She shared her *perceptions* and concerns about the upsides and downsides. Greta showed *discipline* (that is, capability and commitment) when she negotiated with her boss, and was able to secure at least ten days home out of every month. By working with her family and her boss, Greta set realistic expectations and received support from inside and outside the organization. She was able to come up with a plan that had a beneficial impact on all the key players: her current team, the company, and her family.

Case Study #1: Action Steps

Perception: Greta needed to *reflect* on her beliefs. She had to decide if her new role held real value and was worth the sacrifices. She also had to overcome traditional female concepts, such as perceiving her value through her support of others.

Performance: Once she had clarified her vision and anchored it to her values, Greta realized she was trying too hard to be everything to everybody. She had to change her practices, no longer trying to be all things to all people and seek support. She expanded the *reflection* process to include her primary stakeholders.

Together they discussed pros and cons and formulated a common vision.

Discipline: The coach helped to achieve this by supporting Greta and holding her accountable for executing a strategy that would align her practices and her vision.

Practice: The family devised an action plan defining expectations and responsibilities. This included details such as who would be responsible for which chores, and how the bonus would be split.

Partnership: She set up a process for continuous feedback, to make sure the arrangement was working for everybody, and to provide a means for continuous improvement.

Case Study #2: Donna's Story

Donna worked for a large health care organization. She began as an administrative assistant and, over a thirty-year career, worked her way up the corporate ladder to be head manager overseeing services and support. Although this was a high rank, she had always worked in support positions and even as a manager was still in a service-oriented department.

Donna's niche seemed natural to her, as it reflected what she observed in her early life. Donna's mother was a renowned hostess who made everybody feel loved and cared for. In her job, Donna found herself valued for filling a similar role. Like her mother, she was adept at navigating relationships and making sure everybody was comfortable and happy.

But Donna secretly yearned to work in a role involving creativity and innovation. Because she had only shown off some of her talents, she was slotted into a track that allowed for little creativity. She did well in her position, keeping quiet about her other talents because she believed her company valued her for her ability to execute other people's plans, not to formulate her own. Every time she had a performance review and was asked about her interests and next steps, she concealed her true desire. She assumed that, since her coworkers already held a strong *perception* of her in her current role, that her desire to refocus on innovation and strategy would not be appreciated, acknowledged, or even viable. Donna had fallen into the trap that many high-potentials do of failing to *reflect* on her own self-limiting beliefs. Traditionally, women have been valued for supporting others. Putting oneself first is not in the female lexicon. Many women leaders question whether it's right to prioritize their own needs and desires.

Donna needed to change her *perception* of herself, and to teach others to change the way they viewed her. During coaching sessions, we worked on bringing out Donna's hidden facets. She had to change her *practice* of staying silent in strategy meetings. After many years of only speaking up about issues related to her ability to execute on other people's plans, she had to exercise *discipline* by finding the courage to voice her ideas and show her capacity for innovation.

To make this shift, Donna learned to traverse the territory of *partnerships.* She did her research, identifying key players in the company who were involved in strategy and innovation. She prepared for moments when she could connect to these potential supporters, either in formal situations like strategy meetings, or informal chance meetings in the elevator. She practiced how she would share ideas that exposed her creative and innovative side.

Donna's rebranding campaign changed her *perception* of herself, and how others perceived her. Instead of sitting back in silent support, she focused on new competencies of communication and influencing others. By being willing to take a risk and put ideas out there, she demonstrated her strategic side and taught other people to look at her as a resource.

Donna's work paid off. She won over her boss, who is currently championing her efforts and helping her find an opportunity on the innovation and strategy side.

Case Study #2: Action Steps

Reflection: We reflected on what Donna valued most. We addressed her fears about changing her *perception* and *performance,* and understanding the obstacles to her self-confidence.

Practice: We used her practice to change people's *perceptions.* In this case, that meant preparing her strategies and finding the courage to voice them during meetings and in informal settings. We honed her ability to influence others.

Partnerships: We identified key players who could help her get where she wanted to go. It's crucial for coaches to help their clients determine who will stand in support, and who's going to obstruct transformation. High-potential women leaders must learn how to engage their potential champions.

Conclusion

High-potential women and their coaches have exciting opportunities to influence the world and expand the way that women are perceived. As Baby Boomers retire and workforce statistics shift, women will be called into more leadership roles. Coaches must be sensitive to these leaders' unique needs, and be prepared to help them overcome the obstacles that stand in their way. They must understand that women's self-perception and others' perceptions of them have been constrained by culture, impacting their courage to envision the possibilities. As more high-potential women and the organizations and leaders they work with step up to the responsibility of examining the areas of perspective, practice, partnership, and performance, and combine this examination with healthy doses of reflection and discipline, we will see more executive roles being filled with smart and savvy female leaders.

A Call to Action

To any leader who (1) has experience and understanding for the challenges presented and (2) resonates with the Six Points of Influence Model and the possibilities it creates, let me offer you the ultimate challenge in the form of two remaining questions:

1. What can an individual leader within an organization do to create momentum for propping open doors?
2. What do organizations need to do to prop open more doors for high-potential women?

Or, in the words of Rabbi Hillel some two thousand years ago,

"If I am not for myself, who will be for me?"
"If I am only for myself, what am I?" and
"If not now, when?"

Barbara Mintzer-McMahon is an executive coach and consultant who lives in the San Francisco Bay Area. She specializes in leadership development, team building, change management, and strategic partnerships. In 1989 she founded the Center for Transitional Management. She was senior lead for the coaching faculty for the Global Institute for Leadership Development for Linkage Inc. from 2003 to 2011. She has keynoted and developed training programs for Shell International, Intel, Pella Corp., Nektar Therapeutics, University Polytechnic Madrid, and many others. Ms. McMahon is partnered with Alexcel and Institute of Executive Development researching Best Practices of Executives in Transition. She is frequently called on to speak and consult on this topic.

PART VII

COACHING FOR LEADERSHIP—PREMIUM WEB CONTENT

Part VII: Coaching for Leadership: Premium Web Content, is the final section of *Coaching for Leadership* 3e. You won't find these chapters in the printed book, but you will find them at www.pfeiffer.com/go/GoldsmithCF3. We recommend that those new to the subject of leadership coaching peruse these chapters. Beginning this section is "Ten Suggestions for Successful Peer Coaching," by Robert M. Fulmer and John E. Brock, in which the authors lay the groundwork for peer coaching as a viable alternative to professional coaching, then provide concrete suggestions on how to make the process run more efficiently. In "Coaching Executives for Succession," Linda D. Sharkey explores succession planning and how a skilled coach can help the organization assess high-potential successors for executive positions and also assist the new leader as he or she transitions into the new role. In the field of executive coaching, multi-rater feedback report is crucial. In their article, "Why 360s Don't Work and How They Can," Marc Effron and Miriam Ort examine this sixty-year-old performance tool and point out its shortcomings. Originally published in *Coaching for Leadership* (1e), Bruce Lloyd's "Leadership and Power: Where Responsibility Makes the Difference" discusses the coach's role in managing the relationships between responsibility, leadership, and learning, and shows how the nature and role of power and its abuse can change the dynamics of these relationships within a situation or organization. The classic Nancy Adler piece, "Coaching Executives: Women Succeeding Globally," takes an international view on women leaders and shows how issues in their career development may be addressed through coaching. Finally, in his article "Coaching the Coaches," Dave Ulrich illustrates an important philosophy of coaching: "Coaching does not mean doing for others, but means helping others to get things done."

NOTES

Chapter One

1. For a study on the effectiveness of this process with internal coaches in GE Financial Services, see Linda D. Sharkey, "Leveraging HR: How to Develop Leaders in 'Real Time,'" in *Human Resources in the 21st Century*, ed. M. Effron, R. Gandossy and M. Goldsmith (New York: Wiley, 2003).

2. H. Morgan and M. Goldsmith, "Leadership Is a Contact Sport," in S*trategy+Business*, Fall 2004 (republished in Fall 2010 as one of nine outstanding articles in the history of the journal).

3. This process is explained in more detail in Marshall Goldsmith, "Recruiting Supportive Coaches: A Key to Achieving Positive Behavioral Change" in *The Many Facets of Leadership*, eds. M. Goldsmith, V. Govindarajan, B. Kaye, and A. Vicere, (New York: Prentice Hall, 2003).

4. M. Goldsmith, "Try Feed*forward*, Instead of Feedback" originally published in *Leader to Leader*, Summer 2002.

5. For a great description of the impact of coworkers' focusing on their own improvement, read Marshall Goldsmith, "Expanding the Value of Coaching: from the Leader to the Team to the Organization," in *The Art and Practice of Leadership Coaching*, ed. H. Morgan, P. Harkins, and M. Goldsmith (New York: Wiley, 2004).

Chapter Three

1. T. F. Gilbert, *Human Competence: Engineering Worthy Performance* (New York: McGraw-Hill, 1978).

2. R. D. Chevalier, "Updating the Behavior Engineering Model," *Performance Improvement* 42 no. 5 (2003): 8–14.

3. P. J. Dean (Ed.), *Performance Engineering at Work,* 2nd ed. (Silver Spring, MD: International Society for Performance Improvement, 1999).

Chapter Four

1. E. H. Schein, *Process Consultation: Its Role in Organization Development* (Reading, MA: Addison-Wesley, 1969).
E. H. Schein, "Empowerment, Coercive Persuasion and Organizational Learning: Do They Connect?" *The Learning Organization* 6, no. 4 (1999): 163–172.

2. Schein, *Process Consultation Revisited: Building the Helping Relationship* (Reading, MA: Addison-Wesley-Longman, 1999).

3. Schein, *Process Consultation.*
E. H. Schein, *Process Consultation, Vol. II: Lessons for Managers and Consultants* (Reading, MA: Addison-Wesley, 1987).
E. H. Schein, *Process Consultation, Vol. I: Its Role in Organization Development,* 2nd ed. (Reading, MA: Addison-Wesley, 1988).
Schein, *Process Consultation Revisited.*

4. E. H. Schein, *The Corporate Culture Survival Guide* (San Francisco: Jossey-Bass, 1999).
E. H. Schein, *Organizational Culture and Leadership,* 3rd ed. (San Francisco: Jossey-Bass, 2004).

5. J. Flaherty, *Coaching: Evoking Excellence in Others* (Boston: Butterworth-Heinemann, 1999).

6. Schein, *Process Consultation Revisited.*

7. Flaherty, *Coaching.*

8. Schein, *Organizational Culture and Leadership.*

Chapter Five

1. See Dave Ulrich, "Coaching for Results," *Business Strategy Series* 9, no. 3 (2008): 104–114.

2. A review of this work was presented at 21st Annual SIOP (Society of Industrial and Organizational Psychology), Dallas, Texas April 2006, in a paper by Richard Arvey, Maria Rotundo, Wendy Johnson, Zhen Zhang, Matt McGue entitled "Genetic and Environmental Components of Leadership Role Occupancy." The nature/nurture debate is also dealt with in the following:
Thomas J. Bouchard Jr., David T. Lykken, Matthew Mcgue, Nancy L. Segal, and Auke Tellegen, "Sources of Human Psychological Differences: the Minnesota Study of Twins Reared Apart," *Science Magazine* (October 12, 1990).
Judith Rich Harris, *The Nurture Assumption: Why Children Turn Out The Way They Do* (New York: The Free Press, 1998).
Judith Rich Harris, "Where Is the Child's Environment? A Group Socialization Theory of Development," *Psychological Review* 102, no. 3 (July 1995): 458–489.
M. Mcgue, T. J. Bouchard, Jr., W. G. Iacono, and D. T. Lykken, "Behavioral Genetics of Cognitive Ability: A Life-Span Perspective," in *Nature, Nurture, and Psychology,* ed.

R. Plomin & G. E. Mcclearn (Washington, DC: American Psychological Association, 1993), 59–76.

3. The work on changing habits comes from Joseph Grenny at VitalSmarts who found that 73 percent of executives know they need to change, but don't. M. J. Ryan in *This Year I Will . . .: How to Finally Change a Habit . . .* found that 8 percent kept New Year's resolutions and 90 percent of our lives are daily routines, most of which do not change.

4. The work on personal brand has been discussed by Tom Peters, *The Brand You 50: Or Fifty Ways to Transform Yourself from an "Employee" into a Brand That Shouts Distinction, Commitment, and Passion!* (New York: Knopf, 1999).

    Turning this personal brand into a leadership brand can be found in Dave Ulrich and Norm Smallwood, *Leadership Brand; Developing Customer Focused Leaders to Drive Performance and Build Lasting Value* (Cambridge, MA: Harvard Business Press, 2007).

5. An overview of the social network village for retired individuals can be found in: Martha Thomas, "The Real Social Network," *AARP (American Associate of Retired Persons), The Magazine* (April 2011).

6. Michael M. Lombardo and Robert W. Eichinger, *FYI: For Your Improvement, A Guide for Development and Coaching,* 4th ed. (Minneapolis: Lominger, 2004).

Chapter Seven

1. Amazon.com accessed 08–27–11. http://www.amazon.com/gp/search/ref=sr_nr_n_2?rh=n%3A283155%2Cn%3A%211000%2Cn%3A3&bbn=1000&ie=UTF8&qid=1314840567&rnid=1000.

2. See L. S. Lyons, *The Coaching for Leadership Case Study Workbook: Featuring Dr. Fink's Leadership Casebook* (San Francisco: Jossey-Bass, 2012).

3. Note: You should be aware that electricity was known to the Greeks and is often attributed to Gilbert in the 1600s. Franklin is famous for flying a kite in a thunderstorm and making the connection with electricity. Don't try this at home!

4. M. Goldsmith, "Ask, Learn, Follow-up, and Grow," in *The Leader of the Future*, eds. F. Hesselbein, M. Goldsmith, R. Beckhard (San Francisco: Jossey-Bass, 1996), 227–237.

Chapter Nine

1. Tom Wolfe, *The Right Stuff* (New York: Farrar, Straus and Giroux, 1979).

2. James MacGregor Burns, *Leadership* (New York: Harper Perennial, 1982). Burns is a presidential historian by trade but has become a seminal thinker in leadership thought circles. He writes about transformational leadership and in some circles the term is attributed to him. Wikipedia, "James MacGregor Burns," http://en.wikipedia.org/wiki/James_MacGregor_Burns.

3. Based on an author interview with Paul Spiegelman, CEO and founder of the Beryl Company, on September 1, 2010.

4. Adapted from John Baldoni, *12 Steps to Power Presence* (New York: Amacom, 2010).

Chapter Ten

1. R. K. Greenleaf, *Servant Leadership: A Journey into the Nature of Legitimate Power and Greatness* (New York: Paulist Press, 1977), 26.
2. Greenleaf, *Servant Leadership*, 28.
3. Greenleaf, *Servant Leadership*, 27.
4. Steven Covey, *The 7 Habits of Highly Effective People* (New York: Free Press, 2004), 128.
5. Viktor Frankl, *Man's Search for Meaning, rev. ed.* (New York: Pocket Books, 1997), 172.
6. E. B. White, quoted in profile by Israel Shenker, "E. B. White: Notes and Comment by Author," *The New York Times* (July 11, 1969).

Chapter Eleven

1. Telephone interview with Jodi Taylor, PhD, on Center for Creative Leadership, April 1998. Taylor is now with Summit Leadership Solutions.
2. C. C. Araoz, personal interview. Also see C. C. Araoz, "The Challenge of Hiring Senior Executives," in *The Emotionally Intelligent Workplace: How to Select for, Measure, and Improve Emotional Intelligence in Individuals, Groups, and Organizations*, eds. C. Cherniss & D. Goleman (San Francisco: Jossey-Bass, 2001).
3. "Where Are We on the Web?" *Fast Company* (October 1999): p. 306.
4. Kouzes and Posner, *Encouraging the Heart*.
5. J. M. Kouzes and B. Z. Posner, *Credibility: How Leaders Gain and Lose It, Why People Demand It*, rev. ed. (San Francisco: Jossey-Bass, 2003).
   B. Z. Posner and W. H. Schmidt, "Values Congruence and Differences between the Interplay of Personal and Organizational Value Systems," *Journal of Business Ethics*, 1993, 12: 171–177.
6. M. Csikszentmihalyi, *Finding Flow: The Psychology of Engagement with Everyday Life* (New York: Basic Books, 1997), 23.
7. J. M. Kouzes and B. Z. Posner, *The Leadership Challenge*, 3rd ed. (San Francisco: Jossey-Bass, 2002).
8. Kouzes and Posner, *Credibility*.
9. Kouzes and Posner, *Credibility*.

Chapter Thirteen

1. I struggled with how to label what I am calling "Execution Coaching." Other options considered were "Prescriptive Coaching" and "Directive Coaching."
2. The following two articles provide good discussions of the Triangle Offense:
   "In Triangle Offense, Cuts Are Sharp and So Is Learning Curve," available from http://www.nytimes.com/2009/12/14/sports/basketball/14triangle.html
   "The High Priest of the Triangle Offense, Phil Jackson," available from http://sports illustrated.cnn.com/vault/article/magazine/MAG1017460/index.htm
3. "The High Priest of the Triangle Offense, Phil Jackson," 2.

4. Here, I provide a brief overview of the Strategic Diversity Management Process™ for the purpose of giving a feel for the empowering framework I use. A more complete account can be found in my most recent book: R. Roosevelt Thomas Jr., *World Class Diversity Management: A Strategic Approach* (San Francisco: Berrett-Koehler, 2010).

Chapter Sixteen

1. Article originally published in *Journal of Business Strategy* 31, no. 4 (2010): 90–99.
2. The opening section based on Adler's (2006) "The Arts and Leadership: Now That We Can Do Anything, What Will We Do?" *Academy of Management Learning and Education Journal* 5, no. 4 (2006): 486–499.
3. Note that all page numbers refer to the original first edition published by Circumstantial Productions.
4. Paraphrase of Sir Isaac Newton's "If I have seen further it is by standing on the shoulders of giants" in Newton's February 15, 1676 letter to Robert Hook.
5. Address by Kofi Annan at the World Economic Forum in Davos, Switzerland, in 1999.
6. Rumi from his poem "Spring Giddiness" as translated by C. Barks and J. Moyne (Rumi, 1995).
7. Fuller as cited at Wisdom Quotes: www.wisdomquotes.com/000976.html.
8. As cited at The School for Mindful Living website: www.schoolofmindfulliving.org/quote/quote.html.
9. Reverend Martin Luther King's famous plea of "the fierce urgency of now" was often quoted by President-Elect Barack Obama when describing the importance of Americans realizing that we are at a defining moment in our nation's history.

Chapter Eighteen

1. For background information, the author is indebted to Dean George Johnson; faculty members Faith Rivers James and Roland Smith; and coaches William Eagles, Ronnie Grabon, Chris Leupold, Bonnie McAlister, Patricia Perkins, Marty Peters, Chris Smith, and Jonathan Wall.
2. In the third year, students may elect a Capstone Leadership course in which one or more students may pursue an independent project or studies in leadership.
3. William M. Sullivan, Anne Colby, Judith Welch Wegner, Lloyd Bond, and Lee S. Shulman, *Educating Lawyers: Preparation for the Profession of Law* (San Francisco: Jossey-Bass, 2007).

Chapter Nineteen

1. The article was modified in 2011. The original version was published in: *Coaching for Leadership: How the World's Greatest Coaches Help Leaders Learn,* eds. Marshall Goldsmith, Laurence Lyons, and Alyssa Freas (San Francisco: Jossey-Bass, 2000), 103–109.
2. Marshall Goldsmith and Howard Morgan, "Leadership Is a Contact Sport," *Strategy+Business* 36 (2004).

Chapter Twenty

1. Adapted from Shannon Wallis, Brian O. Underhill, and Carter McNamara, "Microsoft Corporation" in *Best Practices in Talent Management: How the World's Leading Corporations Manage, Develop and Retain Talent*, eds. M. Goldsmith and L. Carter (San Francisco: Pfeiffer, 2010).

2. Corporate Leadership Council, "Realizing the Full Potential of Rising Talent" (volume 1). *HR Intelligence Quarterly* (2005).

3. M. W. McCall and G. P. Hollenbeck, *Developing Global Executives* (Cambridge, MA: Harvard Business School Press, 2002).
   M. W. McCall, M. M. Lombardo, and A. M. Morrison, *Lessons of Experience: How Successful Executives Develop on the Job* (New York: The Free Press, 1998).

4. B. Underhill, K. McAnally, and J. Koriath, *Executive Coaching for Results: The Definitive Guide to Developing Organizational Leaders* (San Francisco: Jossey-Bass, 2007).

Chapter Twenty-One

1. Miguel Helft, "For Buyers of Web Start-Ups, Quest to Corral Young Talent," *New York Times* (May 17, 2011).

2. Corporate Executive Board Learning and Development Roundtable, "Setting *Leaders Up to Succeed: Tactics for Navigating Leaders Across Critical Upward Career Transitions*" (Washington, DC: Corporate Executive Board Company, 2004), 3.

3. Michael Watkins, *The First 90 Days: Critical Success Strategies for New Leaders at All Levels* (Boston: Harvard Business School Publishing, 2003), 12.

4. Corporate Executive Board Learning and Development Roundtable, "Setting *Leaders Up to Succeed*, 41.

5. Vanessa Urch Druskat and Steven B. Wolff, "Building the Emotional Intelligence of Groups," *Harvard Business Review* (March 1, 2001). Online. http://books.google.com/book s?id=BuSUCK19ZggC&pg=PA175&dq=Building+the+Emotional+Intelligence+of+Gr oups&hl=en&ei=gYvJTp-LPOaTiAL-zYTMDw&sa=X&oi=book_result&ct=result&re snum=1&ved=0CDUQ6AEwAA#v=onepage&q=Building%20the%20Emotional%20 Intelligence%20of%20Groups&f=false.

6. William Shakespeare, *Hamlet*, V, ii, 234–237.

7. Jose Antonio Vargas, "The Face of Facebook." *The New Yorker* (September 20, 2010).

Chapter Twenty-Three

1. Peter Drucker, *The Essential Drucker* (New York: Harper Collins, 2003), 207.

2. Chris Argyris, *Behind the Front Page: Organization Self-Renewal in Metropolitan Newspapers* (San Francisco: Jossey-Bass, 1974).

3. Drucker, *The Essential Drucker*, 212.

Chapter Twenty-Four

1. Paul Hyde, Roman Regelman, John Rolander, et al., "Five Industries Hit the Reset Button," *Strategy + Business,* (Jan. 14, 2011). http://www.strategy-business.com/article/00060?pg=0.
2. Towers Watson, "Strategies for Growth," white paper, (December 2010). http://www.towerswatson.com/assets/pdf/3371/Towers-Watson-Strategies-Growth.pdf.
3. Alexcel Group and the Institute of Executive Development "Executive Challenges Remain Challenging," white paper, (2010). http://leadingnews.org/TransitionStudyReq.htm.
4. M. Goldsmith, *What Got You Here Won't Get You There* (New York: Hyperion, 2007).
5. Ram Charan, Stephen Drotter, and James Noel, *The Leadership Pipeline* (San Francisco: Jossey Bass, 2006).
6. L. Levin, *Top Teaming: A Roadmap for Navigating the Now, the New and the Next* (Bloomington, IL: iUniverse, 2011).

Chapter Twenty-Five

1. Mickey Connolly & Richard Rianoshek, *The Communication Catalyst: The Fast (But Not Stupid) Track to Value for Customers, Investors, and Employees* (Chicago: Dearborn Trade, 2002), 145.
2. Marshall Goldsmith, *What Got You Here Won't Get You There* (New York: Hyperion, 2007).
3. Jim Collins, *Good to Great: Why Some Companies Make the Leap . . . and Others Don't* (New York: HarperCollins, 2001).

Chapter Twenty-Seven

1. Stephen A. Miles is vice chairman at Heidrick & Struggles. Nathan Bennett is the Wahlen Professor of Management at Georgia Tech. The two are coauthors of the 2010 book, *Your Career Game: How Game Theory Can Help You Achieve Your Professional Goals* (Stanford, CA: Stanford Business Books, 2010).

Chapter Twenty-Eight

1. Michael Watkins, *The First 90 Days* (Boston: Harvard Business Press, 2003).
2. See Scott Blanchard and Madeleine Homan, *Leverage Your Best, Ditch the Rest: The Coaching Secrets Top Executives Depend On* (New York: William Morrow, 2004).
3. See Ken Blanchard and the Founding Associates and Consulting Partners of The Ken Blanchard Companies, *Leading at a Higher Level: Blanchard on Leadership and Creating High Performing Organizations* (Upper Saddle River, NJ: FT Press, 2009 and 2010).
4. Noel Tichy, *The Leadership Engine: How Winning Companies Build Leaders at Every Level* (New York: HarperCollins, 1997).
5. Harper Lee, *To Kill a Mockingbird* (Philadelphia: Lippincott, 1960).

Chapter Twenty-Nine

1. Copyright © 2005 by Marshall Goldsmith. Adopted from an article of the same name in *Leader to Leader* by Marshall Goldsmith, Fall 2002. The term "feed*forward*" was coined in a discussion I had with Jon Katzenbach, author of *The Wisdom of Teams, Real Change Leaders,* and *Peak Performance.*

Chapter Thirty

1. C. S. Dweck, *Mindset: The New Psychology of Success* (New York: Ballantine Books, 2007).
2. P. R. Clance and S. A. Imes, "The Impostor Phenomenon Among High Achieving Women: Dynamics and Therapeutic Intervention," *Psychotherapy: Theory, Research and Practice* 15 no. 3 (1978): 241–247.
3. J. Collins, *Good to Great: Why Some Companies Make the Leap . . . and Others Don't* (New York: HarperCollins, 2001).
   D. Vera, and A. Rodriguez,-Lopez, "Strategic Virtues: Humility as a Source of Competitive Advantage," *Organizational Dynamics* 33 no. 4 (2004): 393–408.
4. Further information on the Realise2 Team Profile is available from: http://www.cappeu .com/Realise2/TeamProfile.aspx.
5. Further information on the Realise2 4M Model and Realise2 strengths assessment tool is available from: http://www.cappeu.com/Realise2.aspx.
6. L. S. Lyons and A. Bateson, "How to Crack the Toughest Leadership Challenge of All," *A Lyons-Bateson Summit Paper* (2009), www.lslyons.com.
   L. S. Lyons and P. A. Linley, "Situational Strengths: A Strategic Approach Linking Personal Capability to Corporate Success," *Organisations and People* 15 no. 2 (2008): 4–11.
   L. S. Lyons, The Situational Intelligence Tetrad (Lyons-Bateson Reference Model), in *The Coaching for Leadership Case Study Workbook: Featuring Dr. Fink's Leadership Casebook* (San Francisco: Jossey-Bass, 2012).

Chapter Thirty-One

1. The Six Points of Influence Model for Transformational Change (formerly called the Four Ps Model of Coaching) has been developed by Barbara McMahon through her practice as an executive coach over the last thirty years.
2. http://www.dol.gov/wb/stats/main.htm. Accessed July 24, 2011.
3. Faith Popcorn, *EVEolution: The Eight Truths of Marketing to Women* (New York: Hyperion, 2000).
4. For the purposes of this article, I will use the following definition of high potential by Jay Conger, Douglas Ready, and Linda Hill, "High potentials consistently and significantly outperform their peer groups in a variety of settings and circumstances. While achieving these superior levels of performance, they exhibit behaviors that reflect their companies' culture and values in an exemplary manner. Moreover, they show a strong capacity to grow and succeed throughout their careers within an organization—more quickly and

effectively than their peer groups do." http://hbr.org/2010/06/are-you-a-high-potential/ar/1 accessed July 24, 2011.

5. McKinsey Company, "Women Matter" report, 2010. http://www.mckinsey.com/careers/women/insights_and_publications/women_matter.aspx.

6. Demast, A. "For Chinese Women U.S. MBAs Are All the Rage," *Bloomberg Business Week* (May 5 2011).

7. *2010 Catalyst Census: Fortune 500 Women Executive Officers and Top Earners.* http://www.catalyst.org/publication/459/2010-catalyst-census-fortune-500-women-executive-officers-and-top-earners.

8. Demast, A. "For Chinese Women U.S. MBAs Are All the Rage."

INDEX

Page references followed by *fig* indicate an illustration; followed by *t* indicate a table; followed by *e* indicate an exhibit.